Client Assessment in Therapeutic Recreation Services

Client Assessment in Therapeutic Recreation Services

Norma J. Stumbo, PhD, CTRS

Venture Publishing, Inc.
State College, PA

Copyright © 2002

Venture Publishing, Inc.
1999 Cato Avenue
State College, PA 16801
Phone: (814) 234-4561
Fax: (814) 234-1651

Production Manager: Richard Yocum
Manuscript Editing: Valerie Paukovits
Cover Design by Echelon Design

Library of Congress Catalogue Card Number 2002104947
ISBN 1–892132–32–X

Table of Contents

Summary
References

List of Tables and Figures

Preface

While professionals primarily enter the field of therapeutic recreation with a desire to help individuals with disabilities and/or illnesses lead healthy, more satisfying lives and "do good," many forces have united recently to encourage us to "do better." Accountability. Outcomes. Performance improvement. Measurement. Quality. Standards. Competencies. Stakeholders. These buzzwords have entered into the language of health care and human services providers in every corner of the country. "Doing good" is no longer good enough. Now is the time to meet the challenge of "doing better."

For the past several decades, client assessment has been a source of concern for many professionals in therapeutic recreation. We have known that our client assessment instruments and procedures could be improved and many have worked to this end. Gary D. Ellis and Julia K. Dunn are two notable examples of individuals who have charted the therapeutic recreation assessment waters. This book intends to add to those efforts and to improve the competence of new and continuing professionals in therapeutic recreation assessment. It aims to solidify in the reader's mind the relationship between intervention programming and assessment and the important place assessment holds in the overall context of accountable service provision.

My many thanks to individuals who provided invaluable feedback on the original outline: Drs. Patricia Malik (RPMalik, Inc.), Nancy Navar (University of Wisconsin-LaCrosse), Cynny Carruthers (University of Nevada-Las Vegas), Jo-Ellen Ross (Chicago State University), Jan Sneegas (formerly of the American Therapeutic Recreation Association), and Peggy Holmes-Layman (Eastern Illinois University). I owe Nancy and Jo-Ellen a very special thanks to reviewing chapter drafts and improving the readability of the text. My thanks to Randy Duncan for unbelievable, enduring patience, and my sisters, Nancy Lockett and Barb Busch, for being among the most wonderful women I know.

Chapter 1
Introduction to Client Assessment

Client assessment plays an important role in the placement of clients into therapeutic recreation programs appropriate to meet their needs. Therapeutic recreation programs intended to be interventions have as their purpose to change some aspect of client behavior (including attitudes, knowledges, skills, and abilities). One of assessment's contributions to the therapeutic recreation intervention process is its ability to place the right clients in the right intervention programs that have been designed specifically to address their leisure-related needs. The ideal intervention process starts with an assessment effective at helping the specialist match the right client with the right program that will in turn assist the client in achieving his or her targeted outcomes. However, this placement process—including designing and delivering quality programs and selecting or developing quality assessment tools—takes a great deal of energy, thought, and problem solving on the part of the therapeutic recreation specialist. Some steps in the process are intuitive and some are not. Some principles surrounding assessment are more difficult to grasp than others. Some commercial assessments are of high quality and some are little better than tree pulp.

This book intends to aid the therapeutic recreation specialist in learning, understanding, and applying information about client assessment for use in therapeutic recreation intervention services. Every therapeutic recreation specialist needs to become a knowledgeable and informed consumer and user of client assessment processes, procedures, and instruments. In some settings, the therapeutic recreation specialist is independent in making decisions about the content and process used for client assessment. In other settings, the therapeutic recreation specialist may be one of many professionals who collaborate on a single agency assessment. This chapter covers foundational material and serves as a springboard to the remaining chapters.

Purposes and Uses of Client Assessment

There are numerous reasons for conducting and numerous ways to use client assessments. **Table 1.1** (p. 2) provides an illustration of the potential purposes of client assessment.

The first purpose is to identify the problem(s) of the client so that appropriate interventions can be designed, monitored, and evaluated. Client assessment is clearly important to determining clients' needs for placement into therapeutic recreation intervention programs. Without appropriate client assessment, clients are likely to be placed into programs not designed to meet their needs, and therefore not produce the outcomes intended from participation (Palmer & McMahon, 1997; Peterson & Stumbo, 2000). On the other hand, quality assessment processes can lead to appropriate placement into programs designed to address the clients' needs and move them toward valued outcomes. Quality assessment procedures are a must for changing client behavior in desired and predictable ways.

Within the first purpose of identifying client problems and needs, additional uses of assessment are appropriate. As noted by Gronlund (1993), Hoy and Gregg (1994), Ward and Murray-Ward (1999), and Salvia and Ysseldyke (1998), assessment information can be used for: (a) placement decisions, (b) formative (ongoing progress) decisions, and (c) summative (end-of-services) decisions. Client assessment provides baseline information about the attitudes, knowledges, skills, and abilities that clients possess prior to receiving intervention. That baseline information is important for (a) establishing what programs should be selected for clients; (b) monitoring and reporting on clients' status (progression or regression) as they participate in the program; and (c) comparing clients' attitudes, knowledges, skills, and abilities as they exit the program or intervention. *Placement, monitoring, and evaluation depend on collecting the right baseline information accurately.*

For placement decisions, assessment needs to be fine-tuned enough to distinguish client problems and needs and match those problems and needs with the appropriate intervention programs. In this case, the assessment procedure must detail the problems and needs of the client so that the most efficient yet effective intervention can be provided. In speaking about psychology, Palmer and McMahon (1997) explained:

Table 1.1
Purposes and Uses of Client Assessment

Individual client information
    Initial baseline assessment (treatment planning/program placement)
    Monitoring progress (formative information)
    Summarizing progress (summative information)
Research on program efficacy and effectiveness
Communication within and among disciplines
Administrative requirements

Diagnosis involves matching signs and symptoms of [the] client with a known cluster of symptoms (a syndrome)...The purpose of making a diagnosis is to allow the counselor to intervene in the most effective way possible...[However] change is only possible within the limitations set by the system or systems of which the person is a part and with the resources at the person's disposal. (Palmer & McMahon, 1997, pp. 7–8)

Obviously, assessment decisions closely parallel the program planning and implementation process. During the course of the intervention and at the end of services, the specialist can use a well-designed assessment that produces valid and reliable results for measuring the client's progress during and after the end of the client's participation in the program. While shortened lengths of stay and the sheer volume of clients affect how well this can be accomplished, the fact remains that a measurement process that produces valid and reliable results can be used at different intervals to measure a person's movement toward and at a final outcome.

The second major reason for assessment is for research purposes—to ascertain the most effective interventions possible for future clients. Baseline assessment data can be used for quality improvement and research purposes (Palmer & McMahon, 1997; Peterson & Stumbo, 2000; Sneegas, 1989). Beyond the implications for programming, baseline assessment data can be used to monitor the overall efficacy or effectiveness of the therapeutic recreation intervention program for a client, a particular group of clients, or all clients entering and exiting the program. This data can assist with performance improvement efforts as well as result in research to determine for whom which programs are most effective. Starting with an effective assessment is one of the easiest ways to determine client outcomes that result from program participation.

The third major reason is for "knowledge, communication, and memory" (Palmer & McMahon, 1997, p. 11), so that people within the discipline may be able to communicate with each other as well as with other professionals. Professionals within a discipline need a common language to communicate, and therefore, need a common knowledge base and common definitions of professional terms. In therapeutic recreation, such terms as *leisure barriers, leisure education, leisure awareness, perceived freedom, client assessment, leisure lifestyle*, and even *therapeutic recreation* need to have common meanings for professional understanding to occur. These definitions and understandings sometimes may be specialized to the discipline and sometimes must be in alignment with those used by other disciplines (Palmer & McMahon, 1997).

A fourth major purpose relates to administrative requirements from external and professional bodies as well as local agency mandates. Three organizations have significant influence on the therapeutic recreation profession at the national level: (a) the Joint Commission on Accreditation of Healthcare Organizations (JCAHO), (b) the Rehabilitation Accreditation Commission (CARF), and (c) the Centers for Medicare and Medicaid Services (CMS, formerly the Health Care Financing Administration HCFA). These three organizations affect all health care professions as they set standards for health care quality that in turn affects reimbursement for services. All three of these organizations monitor specific requirements for client assessment that affects therapeutic recreation services. Since JCAHO, CARF, and CMS standards are updated frequently and since JCAHO and CARF have multiple manuals that apply to different settings, readers are encouraged to view the latest information on their individual websites: http://www.jcaho.org   http://www.carf.org   http://www.hcfa.gov

The two national professional organizations for therapeutic recreation, the National Therapeutic Recreation Society (NTRS) and the American Therapeutic Recreation Association (ATRA), each have standards of practice and codes of ethics that contain important information about client assessment and expectations for professional behavior related to client assessment. Those can be found at http://www.nrpa.org and http://www.atra-tr.org, respectively.

NTRS's *Standards of Practice* (1995) assume client assessment is conducted, although the document does not contain a specific assessment standard. The following standard applies:

Standard IV: Documentation
The therapeutic recreation specialist records specific information based on client assessment, involvement, and progress. Information pertaining to the client is recorded on a regular basis as determined by agency policy and procedures and accrediting body standards (NTRS, 1995).

ATRA's *Standards of Practice* (1993) directly address client assessment and contain the following standard:

Standard 1: The therapeutic recreation specialist conducts an individualized assessment to collect systematic, comprehensive and accurate data necessary to determine a course of action and subsequent individualized treatment plan (ATRA, 1993).

In addition, in 1997 ATRA published a set of *Guidelines for Competency Assessment and Curriculum Planning in Therapeutic Recreation: A Tool for Self-Evaluation* (Kinney & Witman, 1997). This document contains "a well organized and thoughtful approach to delineating the complex matrix of knowledge kills, and abilities which must be mastered to deliver quality therapeutic recreation services" (p. vi). These competencies are organized under the following headings: (a) foundations of professional practice, (b) individualized patient/client assessment, (c) planning and development of treatment/program plans, (d) implementation of the treatment/program plan, (e) evaluation of patient/client functioning and interventions/program, (f) organizing and managing therapeutic recreation services, and (g) support competencies. The list of competencies found under individualized patient/client assessment is located in **Table 1.2** (p. 6)

The National Council for Therapeutic Recreation Certification (NCTRC®), the national credentialing body for therapeutic recreation specialists, provides a list of knowledge areas/competencies used as the basis for the national examination. See **Table 1.3** (p. 7) for a listing of the Job Tasks of the Therapeutic Recreation Specialist as related to client assessment, according to the NCTRC Job Analysis (1997). **Table 1.4** (p. 8) contains the Knowledge Areas related to client assessment, also according to the NCTRC Job Analysis (1997). Recent information about the competencies related to client assessment can be found at http://www.nctrc.org.

Many health care organizations and other agencies also have mandates related to the delivery of services that include client assessment. Each specialist should check with the agency's central or corporate administration to determine local mandates or standards for client assessment and the delivery of services.

The purposes and uses of client assessment are universal, regardless of the profession being discussed. Assessment involves collecting data and using that data appropriately to help individual clients make progress toward useful outcomes. Other professions, such as medicine, nursing, psychology, education, and physical therapy share with therapeutic recreation the same basic measurement and application concerns for assessment. The following section provides a closer examination of assessment within therapeutic recreation.

Definition of Client Assessment in Therapeutic Recreation Services

The focus on client assessment within therapeutic recreation services more often than not has been on placement of clients into programs. Although the other purposes mentioned are implied and are of importance, at the present time client placement into programs remains the primary focus of the literature and in practice.

Peterson and Stumbo (2000, p. 200) defined client assessment as "*the systematic process of gathering and analyzing selected information about an individual client, and using the results for placement into a program(s) that is designed to reduce or eliminate the individual's problems or deficits with his/her leisure, and that enhance the individual's ability to independently function in leisure pursuits."* **Table 1.5** (p. 9) provides a listing of other definitions of assessment found in the literature. Note that these

Table 1.2
Competencies for Individualized Patient/Client Assessment
(Kinney & Witman, 1997, p. 9)

B. Individualized Patient/Client Assessment

The curriculum should provide students with the opportunity to develop competence to individually screen, assess, and systematically collect comprehensive and accurate data in an efficient and effective manner to determine the course of actions subsequent to an individualized treatment/program plan.

Specific competencies should include:

1. Knowledge to assess physical, cognitive, social, emotional, and behavioral functioning, as it relates to leisure behavior, leisure knowledge, and skills, and functional independence in life activities.

2. Knowledge of psychometric properties of tests and measurements, and how those properties are affected by cultural diversity.

3. Knowledge of computer applications in patient/client assessment.

4. Knowledge of various techniques and systems used to document assessment results.

5. Skill in behavioral observation.

6. Skill in interview techniques.

7. Skill in functional performance testing.

8. Skill in use of standardized and nonstandardized instruments/batteries/rating systems.

9. Skill in use of relevant information from records, charts, other professionals and family/significant others.

10. Ability to analyze, interpret, and summarize data to determine patient/client strengths and limitations.

11. Ability to determine need for assistive devices and technologies to achieve maximal independence and functional capacity to maintain optimal health and leisure functioning.

12. Ability to involve clients, families, significant others in the assessment process.

definitions have several key features in common. These key assessment features include:

- Gathering selected pieces of data
- About an individual, involving a
- Systematic process of collecting, analyzing and reporting which
- Results in the ability to make decisions for placement into therapeutic recreation programs that
- Have been designed to reduce or eliminate problems so that the
- Individual can independently function in his/her leisure

Table 1.3
NCTRC Job Tasks of the Therapeutic Recreation Specialist Related to Client Assessment

- Request and secure referrals.
- Obtain and review pertinent background information about the person served, as available from records or charts, from other professional staff, and from relevant others.
- Select assessment instruments and procedures based on the needs of the person served.
- Interview the person served and relevant others to assess physical, social, emotional, cognitive, leisure, and lifestyle needs and functioning.
- Administer instruments to assess physical, social, emotional, cognitive, leisure, and lifestyle needs and functioning.
- Observe behavior of the person served to assess physical, social, emotional, cognitive, leisure, and lifestyle needs and functioning.
- Analyze and interpret results from assessment procedures.
- Integrate the information collected for use in planning services for the person served and report results to the treatment team.
- Discuss results of assessment and involve the person served or relevant others in the design of an individualized treatment plan.
- Develop and document individualized intervention goals and plan based on assessment, consistent with legal requirements and professional guidelines.

These characteristics imply that the specialist must be knowledgeable about client characteristics (disability or illness information as well as typical attitudes, knowledges, skills, and abilities), assessment processes, and program possibilities (Palmer & McMahon, 1997). Assessment becomes one tool in the decision-making process. For example, the specialist needs to decide:

- What *information* is important for program placement
- What *data collection technique* (e.g., observations, interviews) is best to gather the information
- How the data *will be interpreted* for decisions about program placement

Table 1.4
NCTRC Knowledge Areas Required for Therapeutic Recreation Specialist Related to Client Assessment

- Assessment procedures: Behavioral observations
- Assessment procedures: Interview
- Assessment procedures: Functional skills testing
- Assessment procedures: Current therapeutic recreation/leisure assessment instruments
- Assessment procedures: Other inventories and questionnaires
- Assessment process: Other sources of assessment data (e.g., records, other professionals)
- Assessment process: Selection (e.g. reliability, validity, practicality, availability)
- Assessment process: Implementation
- Assessment process: Interpretation
- Sensory domains of assessment (e.g., vision, hearing, tactile)
- Cognitive domains of assessment (e.g., memory, problem solving, attention span, orientation, safety awareness)
- Social domains assessment (e.g., communication/interactive skills, relationships)
- Physical domains assessment (e.g., fitness, motor skill functioning)
- Emotional domains of assessment (e.g., attitude toward self, expression)
- Leisure domains of assessment (e.g., barriers, interests, attitudes, patterns/skills, knowledge)

Table 1.5
Definitions of Assessment

Assessing is collecting, verifying, and organizing data about the consumer or group. Data is obtained from a variety of sources (e.g., formal or informal interviews, assessment instruments) and is the basis for decisions made in subsequent phases [of planning, implementation, and evaluation]. Skills of observation, communication, and interviewing are essential to perform this phase of the therapeutic recreation process. Once data are collected, problems or potential problems can be identified, and goals for the consumer be developed. (O'Morrow & Carter, 1997, pp. 295–296; clarification added)

For therapeutic recreation, **assessment** can be defined as a systematic procedure for gathering select information about an individual for the purpose of making decisions regarding that individual's program or treatment plan. (Dunn, 1984, p. 268)

Assessment is the critical link in the testing process that renders worthwhile the time spent gathering data. Assessment also provides the basis for what instruction should follow. (Horvat & Kalakian, 1996, p. 9)

Resident **assessments** are the first step in understanding individuals. Assessments viewed as mere paperwork miss the point at which the activity program can make real differences in individual lives. Residents' interactions in the activity program provide ongoing information about abilities, preferences, desires, dreams, aspirations, and hopes. Keen observations are necessary to the development of meaningful and effective resident assessments and lead to viable care plans. (Perschbacher, 1993, p. 1)

Assessment represents a systematic procedure of gathering essential information about a person or client that will be used in developing treatment plans and counseling the individual. (Kraus & Shank, 1992, p. 96)

The first phase in the TR process is **assessment**. It is the foundation of all that follows. A sound assessment identifies the client's health status, needs, and strengths. In doing so, the assessment provides direction for the planning phase by developing pertinent data about the client. Assessment is a critical dimension because without adequate and valid data on which to base TR interventions, much time may be lost in effecting treatment and rehabilitation programs. (Austin & Crawford, 1996, p. 47)

Assessment is the process of collecting data for the purpose of making decisions about individuals and groups, and this decision-making role is why it touches people's lives. Assessment in educational settings is a multifaceted process that involves far more than administering a test. When we assess students, we consider the way they perform a variety of tasks in a variety of settings or contexts, the meaning of their performance in terms of the total functioning of each individual, and the likely explanations for those performances. High-quality assessment procedures take into consideration the fact that anyone's performance on any task is influenced by the demands of the task itself, by the history and characteristics the individual brings to the task, and by the factors inherent in the context in which the assessment is carried out." (Salvia & Ysseldyke, 1998, pp. 5–6)

- How the assessment and program placement *relate to the individual's future lifestyle*

These concepts will be repeated in the remaining chapters, as assessment decisions cannot be separated from intervention programming decisions. The next section introduces the concept of intervention programming.

Intervention and Nonintervention Therapeutic Recreation Programs

Perhaps it is appropriate here to introduce the differences between intervention and nonintervention therapeutic recreation programs, as these differences impact the way in which assessment is used. Intervention programs have a very well defined and systematic plan for getting clients with a specific need from Point A (entry into the program) to Point B (exit from the program).

> A program that is designed and implemented to be intervention has as its outcome some degree of client behavioral change (i.e., behavioral change is the purpose of the program). This may mean an increase in knowledge, an increase in skill, a decrease in some behavior, and so on. To be considered intervention, a program has to be well designed and implemented according to a plan that specifically addresses participant change. On the other hand, *diversional* [or nonintervention] activities are provided for fun, enjoyment, or relaxation (i.e., fun, enjoyment, and relaxation are the purpose of the programs) (Peterson & Stumbo, 2000, p. 61; clarification added)

Client assessment is crucial to intervention programs and incidental to nonintervention programs. If a therapeutic recreation intervention program has the goal of improving clients' understanding of leisure barriers, then a baseline assessment that can measure the clients' understanding of leisure barriers is crucial. If a therapeutic recreation program has the goal of entertaining clients with a music performance program, then an assessment is unnecessary. This book is intended primarily for those therapeutic recreation specialists involved in providing intervention programs designed to produce predictable and desired client outcomes. Chapter 3 discusses therapeutic recreation intervention programming as it relates to client assessment.

Principles of Therapeutic Recreation Client Assessment

Client assessment provides a strong link between clients and programs. Like activity analysis that provides a breakdown of *program* characteristics and capabilities (see Peterson & Stumbo, 2000, Chapter 6), assessment provides a breakdown of *client* characteristics and capabilities. The interaction between these two types of analyses is vital if the intention is to deliver intervention programs that change some aspect of client behavior. Before discussing more technical aspects of assessment, some basic principles of client assessment are presented to gain a clearer rationale and understanding of the purpose of assessment. Peterson and Stumbo (2000, pp. 202–205) provided the following five principles that are useful as a launch pad for the more technical discussions that follow.

Principle #1: Client assessment is not just a piece of paper, but a systematic process of deciding what information is important to gather, how to collect the information, how to analyze the results, and what kind of decisions are made appropriately from the data gathered.

Client assessment involves a series of decisions on the part of the specialist. What are the outcomes expected of programs? What are the typical needs of the clients? What is the best way to gather information from or about clients? How can results be analyzed for their fullest benefit? What types of program placement decisions should be and can be made from the results? How systematic are the processes used to make these decisions?

Client assessment is an evolving process that allows clients to receive the maximum benefit from their involvement in therapeutic recreation programs. The decisions mentioned previously are most likely to have positive impacts on the clients' outcomes when they are made systematically, logically, and with great care. Assessment is a systematic and deliberate process that requires a great deal of attention from the specialist. The difference between a good assessment and poor assessment could mean the difference between clients achieving or not achieving intended outcomes. As such, valid and reliable assessment results are essential to the intervention delivery process.

Principle #2: There must be a logical connection between the assessment and programs delivered to clients.

One basic principle that provides the foundation for all assessment development and implementation is that *the content of the assessment must match the content of the program.* First of all, the program is built upon the deficits or needs of the generic characteristics of clients. For example, individuals with depression as a group have these common deficits: low energy, poor eating patterns, poor concentration, difficulty making decisions, sense of hopelessness, and loss of interest in daily events. Program offerings then reflect these areas of need and specific programs are designed to meet these needs, for example, Fitness and Exercise; Nutrition and Foods; Decision Making and Planning; and Concentration Skills. The comprehensive therapeutic recreation program design is created prior to clients entering the programs. The client assessment, used to identify *specific, individual* client needs, must align with these specific program offerings. The client assessment would cover content related to fitness and exercise, nutrition and foods, decision making and planning, ability to concentrate, and the like.

If, on the other hand, the programs provided include Fitness and Exercise; Nutrition and Foods; Decision Making and Planning; and Concentration Skills, and the assessment content focuses on past leisure involvement, leisure interests, and family history, the assessment results will not provide adequate information to place clients into appropriate programs or monitor their progress. The content of the assessment would not match the content of the programs. The remainder of this text explores this principle.

Table 1.6 shows examples of matched and mismatched assessment and program content. In the top example, the assessment content *does not* match the program content. In this case, it will be highly unlikely that the results of the assessment can be used systematically and logically for client placement into programs. The results will not lend themselves to making the dependable, worthwhile decisions. In the bottom example, the assessment content *does* match the program content. Although there are other factors to consider, the results of an assessment that contain content matching that of programs are much more likely to help place clients into the programs they need. The match between assessment and program content is a basic element to produce valid and reliable assessment results. This is true for both assessments that are "self-developed" by a specialist or commercial assessments purchased from a vendor. If the content of the assessment and the overall program does not match, the likelihood of correct placement into programs is minimized.

Principle #3: The assessment process must yield dependable and consistent results to be useful.

The assessment procedure must be standardized enough to be able to yield dependable and accurate results between specialists, between clients, between administrations, and over time. The tool and procedure need to be developed and tested to the point that all specialists administer the assessment in the same way, for example, using the same questions, the same phrasing, and the same probes. If this is not true, then differences in the clients' scores or results are likely due to the specialists and not the clients. In addition, each specialist also needs to be consistent when he or she administers the tool or procedure to clients. For example, if a specialist takes 20 minutes for one client's assessment and 2 hours for another, the differences in results may be a result of the administrations and not the

Table 1.6
Examples of Assessment Content Matching and Not Matching Program Content (Adapted from Stumbo, 1997, 2001)

Poor example: The content of the assessment does not match the content of the program

Program Content	Assessment Content
Functional Intervention	Leisure Interest Inventory
Physical functioning	Leisure history
Social functioning	Self-esteem
Leisure Awareness	
Leisure attitudes	
Self-awareness	
Leisure barriers	
Leisure Resources	
Personal resources	
Home resources	
Community resources	

Better example: The content of the assessment does match the content of the program

Program Content	Assessment Content
Functional Intervention	Functional Intervention
Physical functioning	Physical functioning
Social functioning	Social functioning
Leisure Awareness	Leisure Awareness
Leisure attitudes	Leisure attitudes
Self-awareness	Self-awareness
Leisure barriers	Leisure barriers
Leisure Resources	Leisure Resources
Personal resources	Personal resources
Home resources	Home resources
Community resources	Community resources

clients. Lastly, we need to know that if the same assessment were given twice to the same client in a relatively short period of time, the results would remain relatively consistent.

Two concerns here are the actual tool (e.g., the content, the number and types of questions, and the length) as well the procedure used to administer the tool (e.g., the assessment environment or whether the assessment is an interview and observation). Both assessment tools and procedures will be discussed more fully in the sections on validity and reliability, as well as the development of assessment protocols.

Principle #4: Client placement into programs should be based on assessment results, not just opinions or judgments of the specialist.

When client assessment is done poorly, the specialist is left with problematic, sketchy, or misleading results that tell very little about the client's need for programs. Typically the specialist has little choice but to "make it up as he or she goes" and place clients into programs without the benefit of systematic data and results. This total reliance on judgment is a concern because of the high likelihood of mistakes and inaccurate program placements. Errors of this nature almost guarantee that client outcomes will not be achieved, because clients are most likely placed in the wrong programs or ones that do not meet their needs.

Table 1.7 displays the relationship between client needs and client program placement (Stumbo, 1997, 2001). Assessment decisions can and will affect the treatment or intervention received by clients. So whether these decisions are made with care or made capriciously, the client and his or her ability to attain the targeted outcomes will be affected.

Down the left side of Table 1.7 are two decisions about whether the client does or does not need the program (based on assessment results). Across the top are the two decisions of whether a client is actually placed in the program or not (matching client needs with the potential of the program to meet those needs). The four quadrants provide a quick view of the potential results of assessment and placement decisions.

Quadrants I and IV indicate correct decisions—the match between the client needs (from assessment results) and their placement into programs is correct. Clients who need programs receive services, while clients without need do not. In Quadrant II the assessment results indicate needed program involvement that is not realized—an incorrect decision. The end result is that clients involved with erroneous Quadrant II decisions do not receive the necessary services. Quadrant III also indicates faulty matches or decisions. In these cases, clients receive services that do not match their needs. Programs provided in Quadrant III are likely to be misdirected in that clients without need are involved in programs without clearly defined outcomes. Whether this is due to agency mandates, high staff/client ratios, client diversity or other reasons, the specialist often resorts to "smorgasbord" programming, often with the intent of keeping clients busy without concrete goals for improving behavior. Or worse, the specialist creates misdirected goals and outcome statements that are not likely for a certain program, for example, stating that participation in bingo or volleyball will improve social skills. (An activity analysis would show that these programs do not *teach* specific social skills.) Producing meaningful and reliable client outcomes is less likely in situations where clients with widely varying characteristics and needs are placed into one program or clients are placed into programs which have not been analyzed correctly for their potential to address client needs.

Let's use the example of surgery to make the utility of the quadrants apparent. In Quadrant I, the client needs and receives the right surgery (good decision). In Quadrant IV, the client does not need surgery (based on assessment results) and, therefore, does not have it (also a good decision). In these two cases, both the patient and surgeon should be satisfied that the correct decisions were made. The client "placement" as a result of the systematic assessment decision matched the client needs. Both the client

Table 1.7
Relationship between Client Placement into Programs and Client Needs

	Client placed into program	Client not placed into program
Client needs program	**I. Correct Decision** Client receives necessary services; likely to be an intervention program	**II. Incorrect Decision** Client does not receive necessary services; no or unnecessary program involvement
Client does not need program	**III. Incorrect Decision** Client receives unnecessary services; not likely to be an intervention program	**IV. Correct Decision** Client does not receive services; program involvement not necessary

Stumbo, N. J. (1997). Issues and concerns in therapeutic recreation assessment. In D. Compton (Ed.), *Issues in therapeutic recreation: Toward a new millennium.* (2nd ed., pp. 347–372). Champaign, IL: Sagamore Publishing, Inc. Reprinted with permission.

and surgeon would be less happy with decisions falling into Quadrants II and III. In Quadrant II, the patient needed surgery and did not receive it. Obviously, depending on the condition, this could be life threatening. In Quadrant III, the patient did not need surgery but received it anyway (probably to keep the patient busy). Few of us would tolerate medical services that did not meet a specific need or were performed without a clear need for services.

Similar parallels can be drawn for therapeutic recreation services. Part of being accountable for outcomes means providing the appropriate services to affect client behavior. Clearly, Quadrant I contains the "right" programs in which the "right" clients are placed. As such, it has the greatest likelihood to be outcome-based intervention—that is, produce measurable, predetermined client outcomes. It requires the mix of an appropriate assessment procedure able to produce valid and reliable assessment results and appropriate programs designed on common client needs. This match is essential for correct client placement decisions.

Principle #5: The assessment process should provide baseline information from which a client's progression or regression as the result of participation in programs can be judged.

This principle addresses the need for the assessment results to be valid and reliable for the intended purpose. The results of the assessment should offer enough precision about important client characteristics and needs that it not only directs decisions for appropriate program placement, but also for the evaluation of client outcome attainment at the end of program involvement. If the assessment results are specific enough about the areas deemed to be important, then it can also be used later to determine the effects of the program on the client. Where did the client start and what changes have occurred as the result of his or her involvement in the program?

It is clear that these principles relate to one another. Each decision connects to all other decisions. Each decision about client assessment is affected by and affects decisions about program delivery. These relationships are important because they highlight the interconnectedness of quality program delivery. No decision or action occurs without considering its impact on other decisions or actions (Stumbo & Rickards, 1986).

Assumptions about Client Assessment

Sometimes without realizing it many tacit assumptions are made about client assessments, clients, intervention programs, and the therapeutic recreation specialists who provide them. These assumptions (some true and some not true) have profound effects on how clients are treated, how assessments are selected and administered, and how therapeutic recreation specialists perform. Following are some assumptions common throughout the profession. As you read each of them, think about how they affect the assessment and service delivery process, and whether you personally believe these assumptions.

Assumptions about Assessment Instruments and Procedures

The following are assumptions often made about client assessments in therapeutic recreation services:

- Information about behavior, knowledges, attitudes, skills, and abilities can be assessed through an assessment instrument/ procedure.
- An assessment can gather only a limited amount of information about a client.
- An assessment can gather an adequate amount of information about the client to make decisions about program placement.
- An assessment can gather the right information about the client to make decisions about program placement.
- An assessment is sensitive and finely tuned enough to "detect" client problems and needs.
- An assessment is available for any and every type of therapeutic recreation program offered to clients.
- An assessment is appropriate for any and every type of therapeutic recreation program offered to clients.
- An assessment produces results that have meaning and validity in the client placement process.
- The assessment results yield reliable/consistent information across clients, administrations, and specialists and over time.
- The assessment is administered in the most efficient and effective manner possible.
- The assessment is sensitive to cultural, gender, disability or illness, age, or ethnic differences among individuals being evaluated.
- Information to be gathered by therapeutic recreation assessments is unique from assessments used by other professions.

- If an assessment is available for purchase, it must be good and it can be used for any population and any therapeutic recreation program.

Which of these assumptions do you hold? Why do you believe them to be true? Which do you think are faulty? Why do you think they are false? What are other common assumptions not mentioned on this list? For each assumption, think how it may lead the specialist to make certain decisions or act in certain ways. What would be the consequences of these decisions and/or actions?

Assumptions about the Individual Client

Often a variety of assumptions are made about the clients before, during, and after the assessment process, including the following:

- Clients need to be assessed before being placed into intervention programs.
- The characteristics, traits, and functioning levels to be measured are relatively stable over time.
- Clients or relevant others are credible and reliable sources of information.
- The individual understands the importance of and is cooperative to the assessment process.
- The individual understands and has the ability to communicate his or her needs, interests, attitudes, knowledges, skills, and abilities.
- The individual believes that therapeutic recreation may be a necessary part of his or her treatment.
- The "selected information" gathered is representative of the totality of the client's attitudes, knowledges, skills, and abilities.
- The totality of the client' attitudes, knowledges, skills, and abilities can be measured accurately by interviews, observations, self-administered surveys, and/or records reviews.
- Clients with different backgrounds, ethnicities, genders, personalities, cultural differences, and preferences respond in the same ways or nearly the same ways to assessment questions.

Which of these assumptions do you hold? Why do you believe them to be true? Which do you think are faulty? Why do you think they are false? What are other common assumptions not mentioned on this list? For each assumption, think how it may lead the specialist to make certain decisions or act in certain ways. What would be the consequences of these decisions and/or actions?

Assumptions about the Therapeutic Recreation Intervention Program

Therapeutic recreation specialists may operate with a variety of assumptions. Some of those targeted to therapeutic recreation programs include:

- The department has a well-rounded, systematically designed program based on a sound philosophy (e.g., Leisure Ability) and theory (e.g., self-efficacy).
- The programs have been designed to lead to specific, targeted, and desired client outcomes and that the outcomes are meaningful and measurable.
- The intent and content of the therapeutic recreation program is consistent over time and between clients with similar needs.
- The content of the program is suitable for client participation.
- The best programs are those designed with a specific purpose or outcome in mind, and for a specific cluster of client needs.
- There is a strong correlation/connection between the content that the assessment measures and the goals and content of the therapeutic recreation intervention program.
- The therapeutic recreation program contributes to the outcomes of the individual valued by the agency and by society at large.

Which of these assumptions do you hold? Why do you believe them to be true? Which do you think are faulty? Why do you think they are false? What are other common assumptions not mentioned on this list? For each assumption, think how it may lead the specialist to make certain decisions or act in certain ways. What would be the consequences of these decisions and/or actions?

Assumptions about the Therapeutic Recreation Specialist

In addition to assumptions about assessments, clients, and programs, therapeutic recreation specialists hold a number of assumptions about themselves in relation to assessment and their practice, including:

- The specialist understands the close relationship between client assessment, intervention programs, and client outcomes.
- The specialist understands measurement characteristics (validity, reliability, fairness, usability) that affect the quality of a client assessment.
- The specialist has access to a wide variety of assessments/ resources from which to choose and can do so skillfully.
- The specialist has the ability to select the most appropriate assessments according to the clients' and program's needs.
- The specialist has skills in collecting information for assessment purposes through interviews, observations, self-administered surveys, and records reviews.
- The specialist has the ability to accurately administer, interpret, analyze, and report assessment results in a meaningful way.
- The specialist has competence to make judgments and place clients into programs, using assessment information.
- The specialist is invested enough in the assessment process to skillfully and ethically carry out the process of assessing, documenting, and evaluating.
- The specialist values lifelong learning that will be necessary to continually improve performance and practice.

Which of these assumptions do you hold? With which of these assumptions do you disagree? How does each of these assumptions affect how assessment and intervention services will be provided to clients? What are the consequences of holding these assumptions if they are indeed faulty? What other assumptions about clients, assessments, programs, or professionals are not listed here you can think of?

What Should an Assessment Measure?

The question of "What should an assessment measure?" has a simple yet dauntingly complex set of answers. On one hand, there seems to be some agreement about the content side of that question. For example, here are some comments from experts in the field:

The current, future, and oftentimes past leisure behavior of the client are important areas of focus for the therapeutic recreation specialist. Relevant information to be gathered may include leisure interests, use of leisure time, ability to participate in individual or group activities, ability to experience fun and enjoyment, leisure skills, leisure attitudes and awareness, and knowledge of leisure resources as well as any physical, cognitive, or social limitations affecting leisure lifestyle. (Sneegas, 1989, p. 223–224)

Others describe leisure assessment as a process of systematic inquiry about client attitudes, needs, interests, values, behaviors, and patterns where some type or degree of intervention is desired. (Howe, 1989, p. 209)

Assessment should aid us to determine client strengths, interests, and expectations and to identify the nature and extent of problems or concerns. Determining client strengths and interests will allow us to construct a strengths list on which to base interventions during the planning phase. Identifying client expectations helps us to determine treatment or rehabilitation goals. (Austin, 1997, p. 153)

A sound assessment identifies the client's health status, needs, and strengths. (Austin & Crawford, 1996, p. 47)

Therapeutic recreation specialists "assess physical, cognitive, social, emotional, and behavioral functioning, as it relates to leisure behavior, leisure knowledge and skills, and functional independence in life activities." (Kinney & Witman, 1997, p. 9)

Some of the generic commonalties among these insights include: (a) functional abilities; (b) clients' strengths and limitations; and (c) leisure patterns, attitudes, knowledges, skills, and abilities. Although several taxonomies have been suggested to classify client assessments within therapeutic recreation (cf. Burlingame & Blaschko, 1990; Howe, 1984; Stumbo, 1991, 1992; Stumbo & Thompson, 1986), the following will be used for this text:

- Functional abilities
- Leisure attitudes and barriers
- Leisure activity skills
- Leisure interests and participation

Each of these four areas, as well as the 50 to 60 commercial assessments available within these categories, will be discussed in more detail in Chapter 6 as well as the appendix.

At least two factors make this seemingly simple task of classifying and listing assessments more difficult to operationalize. First is the concern over the selection of a theory or set of theories on which to base therapeutic recreation intervention programs, and therefore the client assessment.

Second are the problems associated with measuring the attitudes, knowledges, and behaviors of individuals, especially those with illnesses and/or disabilities.

Caldwell (2001), Ross and Ashton-Shaeffer (2001), and Sylvester, Voelkl, and Ellis (2001) discussed the importance of filtering programming and assessment decisions through a theory or through models of therapeutic recreation practice. For example, choosing a theory (e.g., self-efficacy, intrinsic motivation, resiliency) as the basis of services affects the way in which the therapeutic recreation specialist delivers those services (Caldwell, 2001). Choosing the Leisure Ability Model as the basis for services affects the way in which the therapeutic recreation specialist plans and implemented intervention services (Peterson & Stumbo, 2001; Ross & Ashton-Shaeffer, 2001). So while there is some agreement about the content of assessments (and we would assume the content of therapeutic recreation programs), the filter of theory or models must be explored to best answer the question, "What should an assessment measure?" Although these ideas are revisited in Chapter 3, the reader is encouraged to review Caldwell (2001), Ross and Ashton-Shaeffer (2001), and Sylvester, Voelkl, and Ellis (2001) for a more in-depth coverage of theory and practice models.

Sneegas (1989) and Sylvester, Voelkl, and Ellis (2001) noted that measuring complex phenomena, such as human behavior and attitudes, is difficult at best. How do we adequately measure such a complex phenomena as "leisure behavior" or "leisure attitudes" or "health and well-being?" Addressing the measurement of leisure behavior, Sneegas (1989, p. 225) indicated:

> There is currently a lack of appropriate measurement tools, or instrumentation, which reflect the complexity of leisure behavior. Whereas time diaries and activity checklists provide a measure of time use and activity involvement, they do not generally provide any information detailing the whys and wherefores of the behavior, information on the subjective experience of the individual's involvement.

This quote provides a small indication of some of the difficulties encountered in selecting and developing assessment tools and procedures. More of these issues will be explored in Chapter 2.

At the microlevel, the content of the program remains important in deciding what the assessment should measure. The intent and content of the program and the purpose and function of the assessment both have a large impact on determining what content needs to be included on the assessment instrument. While these decisions are not impossible to make, many find it difficult because a great deal of knowledge, expertise, and professional judgment must accompany these decisions. It is not that the answers are vague and unobtainable, it is that they are often unique to the therapeutic recreation department and program. No single assessment will fit all therapeutic recreation programs, largely because few therapeutic recreation programs across the country are similar.

The reader, at the successful completion of this text, should be able to follow a systematic process for determining the appropriate assessment content relative to the needs of the intended clients and therapeutic recreation program. He or she will be able to answer the question, "What's the best assessment for this therapeutic recreation program and for the clients served by this agency?" for any given therapeutic recreation program across the country.

Summary

This chapter introduced some of the basic concepts related to client assessment. Some of the purposes of assessment include gathering baseline client information that can be used to place clients into programs as well as monitor their progress, data collection and research that improves future intervention programs, and quality and performance improvement issues. For the most part, therapeutic recreation's discussions concerning assessment have centered on client placement functions. For this reason, assessment's connection to intervention programming is important; that is, assessment of baseline information is important to the provision of programs and evaluation of client outcomes. A variety of assumptions (some true and some not) were mentioned so the reader has a better understanding of what may and may not be true about client assessment in therapeutic recreation services. The final discussions within this first chapter included what an assessment should or could measure. The next chapter centers on measurement properties and issues as they relate to therapeutic recreation client assessment.

References

American Therapeutic Recreation Association (1993). *Standards for the practice of therapeutic recreation*. Hattiesburg, MS: Author.

Austin, D. R. (1997). *Therapeutic recreation: Processes and techniques* (3rd ed.). Champaign, IL: Sagamore Publishing.

Austin, D. R. and Crawford, M. E. (1996). *Therapeutic recreation: An introduction* (2nd ed.). Needham Heights, MA: Allyn & Bacon.

Burlingame, J. and Blaschko, T. M. (1990). *Assessment tools for recreational therapy: Red book #1*. Seattle, WA: Frontier Publishing.

Caldwell, L. (2001). The role of theory in therapeutic recreation: A practical approach. In N. J. Stumbo (Ed.), *Professional issues in therapeutic recreation: On competence and outcomes* (pp. 349–364). Champaign, IL: Sagamore Publishing.

Dunn, J. K. (1984). Assessment. In C. A. Peterson and S. L. Gunn (Eds.), *Therapeutic recreation program design: Principles and procedures* (2nd ed., pp. 267–320). Englewood Cliff, NJ: Prentice Hall, Inc.

Gronlund, N. E. (1993). *How to make achievement tests and assessments* (5th ed.). Boston, MA: Allyn & Bacon.

Horvat, M. and Kalakian, L. (1996). *Assessment in adapted physical education and therapeutic recreation* (2nd ed.). Madison, WI: Brown & Benchmark.

Howe, C. Z. (1984). Leisure assessment instrumentation in therapeutic recreation. *Therapeutic Recreation Journal, 18*(2), 14–24.

Howe, C. Z. (1989) Assessment instruments in therapeutic recreation: To what extent do they work? In D. Compton (Ed.), *Issues in therapeutic recreation: A profession in transition* (pp. 205–221). Champaign, IL: Sagamore Publishing.

Hoy, C. and Gregg, N. (1994). *Assessment: The special educator's role*. Pacific Grove, CA: Brooks/Cole Publishing.

Kinney, T. and Witman, J. (1997). *Guidelines for competency assessment and curriculum planning in therapeutic recreation: A tool for self-evaluation*. Alexandria, VA: ATRA.

Kraus, R. and Shank, J. (1992). *Therapeutic recreation service: Principles and practices* (4th ed.). Dubuque, IA: Wm. C. Brown Publishers.

National Council for Therapeutic Recreation Certification. (1997). *Job analysis*. New City, NY: Author.

National Therapeutic Recreation Society (1995). *Standards of practice for therapeutic recreation service*. Arlington, VA: National Recreation and Park Association.

O'Morrow, G. S. and Carter, M. J. (1997). *Effective management in therapeutic recreation service*. State College, PA: Venture Publishing, Inc.

Palmer, S. and McMahon, G. (1997). *Client assessment*. Thousand Oaks, CA: Sage Publications.

Perschbacher, R. (1993). *Assessment: The cornerstone of activity programs*. State College, PA: Venture Publishing, Inc.

Peterson, C. A. and Stumbo, N. J. (2000). *Therapeutic recreation program design: Principles and procedures* (3rd ed.). Needham Heights, MA: Allyn & Bacon.

Ross, J. and Ashton-Shaeffer, C. (2001). Therapeutic recreation practice models. In N. J. Stumbo (Ed.), *Professional issues in therapeutic recreation: On competence and outcomes* (pp. 159–188). Champaign, IL: Sagamore Publishing.

Salvia, J. and Ysseldyke, J. E. (1998). *Assessment* (7th ed.). Boston, MA: Houghton Mifflin Company.

Sneegas, J. J. (1989). Can we really measure leisure behavior of special populations and individuals with disabilities? In D. Compton (Ed.), *Issues in therapeutic recreation: A profession in transition* (pp. 223–236). Champaign, IL: Sagamore Publishing.

Stumbo, N. J. (1991). Selected assessment resources: A review of instruments and references. *Annual in Therapeutic Recreation, 2*, 8–24.

Stumbo, N. J. (1992). Re-thinking activity interest inventories. *Illinois Parks and Recreation, 23*(2), 17–21.

Stumbo, N. J. (1997). Issues in client assessment for therapeutic recreation. In D. Compton (Ed.), *Issues in therapeutic recreation: A profession in transition*. (2nd ed., pp. 347–372), Champaign, IL: Sagamore Publishing.

Stumbo, N. J. (2001). Revisited: Issues and concerns in therapeutic recreation. In N. J. Stumbo (Ed.), *Professional issues in therapeutic recreation: On competence and outcomes* (pp. 215–236). Champaign, IL: Sagamore Publishing.

Stumbo, N. J. and Rickards, W. H. (1986). Selecting assessment instruments: Theory into practice. *Journal of Expanding Horizons in Therapeutic Recreation, 1*(1), 1–6.

Stumbo, N. J. and Thompson, S. R. (1986). *Leisure education: A manual of activities and resources*. State College, PA: Venture Publishing, Inc.

Sylvester, C., Voelkl, J. E., and Ellis, G. D. (2001). *Therapeutic recreation: Theory and practice*. State College, PA: Venture Publishing, Inc.

Ward, A. W. and Murray-Ward, M. (1999). *Assessment in the classroom*. Belmont, CA: Wadsworth Publishing.

Chapter 2
Measurement Characteristics of Client Assessment

Assessment is the process of gathering information about an individual so that the most appropriate therapeutic recreation services may be provided to eliminate, reduce, or compensate for the individual's "problems" with or barriers to meaningful leisure. To identify these problems or barriers, the professional must complete an assessment. To select systematic and useful assessment procedures, the specialist needs to be aware of certain measurement properties: validity, reliability, fairness, and practicality. This chapter will discuss these and other measurement terms as they relate to client assessment.

Reducing Error and Increasing Confidence in Client Assessment

Assessment, because it involves measurement, is largely about *reducing error* and *increasing confidence* in the results. Understanding these two concepts is important to every therapeutic recreation specialist concerned with selecting or developing the best, most appropriate, and most useful assessment instruments and procedures to match the purpose of the program and the needs of the clients (Peterson & Stumbo, 2000; Stumbo, 2001). Error and confidence are at the heart of measurement and underlie the concepts of validity, reliability, fairness, and usability that will be discussed later in this section.

It is important to understand that every score, including those received from therapeutic recreation assessments, has error in it. Measurement of any type, whether assessing blood pressure, weight, height, leisure satisfaction, personality, or depression has some degree of error in it. No score will be 100% valid and reliable. The assessment designer's job is to minimize errors in measurement as much as possible so that assessment scores are as accurate as possible.

Scores vary for many reasons, sometimes for logical, *intentional* reasons, such as the client changing an attitude or mood (or skill) that the scale measures. The client's scores from one administration to another would be expected to change roughly in the amount that the attitude (or skill) changes. However, sometimes variance in scores is caused by *unintentional* or *random error*. The client may misunderstand the question, become fatigued, experience difficulty in communicating an answer, have test anxiety, or not have the cognitive function to answer validly. The room may become hot, noisy, or stuffy. The specialist may ask questions in different ways, become distracted, or be in a rush to complete the interview. Any condition irrelevant to the purpose of the assessment is considered *error variance*. That is, error causes a score to deviate from its *true score*.

In all cases the goal of the specialist is to reduce unintentional error as much as possible so that more of the score is the client's true score, and error is reduced as much as is feasible. For example, efforts to reduce error include making sure that questions are understandable and standardized; that the room is quiet, comfortable, and private; and that all specialists conduct assessments as consistently as possible for every client. When these conditions are standardized and tested according to a defined *protocol*, the results are more likely to reflect the client's true score. Reduction of error is the primary rationale for assessment protocols and periodic staff training and retraining. Reducing error is extremely important; otherwise specialists might as well throw darts at a dartboard to determine in which programs clients are to be placed. Table 1.7 (p. 15) displays the incorrect decisions (errors in program placement) that can occur from poorly designed or implemented assessments.

Another closely related goal of the specialist is to be *confident* that the results of the assessment will lead to the correct placement of the client into the best intervention programs to meet their needs. This relates to making correct placement decisions as shown in Table 1.7. The specialist needs to be confident that the client's needs or deficits will be best met by placement into a certain intervention program(s). Confidence in this placement process (from administration, to scoring, to analyzing, to reporting) increases by using assessments that produce as valid, reliable, and usable results as possible. This in turn means that the specialist needs to become well-versed in the measurement properties of validity, reliability, fairness, and usability. While no assessment will produce 100% valid and reliable results (there will always be some degree of error present), knowing information about measurement properties will help the specialist increase the probability of producing better results and reducing unwanted error. In addition, knowledge of validity and reliability will help the professional become a better consumer of assessments. In this case, knowledge certainly is power (to buy or not to buy).

Gronlund (1993) provided a set of principles to guide development of tests and assessment devices. If followed, these principles help both the designer and user reduce the amount of error in the individual's score as well as increase confidence in the results. These principles have been adapted to client assessment and include:

Principle #1: Client assessments should measure clearly defined client outcomes.

The first step in assessment development is specifying and clarifying what should be measured. In therapeutic recreation this means a clear delineation of what client outcomes are to be achieved through participation in intervention programs. These outcomes are then represented on the client assessment.

Principle #2: Client assessments should be concerned with all intended important client outcomes.

While it may be tempting to remain at a simpler knowledge level, sometimes outcomes focus on attitudes or behavior. If client outcomes include a change in attitude, knowledges, skills, and behaviors, then the assessment should reflect all these outcomes, not just the ones simplest to measure.

Principle #3: Client assessments should measure a representative sample of relevant client outcomes.

Client assessments are limited by time and resources available. However, that does not dismiss the fact that assessments should reflect a representative sample of all outcomes intended for clients. The items on the client assessment should be relatively proportional to the client outcomes intended from involvement in programs.

Principle #4: Client assessments should include the types of test items most appropriate for measuring the intended client outcomes.

More about item writing will be discussed later in this chapter and in Chapter 7, but generally the types of items asked should reflect the types of outcomes to later be achieved.

Principle #5: Client assessment should be based on plans for using the assessment results.

For the most part, client assessments in therapeutic recreation are used to place clients into the right programs that address their needs. Whether developing an agency-specific assessment or selecting a commercial assessment, the specialist should keep in mind how the results will be used to place clients into programs. Even the "best" assessments are not useful if they do not help place clients into the right programs.

Principle #6: Client assessment should provide scores relatively free from measurement errors.

As mentioned earlier, individuals interested in developing assessments need to follow accepted psychometric procedures to ensure the highest validity and reliability of results. Assessment users need to ensure that they follow the documented assessment protocols to reduce error whenever possible.

Introduction To Measurement Terminology

Client assessment instruments are measurement tools. In therapeutic recreation, they help to describe a person's attitudes, knowledges, skills, abilities, and interests with regard to his or her leisure. They are similar to other measurement devices, such as personality tests, personnel screening devices, college entrance exams, and driver's license tests. As such it is important to measure the desired properties well and with accuracy. Because client assessment in therapeutic recreation means that people will be categorized, sorted, and placed into programs based upon their responses to the assessment, it is important to ensure that the process and results represent the person's true leisure attitudes, knowledges, skills, abilities, and interests. This applies to all types of collecting data for assessment purposes, whether through paper-and-pencil instruments, interviews, or observations.

Before we move into the sections on the process of gathering, documenting, and reporting on assessment data, readers must have a clear understanding of measurement terms and concepts. We now explore some terms and definitions associated with measurement.

Norm-Referenced or Criterion-Referenced Results

Test scores can either be norm-referenced or criterion-referenced. *Norm-referenced* means that each individual person's score is compared with a larger sample of scores from a norm group. For example, a first place finisher is compared with others in the same race event and her score is reported relative to others in the group. Thus, she is the first place winner, placing ahead of everyone else in the group. In this instance, her finishing time might not be as important as her comparison to others in the group, as only a limited number of ribbons is given out. Another popular and easily understood example is classroom tests graded on a curve. Each individual is graded compared with others in the class versus a predetermined level of excellence determined by the instructor. Many individuals would rather have their own grade determined by its relation to their peers than by a set standard.

Most individuals in the American school system are acquainted with *norms* and *percentiles* through standardized tests given at certain points during elementary school, middle school, and high school. These tests often are norm-referenced and the scores of individuals are reported in comparison with others. For example, if an individual's score stood at the 95th percentile, he or she scored better than 95% of the individuals (norm group) taking the test during the same administration. Norm-referenced tests report scores about individuals in comparison with others in their peer group. Of particular concern is that the norm group is representative of the test takers for whom the test was designed.

Criterion-referenced tests or measurements, on the other hand, report an individual's score in comparison with a preset standard or criterion. This absolute standard or expected success rate is established ahead of time and is not swayed by the abilities or characteristics of the test group. Using a race example similar to the one above, an individual may not qualify to enter the race because he did not have an adequate score. If runner A did not finish in an acceptable time (predetermined ahead of time by race officials) then he would not qualify to enter the race. The acceptable time would be the criterion he is judged by, not by comparing him with other individuals as in norm referencing.

In the classroom testing example, instead of grading on the curve, the instructor would predetermine the amount of points necessary for an A, B, C, etc. Any and every individual receives a grade based on how many points he or she collected, regardless of how anyone else in the class performs. There may be one person with an A or there may be one hundred. One person's score does not affect the grade received by another person.

It should be noted that norm-referenced and criterion-referenced refers to how the results are interpreted, rather than to the test itself. Both types of interpretation can be applied to the same set of scores. For example, "Jose received a score higher than 90% of the clients (norm-referenced interpretation) by answering correctly 15 questions on leisure resources" (criterion-referenced interpretation). Client assessments in therapeutic recreation can focus on criterion-referenced interpretation (as we focus on mastery of concepts and examples of behavior) or on norm-referenced interpretation (as we determine how individuals respond in comparison to other clients).

Validity

Validity of an assessment refers to the extent to which it meets its intended purpose. It concerns what the test measures and how well it does so" (Peterson & Stumbo, 2000, p. 207). *Validity* refers to the extent to which the results of an evaluation procedure serve the particular use(s) for which it was intended. That is, does the instrument measure what it intends to measure? Validity is always concerned with the specific use to be made of the results and with the soundness of the interpretations. Tests or instruments are used for several types of judgment, and for each type of judgment, a different type of investigation is required to collect evidence of validity.

Six Points about Validity

Gronlund (1993) provided six points related to validity.

1. *Validity is inferred from available evidence (not measured).*

The appropriateness, meaningfulness, and usefulness of specific inferences to be made from assessment results are estimated by accumulating evidence to support these inferences. Test validation results from the collection of different types of evidence to support these claims. The greater the accumulation of validity evidence, the greater the confidence in the results of the assessment.

2. *Validity depends on many different types of evidence.*

Since there are a variety of inferences that can be made from results of a given assessment, there are many ways to gather evidence to support a particular inference or interpretation of an assessment result.

3. *Validity is a matter of degree.*

No measurement tool is perfect. Validity cannot be expressed in absolutes, but rather the degree (high, moderate, or low) to which a tool produces valid results (Gronlund, 1993). Whether a classroom test, certification examination, or client assessment, every measurement tool has some degree of error. Sometimes a lower degree of validity is acceptable, depending on the difficulty of measuring certain content or with certain people (e.g., decision-making skills with clients with brain injuries). Other times, only a very high degree of validity is warranted, depending on the nature of the decision to be made from the results. Much depends on the significance of decisions stemming from the assessment scores. What we look for in client assessment are measurement tools that do the best possible job of reducing error and increasing confidence in our placement of clients into programs.

4. *Validity is specific to a particular use.*

To say "a test is valid" is incorrect. A test's results are only valid for certain groups of people and in situations for which the test was built. An adult IQ test might be well-constructed and have fabulous statistics reporting its validity for measuring adult IQ, but it would make a very poor client assessment for therapeutic recreation. Some assessments are built for children, some focus on people with functional problems, some focus on individuals with communication disorders. A test designed for one specific group of individuals may not be as effective with other samples or groups of individuals until it has been validated (proven to be effective) for that group.

5. *Validity refers to the inferences drawn from the results of a test or evaluation instrument for a given group of individuals, not the instrument itself.*

Each assessment has to be tested for a particular use and for a particular population. For example, to say the Leisure Diagnostic Battery (Witt & Ellis, 1987) is a valid tool because of its significant research history is incorrect. The Leisure Diagnostic Battery, as any other assessment or measurement tool, is likely to produce results that have some degree of validity for some uses and some populations. That is, those purposes, conditions, and populations for which it has been tested and proven to perform well. If the Leisure Diagnostic Battery were to be used for a different purpose or for a different sample from which it was tested, it would produce results that may have a questionable degree of validity. Therefore, it is crucial for the specialist to become fully aware of the purpose, population, and testing procedures used in commercial assessments so that intelligent judgments about appropriateness can be made.

6. *Validity is a unitary concept.*

Gronlund (1993) stated:

Describing validity as a unitary concept is a basic change in how validity is viewed. The traditional view that there were several different types of validity has been replaced by the view that validity is a single, unitary concept that is based on various forms of evidence. The former types of validity (content, criterion-related, and construct) are now simply considered to be convenient categories for accumulating evidence to support the validity of an interpretation. Thus, we no longer speak of "content validity," but of "content-related evidence" of validity. Similarly we speak of "criterion-related evidence" and "construct related evidence." (pp. 160–161)

For some interpretations of test scores only one or two types of evidence may be critical, but an *ideal* validation would include evidence from all three categories. We are most likely to draw valid inferences from test scores when we have a full understanding of: (1) the nature of the test content and the specifications that were used in developing the test, (2) the relation of the test scores to significant criterion measures, and (3) the nature of the psychological characteristic(s) or construct(s) being measured by the test. Although in many practical situations the evidence falls short of this ideal, we should gather as much relevant evidence as is feasible within the constraints of the situation. (p. 161)

Three Aims of Testing and Assessment

There are three basic reasons to develop and administer a test. These reasons relate to what needs to be done to the test to make it as good as it can be. The aims relate to the evidence for validity that needs to be collected before the assessment can be used with confidence.

1. *The test user wishes to determine how an individual performs at present in a universe of situations that the test situation is claimed to represent.*
   For example, most achievement tests used in schools measure the student's performance on a sample of questions intended to represent a certain phase of educational achievement or certain educational objectives. Most client assessments cannot ask all 150 questions we would like to have answered, so we need to streamline the content and yet make sure it is valid for our purposes. We need to make sure the questions or items on the assessment are representative of all the content in which we might be interested. In this case, we are interested in collecting evidence for content validity.

2. *The tester wishes to forecast an individual's future standing or to estimate an individual's present standing on some variable of particular significance that is different from the test.*

For example, an academic aptitude test may forecast grades, the ACT or SAT can be used to predict college success, or a brief adjustment inventory may estimate what the outcome would be of a careful psychological examination. This requires an excellent grasp of the *criterion variable*—the behavior that the test is predicting to (e.g., college success) and the aim would be to establish evidence of criterion-related validity. Of course, there are problems with criteria—for example, they are not the same for all ethnic or age groups.

Most client assessments in therapeutic recreation do not attempt to predict future behavior in the way this aim intends, although we are clearly interested in the future lifestyles of our clients. We are not usually able to say, with confidence, that client X is 85% likely to be successful in the community after discharge. We have generally not built our assessments to be predictors of future success and have not conducted research studies to validate them for this purpose.

3. *The test user wishes to infer the degree to which the individual possesses some hypothetical trait or quality (construct) presumed to be reflected in the test performance.*

For example, the tester wants to know whether the individual rates high on some abstract trait such as *intelligence, creativity, leisure satisfaction,* or *leisure motivation* that cannot be observed directly. This may be done to learn something about the individual, to study the test itself, to study the test's relationship to other tests, or to develop psychological theory. The aim would be to establish evidence of construct validity.

Therapeutic recreation assessments generally have not focused on building or examining constructs (traits not directly observable but believed to exist, such as intelligence) as part of the assessment process. Although some assessments do measure concepts such as *perceived freedom in leisure* or *leisure satisfaction,* most client assessments—because they relate to the programs in which clients are placed—measure the attitudes, knowledges, and skills addressed during the intervention. This primarily may be due to the brevity of most therapeutic recreation intervention programs in today's health care and human service environment.

Regardless of the purpose of the test and evidence of validity collected, the primary concern is the degree to which the assessment meets its intended purpose. How representative is it of the domain being examined?

(Evidence of content validity) How well is the criterion predicted from the test results? (Evidence of criterion-related validity) How well is the construct of interest measured by the test? (Evidence of construct validity) Each of these categories of evidence of validity will be discussed in greater detail in the next section. Remember: a procedure is never valid in general. It is valid for some purpose and for some group. Evidence is collected to infer its usefulness for some purpose(s) and some group(s).

Demonstrating Evidence of Validity

There are three types of evidence of validity: content-related, criterion-related, and construct-related. **Table 2.1** displays the types of evidence of validity and the questions each should address. Each has its own purpose and method of determining to what degree assessment results are valid.

Evidence of *content validity* shows the degree to which assessment content covers a representative sample of the domain in question (Peterson & Stumbo, 2000, p. 208). Evidence of content-related validity is the extent to which a test or instrument measures a representative sample of the domain of tasks or content under consideration. Content validity is important when the user wishes to describe how an individual performs on a domain of tasks that the instrument is supposed to represent. For example,

Table 2.1
Questions Answered by Approaches to Validation
(Adapted from Gronlund, 1993)

Type of Evidence	Question to be Addressed
Content-related evidence	How adequately does the sample of assessment items represent the domain (totality) of content to be measured?
Criterion-related evidence	How accurately does performance on the assessment predict future perfor mance (predictive evidence) or esti mate present performance (concurrent evidence) on some other valued measure called a criterion?
Construct-related evidence	How well can performance on the assessment be explained in terms of psychological characteristics?

if a portion of an assessment is to measure knowledge of community leisure resources, then content validity determines the degree to which it does so. If the assessment is to measure social skills, then content validity helps determine how representative the results are to the entire domain of social skills. It would be difficult to measure all social skills, so the intent is to measure a representative and meaningful subset of the intended content or skills.

Content validity should answer the question: "How well does the content of this procedure constitute an adequate sample of the subject matter?" The primary step in answering this question is making the proper determination of the content of interest. For example, *leisure functioning* is a multidimensional concept and implies more than just activity skills. On the other hand, an assessment process can be unidimensional and measure only knowledge of leisure resources or some other limited content. The correct starting point (based on program content and client outcomes) is fundamental to determining content validity.

To help establish content validity, one must clearly define the domain or area to be measured, then construct or select a representative list of attitudes, knowledges, or skills. This may include a thorough review of the professional literature. It often is useful to make a test blueprint or table of specifications that identifies the numbers and percentages of types of items and content areas. The key task then is to adequately draw a sample from the many questions that might be included (Gronlund, 1993).

This is similar to teachers constructing classroom tests. "To maximize the validity of a classroom test, it should be as reliable as possible and should be explicitly linked, item for item, to what has been taught" (Green, 1991, p. 33). Content validity relies heavily on the use of expert judgment, as there are no statistics to measure content validity.

Evidence of *criterion-related validity* concerns the inferences or predictions made from a person's assessment results in relation to some other variable (an independent criterion). Criterion-related validity describes the extent to which test performance relates to some other valued measure of performance. It is used when one score (predictor) is used to estimate another score (criterion). Most individuals have experience with tests such as the ACT or the SAT (predictor) to predict success in college (criterion).

There are two types of criterion-related validity: concurrent validity and predictive validity. Both use the term "prediction" to examine the relationship of two sets of scores—the difference lies in the amount of time elapsing between the two test occurrences and how many variables are in question. In *concurrent validity*, the desire is to predict one set of scores from another set of scores measuring the same variable, taken at the same or nearly the same time. For example, a professional might want to be able to predict a client's score from one assessment covering leisure awareness (Leisure Awareness Assessment A) by knowing that person's results on a second assessment on leisure awareness (Leisure Awareness Assessment B). Testing could be completed with a sample or samples of clients to establish the concurrent validity of these two sets of assessment results from two different assessments covering approximately the same content or variable, taken at approximately the same time (i.e., concurrently). In both cases, the degree of relationship between the two variables is expressed through a correlation coefficient (r) (Gronlund, 1993).

A correlation coefficient expresses the degree of relationship between two sets of scores. There is a perfect, positive relationship if the person who scores the highest on the first set of scores also scores highest on the criterion set, the person who scores second-best on the first set also scores second-highest on the criterion set, and so on throughout the sample. The correlation between the test scores would have a value of +1.00 (perfect positive relationship). If the person who scores highest on the first set scores lowest on the criterion set, and the person who scores second-highest on the first set scores second-lowest on the criterion set, and on throughout the sample, this is said to have a perfect negative relationship. The correlation between the test scores would have a value of -1.00. A zero correlation indicates a complete absence of a systematic relationship (i.e., a random relationship) and is indicated by a 0.

In most cases for therapeutic recreation, a positive relationship between two sets of scores is desired (as a person's performance on one set of scores goes up, it also goes up on another set of scores). Depending on the purpose and the tests, correlations between r = +.40 to +.70 are within the acceptable range. (Conversely, if negative correlations are sought—as one set of scores goes up, the other set goes down—r values of -.40 to -.70 are acceptable.)

Predictive validity is concerned with how accurately one set of scores measuring one variable predicts a second set of criterion scores measuring a second variable taken at some point in the future. For example, a special-ist may want to know the degree to which future leisure satisfaction (criterion score: Leisure Satisfaction Test B) can be predicted from an assessment of leisure awareness immediately prior to discharge (predictor score: Leisure Awareness Test A). In this case, two variables are measured at different times, to test their predictive relationship. Measuring the predictive validity of these variables assumes many things, such as the reliabilities of the predictor score results and the criterion score results, time elapsed between tests, and value of the criterion. Usually predictive validity of any two sets of scores will be low because of all the possible sources of error likely to be present. Most assessments used in therapeutic recreation do not report criterion-related validity because of the difficulties involved in tracking clients after discharge, as well as the measurement difficulties involved.

One of the most difficult problems that the investigator of such assessments faces is locating or creating a satisfactory criterion measure. Four important characteristics must be present: (a) relevance, (b) freedom from bias, (c) reliability, and (d) availability. Defining and being able to measure a criterion well is important yet difficult. In addition, evidence of criterion-related validity is strengthened if the test sample is heterogeneous (i.e., as diverse as possible).

It should be noted that criterion-related validity is not the same as pretesting and posttesting. In criterion-related studies, one set of test results is used to predict a second set of test results, with the researcher being interested in the relationship between the predictor and the criterion (i.e., Can one set of scores predict the other?). In pretesting and posttesting, almost always the same test is given both before and after an individual or a group of individuals has been exposed to some treatment, such as an exercise program. Normally, the researcher uses the same test, focusing on the change of scores that came about (hopefully) as a result of the treatment (i.e., What effect did the treatment have?). Measuring evidence of criterion-related validity involves calculating the relationship between the scores on a test (assessment) and the criterion measure, using a correlation coefficient.

Evidence of *construct validity* is present when an unobservable trait is being measured to assure that it is being measured adequately (Peterson & Stumbo, 2000, p. 209). Familiar psychological constructs include self-esteem, anxiety, locus of control, extroversion, depression, and intelligence. Constructs in therapeutic recreation may include leisure lifestyle, wellness, leisure satisfaction, perceived freedom, leisure motivation, and quality of life. It is believed that these constructs exist, but they exist only to the degree that they can be described, organized, and tested.

The purpose of construct validity is to accumulate evidence that supports that the measurement tool truly measures the construct in question. Construct validity cannot be established with a single study on a single population; it is accomplished through statistical and rational means. For example, evidence for construct validity can be built through:

- Calculations of correlations with other tests that measure the same trait or construct

- Factor analysis (a statistical procedure)
- Convergent validity (what it measures)
- Discriminant validity (what it does not measure)
- Expert panel reviews of the test content

While not impossible, few therapeutic recreation assessments will utilize construct validity because the content focuses more on *behavior* (e.g., leisure participation patterns, acquiring leisure partners, or social interaction skills) or *knowledge* (e.g., leisure resources in the community, how to find information about leisure events) rather than *constructs* (e.g., leisure satisfaction or leisure motivation). Similarly, most therapeutic recreation programs focus on teaching behaviors rather than teaching constructs.

Typical Validity Questions

There are different methods of gathering evidence of validity, depending on the purpose of the measurement. Following are some questions that address validity.

Does the instrument measure what is needed to place the participant in the best possible program?

If the assessment examines only background information and the program is targeted to improve leisure skills and knowledge, another instrument(s) may be needed to appropriately place participants into programs that will afford them optimal benefits. The match between the content of the client assessment and the content of the therapeutic recreation intervention program was established in Chapter 1. That relationship forms a basis for establishing validity.

Does the assessment instrument yield similar results to what is known about the participant?

We often have the chance to observe participants and to gain information about them from a variety of sources. If the information is not similar, the validity of the instrument is in question. For example, an instrument may require considerable reading ability and cognitive skills, and the low scores of an illiterate individual may reflect reading ability and not leisure skills and knowledge that the instrument is attempting to measure. If the person received a low score, but all other indications were that the person had adequate leisure skills and knowledge, then the test results may have a low degree of validity.

Factors Affecting Validity

A number of factors can lower the evidence of validity in a set of assessment scores. What makes a test administration difficult? When do clients not do their best on the assessment? What factors influence, in a negative way, the scores received by individuals taking the test? Many individuals can think of less than optimal testing conditions, when they were not able to perform at their best, and when they felt they received scores lower than they should have. Below is a partial list of factors that reduce the validity of scores received by test takers, whether a national certification examination or a one-to-one client assessment. These should be avoided, reduced, or eliminated to the greatest extent possible. Doing so will reduce the score's error and improve the specialist's confidence in the results.

Factors in the Test Itself

- Unclear directions (written or oral)
- Reading vocabulary and sentence structure too difficult
- Inappropriate level of difficulty of the test items
- Poorly constructed test items
- Ambiguity or vagueness of the items
- Test items inappropriate for the outcomes being measured
- Test too short (inadequate sample of items)
- Too few items to test the domain
- Improper arrangement of items
- Identifiable pattern of responses

Functioning Content and Teaching Procedure

- Whether the item reflects the level of knowledge at which the content was or will be taught

Factors in Test Administration and Scoring

- Insufficient time to complete the test
- Unfair aid to persons who ask for help
- Cheating during the administration
- Excessive interruptions
- Not following standardized instructions for administration and scoring (e.g., subjective scoring or errors in score computations)
- Adverse physical and psychological conditions at the time of testing

Factors in the Person's Responses

- Personal factors within the individual (e.g., emotional problems)
- Test anxiety
- Lack of motivation
- Response set of the individual (e.g., working for speed rather than accuracy, gambling when in doubt)

Nature of the Group and Criterion

- Influence of such factors as age, gender, ability level, educational background, and cultural background

Each of these has a negative impact on the validity of test results. The person in charge of the testing or assessment process needs to make every effort to reduce error by minimizing the affect of these factors.

Reliability

Reliability "refers to the estimate of the consistency of measurement" (Peterson & Stumbo, 2000, p. 210). Reliability of assessment results means that a sample of persons would receive relatively the same scores when reexamined on different occasions, with a different set of equal items, or under specific conditions. Reliability estimates essentially ask: "How accurately and consistently does the instrument measure what it is intended to measure?" or "To what degree are the assessment scores free from errors of measurement?" The concept of true and error scores plays prominently in reliability. Error of measurement is defined as the degree of difference between a person's observed or obtained score and his or her true score. The goal is to increase the measurement of the true test score and reduce the amount of unintentional or random error (error variance) in the score as much as is possible.

Since a person's absolute true score is difficult to determine, reliability presents an estimate of the effects of changing conditions on the person's score. Reliability of assessment scores can be estimated in three ways:

1. Stability measures (How stable is the instrument over time?)
2. Equivalency measures (How closely related are two or more forms of the same assessment?)
3. Internal consistency measures (How closely are items on the assessment related?)

The type(s) of reliability tested on an assessment depends on the nature of the information needed and the purpose and intended use of the instrument. Methods of determining reliability are essentially means of determining how much error is present under different conditions.

Seven Points about Reliability

Much like the concept of validity, reliability is a measurement property or characteristic of a test or assessment. Reliability statistics provide an estimate of the degree of consistency or dependability of the assessment's results. Following are seven points concerning reliability.

1. Reliability refers to the results obtained with an assessment instrument and not the instrument itself.

Much like validity, to say a test is "reliable" is incorrect. A test's results are only reliable for certain groups of people, over certain periods of time, or between certain forms of a test. Some assessments may have higher degrees of internal consistency but have lower degrees of stability over time.

Again using the Leisure Diagnostic Battery (Witt & Ellis, 1987) as an example, remember that each assessment is tested for a particular use and for a particular population. To say that the LDB is "reliable" even given its long-standing research history is incorrect. As with any other assessment or measurement tool, the LDB is likely to produce results that have some degree of reliability for some uses and some groups of clients. Like validity, the user has to understand the concept of reliability and be able to judge from the information whether reliability might be inferred for the group in question.

2. An estimate of reliability always refers to a particular type of consistency.

There are three basic methods of estimating reliability: stability, equivalence, and internal consistency. Reliability is not a general trait of an assessment or its results; it is reported with regard to the particular estimate of reliability being studied. For example, an assessment may report an internal consistency coefficient of .73. Not surprisingly, that statistic only applies to the internal consistency of the instrument's results, not the equivalence or stability.

> Each of these methods [stability, equivalence, and internal consistency] of obtaining reliability provides a different type of information. Thus, reliability coefficients obtained with different procedures are not interchangeable. Before deciding on the procedure to be used, we must determine what type of reliability evidence we are seeking. (Gronlund, 1993, p. 169; clarification added)

3. *The reliability coefficient tells what proportion of the test variance is nonerror variance.*

The reliability coefficient reflects the proportion of variability in a set of scores that reflects true differences among individuals (Salvia & Ysseldyke, 1998). Because there is measurement error in every score, a certain amount of variation in test scores is expected from one time to another, from one sample of items to another, and from one part of the test to another. Reliability measures report an estimate of how much variation we might expect under different conditions (Gronlund, 1993). If there is relatively little error, the ratio of true score variance to obtained score variance approaches a reliability of 1.00 (perfect positive reliability). If there is a greater degree of error, the ratio of true score variance to obtained approaches zero (total unreliability). A test with a coefficient of .80 has relatively less measurement error and its results are more reliable than one with a reliability coefficient of .30 (Salvia & Ysseldyke, 1998). The acceptability of a reliability coefficient depends on the purpose for which the test is to be used.

4. *The reliability coefficient increases with the length of the test, a relationship that is much less pronounced for validity.*

As one might expect, the more items on a test, the more likely it is to measure the full range of the content in question. Therefore, the final score of an individual or group of individual would be considered more accurate or meaningful in explaining what is known about the content. Take archery as an example. If one arrow is shot into a target, how likely is that to be an accurate, dependable measure of one's ability to shoot an arrow into a target? However, if 15 shots are taken, a greater degree of confidence can be gained in estimating the accuracy of the individual's ability to shoot an arrow. If 100 shots are taken, an even better estimate of the person's true ability can be provided. However, 1,000 shots are probably not needed to get a good idea of the person's true archery ability. Not surprisingly, there is some limit to the length of any test or assessment. There is only so much time or so many resources to devote to the assessment process. The assessment instrument then becomes a trade-off between sampling as many items as possible to measure the content in question and the financial and time limits of its use.

5. *The reliability coefficient increases with the spread or variance of the scores.*

Since reliability indicates the amount of variance in a set of scores that represent individuals' true scores, the results should vary and reflect the range of responses held by the individuals. If some people have a high degree of leisure satisfaction and some people have a low degree of leisure satisfaction, the test results should reflect this variability accurately. The more the assessment reflects this range, the more it represents individual's true answers. If everyone receives the same score even though their true answers vary, the results are not reliable. This is easy to demonstrate on a yes/no type of item. If people actually have a variety of answers but they are forced to respond to a yes/no format, the results will not be reflective of their true scores, and the reliability coefficient will approach zero.

6. *A test may measure reliably at one level of performance and unreliably at another level.*

Items too difficult for some may cause them to guess, yielding unreliable but chance results. Items too easy for others provide reliable but nondiscriminatory information. For example, people with cognitive impairments may have difficulty responding to some items on an assessment; therefore, their results may not be a reliable indication of their true scores. However, for individuals with intact cognitive abilities, the assessment may produce more reliable results. The difficulty level of the assessment must be adjusted to the purposes of the testing and the people taking it.

7. *Reliability is a necessary but not a sufficient condition for validity.*

In addition to being important in its own right, reliability is necessary to obtain validity. After all, if an individual's test score fluctuated widely on a given sample of items, we could not expect the test to provide a valid measure . . . Thus, *reliability provides consistency that makes validity possible.* It should be noted, of course that consistency of results is just one important requirement for validity. We could be consistently measuring the wrong thing or using the scores inappropriately. Thus, reliability is a necessary, but not a sufficient, condition for validity. (Gronlund, 1993, p. 35)

We look for indices of reliability in test or assessment scores so we can generalize those to the person's true attitudes, knowledges, and behaviors. If a test is inconsistent and produces different results each time it is administered, the results cannot be easily generalized (Hoy & Gregg, 1994).

Ways to Estimate Reliability

There are three basic estimates of reliability: stability, equivalence, and internal consistency. **Table 2.2** (p. 46) illustrates the types of reliability estimates and the questions they represent.

Stability of test results is estimated through the use of test–retest correlation coefficients. Test–retest statistics calculate the relationship between scores obtained by a group of people on one administration of a test with their scores on a second administration of the same test. Obviously time lapsing between administrations is important. Too long of a period (months, years) and the change in scores may fluctuate due to error or change in the sample. Too short of a period (hours, days) and the first administration is likely to affect the second administration. The time period between testings should always be reported in test manuals and protocols, and should note any significant events that may have occurred to the sample group between administrations, such as other interventions or developmental growth.

Often the amount of error in reliability coefficients for test–retest procedures is artificially inflated. Any change in the individual's score due to outside influences such as maturation, growth, or learning adds to the error variance instead of the true score, unless each person in the test sample changes in exactly the same way. Any change in the person's true score is incorporated statistically into the error score. Generally then the closer in time the test and retest are given, the higher the reliability is

Table 2.2
Questions Addressed by Reliability Estimates

Type of Evidence	Question to be Addressed
Test–retest (stability)	How stable is the instrument over a given period of time? To what degree are the two sets of scores alike?
Equivalent forms (equivalency)	How closely related are scores from two or more forms of the same assessment? How consistent are test scores from different forms of the test (i.e., different samples of items)?
Internal consistency	How closely related are items on a single assessment related? How consistent are test scores over different parts of the test?

because within a shorter time, there is less chance of true scores changing (Salvia & Ysseldyke, 1998).

Equivalent-form reliability (also called *parallel-form reliability* or *alternative-form reliability*) is used to estimate the consistency between two forms of a test that have similar but not the same items. This condition attempts to reduce some of the time-based errors inherent in the test–retest situation. One group is given one form during one administration and the second form during the same or a soon-to-follow administration. The reliability coefficient is calculated between scores of the two forms. Reliability coefficients determined by this method take into account errors within the measurement procedure and consistency over different samples of items, but they do not include the stability or time factor of the individuals' responses, unless the administrations are staggered (Gronlund, 1993).

Thus, additional information can be obtained by performing a test–retest with equivalent forms. Two different forms of the same test are administered with some time intervening. This method allows an estimate of all possible sources of variation including errors within the testing procedure, consistency over different samples of items, and the stability of the individuals' responses. As such it allows for generalizations about the test results over various conditions. A high reliability coefficient would indicate a test score represents not only present test performance but also test performance at another time or with a different set of equivalent items (Gronlund, 1993).

Most therapeutic recreation assessments do not have identical equivalent forms. Some assessments have *short forms* (e.g., with 30 items) and *long forms* (e.g., with 60 items), but these are not truly equivalent forms. All things being equal, a test with more items will have a higher reliability (simply because it has more items to measure the content in question) and will show higher reliability coefficients.

Internal consistency is important for tests that only have one form and intend to be given only one time. Internal consistency statistics view each test as two halves that measure the same thing and can be compared with one another. Internal consistency estimates error within the testing procedure and consistency over different samples of items, but does not address stability of the individuals' responses (Gronlund, 1993). Similar to the above situation, test length or number of assessment items has an effect on internal consistency coefficient results. Since the two halves contain fewer items that the entire test, reliability coefficients for internal consistency are typically smaller.

There are a number of statistical calculations devised to calculate internal consistency, including (a) Spearman–Brown split-half reliability; (b) Kuder–Richardson's formulas; and (c) Cronbach's alpha.

Spearman–Brown's formula acknowledges that a half of a test will always have lower reliability than the whole test, and corrects for the smaller number of items. It estimates the reliability as if it were being reported for the whole test. The effect of using the Spearman–Brown formula is to increase the estimate of reliability (Kaplan & Saccuzzo, 1982).

Kuder and Richardson have two formulas; *Kuder–Richardson 20* and *Kuder–Richardson 21*. K–R 20 calculates the mean of all split-half coefficients resulting from different splittings of the test but is only appropriate for dichotomously scored answers (yes/no or true/false). K–R 21 is a simplified version that does not require the same complex calculations as K–R 20. It does assume that each item on the test is of equal difficulty and usually provides an underestimate of reliability (Gronlund, 1993; Kaplan & Saccuzzo, 1982).

Cronbach's alpha involves variance of individual test items as well as the total test score, and can be used on both dichotomously scored (yes/no) responses and those that have weighted scales. It also can be used when the two half-tests do not have equal variance (Kaplan & Saccuzzo, 1982). Alpha is considered a robust statistic and can be used in a variety of situations.

Each method has advantages and disadvantages, and is used best for certain types of tests. Those readers interested in more in-depth information are guided to psychological testing and statistics books.

A Special Case of Reliability

The previous discussion of validity and reliability focuses mostly on paper-and-pencil assessments, either conducted through interviews or self-administered. Another method of gathering assessment information is through observations. One of the major sources of error in observations is through the individual(s) performing the observation. In these cases, the specialist(s) can become a source of error because observations require the judgment of the specialist on whether or not the behavior occurred or to what degree the behavior occurred. The more concise and descriptive the behavioral observation tool, the less opportunity for rater error. Interrater reliability is calculated for observational recording.

One caution in calculating interrater reliability: There is a difference between agreement and accuracy. Even though two or more scorers agree, their observations may not be accurate to what actually occurred. Accuracy refers to the extent to which observations scored by an observer match those of a predetermined standard for the same data. Agreement reflects the extent to which observers agree on scoring behavior. Usually there is no firm basis to conclude that the one observer's data should serve as the standard (i.e., is accurate).

Salvia and Ysseldyke (1998) suggested four different methods for calculating interrater reliability: (a) simple agreement, (b) point-to-point agreement, (c) percentage of agreement for the occurrence of target behaviors, and (d) kappa index.

Simple agreement is calculated by first noting how many agreements and disagreements the two observers had in an observation schedule. The smaller number of occurrences (whether agreements or disagreements) is divided by the larger number of occurrences (whether agreements or disagreements) and then the total is multiplied by 100. For example, if there were 8 agreements and 10 disagreements, that would be 8 divided 10 and multiplied by 100 for a reliability coefficient of .80. However, this does not explain on what the observers agreed or disagreed (Salvia & Ysseldyke, 1998).

Point-to-point agreement takes each data point into consideration. It is calculated by adding the frequency of agreement for occurrences and the frequency of agreement for nonoccurrences, dividing this sum by the total number of observations, then multiplying the quotient by 100. For example, if two observers agreed on 3 occasions and disagreed on 7 occasions within a total of 20 observations, 3 plus 7 equals 10, divided by 20 is .50 and when multiplied by 100 equals 50. The reliability coefficient for point-to-point agreement would be .50.

Percentages of agreement for the occurrence of target behavior are calculated by multiplying 100 times the number of agreements on occurrence of the target behavior divided by the number of total observations minus the number of agreements on nonoccurrence. So if the observers agree 6 times on the number of occurrences and 8 times on the number of nonoccurrences within 20 observations, the calculation would be (100 times 6) divided by (20 minus 8) or 600 divided by 12 for a 50% agreement rating or a .50 reliability.

Since both the point-to-point and agreement of occurrence indexes can be affected by chance agreement, the *kappa index* was developed (Salvia & Ysseldyke, 1998). Although much more complex than the previous calculations, the kappa index represents the proportion of occurrences in relation to the proportion of expected occurrences. The formula is (proportion of occurrences minus the proportion of expected occurrences) divided by (1 minus the proportion of expected occurrences). The progression of these four formulas attempts to take into account the difference between agreement and accuracy.

Error Variance and True Score Variance

Table 2.3 displays the different ways to estimate reliability, depending on the number of tests and test administrations. **Table 2.4** describes the type of error variance examined by each type of reliability estimate. A reliability coefficient may be interpreted directly in terms of the percentage of score variance attributable to different sources. That is, a reliability coefficient of .85 signifies 85% of the variance in test scores depend on true variance of the trait measured and 15% is error variance (Anastasi, 1968). The developer and user are concerned with lowering error variance and increasing true score variance. Therefore, depending on the nature and the intended use of the test, a developer may choose to estimate several types of reliability, thereby analyzing the total score variance from different perspectives. Of course, this depends on the kind and purpose of the assessment.

Also, regardless of the type of reliability tested and reported, a well-constructed assessment with reasonable reliability indices can be made unreliable if standardized procedures are not followed. It remains extremely important to administer the test in the same manner it was given to the norm group (and reported in the assessment manual), and to keep the assessment environment free of unnecessary distractions that would introduce error (Hoy & Gregg, 1994). After an introduction to typical reliability questions, more information about ways in which reliability is lowered will be discussed.

Table 2.3
Ways to Estimate Reliability Considering Test Forms and Test Administrations (Adapted from Anastasi, 1968)

Test Administrations	Test Forms Required	
	One	Two
One	Internal consistency Interrater	Equivalent forms (immediate)
Two	Test–retest	Equivalent forms (delayed)

Typical Reliability Questions

There are several ways to estimate an assessment's reliability. Each depends on the nature and purpose of the assessment. Following are some questions that address reliability.

If the instrument is administered two or more times, with a short time between administrations, will the results be similar?

In a test–retest situation, it is hoped that nearly identical scores will be obtained by all individuals in the group, thereby, increasing the reliability coefficient (1.00 would mean the scores did not vary at all between the two administrations.) The lower the reliability coefficient, the greater the error variance, and the greater the instability of the test over time. When traits change little over time, test scores should reflect that minimal change and yield nearly the same results at multiple administrations.

If the participant is given two forms of the same instrument, will both yield similar results?

Sometimes the reliability of one instrument may be checked by administering another form of the same instrument. The purpose here would be to prove that the two forms of the test are equivalent or nearly equivalent, so that individuals receive nearly the same score from both tools. The reliability

Table 2.4
Sources of Error Variance
(Adapted from Gronlund, 1993)

Type of Reliability Coefficient	Error Variance
Test–retest	Time sampling
Equivalent forms (immediate)	Content sampling
Equivalent forms (delayed)	Time sampling and content sampling
Internal consistency (split half)	Content sampling
Internal consistency (Kuder–Richardson)	Content sampling and content heterogeneity
Interrater reliability	Interrater differences

coefficient explains the amount of variance between the two sets of scores, that indicates how different the forms of the tests are from one another. Most developers want the forms to be equal, and therefore want a high reliability coefficient between the two sets of scores.

How internally consistent is the test within itself? How well do items on the test converge to measure the same thing?

When only one test is given in one administration, it is important to test the internal *goodness* or *interitem consistency* (Anastasi, 1968) of the instrument. Since there is only one administration of one test to one group, the test is "split" into halves to determine how well the halves match or contribute to measuring the trait at hand. The different reliability coefficients used to measure internal consistency essentially split the test in different ways. For example, the Kuder–Richardson reliability coefficient is actually the mean of all split-half coefficients resulting from different item combinations of the test (Anastasi, 1968).

If two people administer the same instrument or observe the same event, will they record the results in the same way?

Instruments that have several open-ended questions and leave room for considerable variation in recording and interpretation are open for questions about reliability. Generally, instruments (including observations and checklists) should leave little room for individual judgments so that different observers always record the same behaviors in the same ways. In that way observations can become more accurate and more dependable.

Factors Influencing Reliability Measures

Like validity, a number of factors influence and sometimes artificially lower the reliability of an assessment's results. In many cases, these factors introduce unwanted error variance. Some of these factors include:

Length of Test. In general, the longer the test, the higher the reliability. A longer test also tends to lessen the influence of chance factors such as guessing.

Spread of Scores. Other things being equal, the larger the spread of scores, the higher the estimate of reliability. (Arbitrarily manipulating the wording of test items, simply to make them more difficult, is likely to result in increased reliability at the expense of validity.)

Difficulty of Items. Norm-referenced tests that are too easy or too difficult for the group members taking it will tend to provide scores of low reliability. This is because both easy and difficult tests result in a restricted set of scores. As noted earlier, the bigger the spread of scores, the greater the likelihood that the measured differences are reliable.

Objectivity. The objectivity of a test refers to the degree to which equally competent scorers obtain the same results. A desirable solution is to select the evaluation procedure most appropriate for the behavior being evaluated and then to make the evaluation procedures as objective as possible.

Lasting and General Characteristics of the Individual. Sometimes the individual has a general set of skills or behaviors that influences how he or she completes the assessment. These might include general skills (e.g., reading), general ability to comprehend instructions (e.g., testwiseness, techniques for taking tests), ability to solve problems of the general type presented on this assessment, and attitudes, emotional reactions, or habits generally operating in assessment situations (e.g., self-confidence).

Lasting and Specific Characteristics of the Individual. Sometimes an individual also has specific responses to certain stimuli, such as knowledge and skills required by particular problems in the test, and attitudes, emotional reactions or habits related to particular test stimuli (e.g., fear of high places brought to mind by an inquiry about such fears on a personality test).

Temporary and General Characteristics of the Individual. These characteristics systematically affect performance on various assessments at a particular time, including: (a) health, fatigue, and emotional strain; (b) motivation and rapport with examiner; (c) testing conditions (e.g., effects of heat, light, and ventilation); and (d) present attitudes, emotional reactions, or strength of habits (insofar as these are departures from the person's average or lasting characteristics—e.g., political attitudes during an election campaign).

Temporary and Specific Characteristics of the Individual. These might include: (a) changes in fatigue or motivation developed by this particular test (e.g., discouragement resulting from failure on a particular item); (b) fluctuations in attention, coordination or standards of judgment; (c) fluctuations in memory for particular facts; (d) level of practice on skills or knowledge required by this particular test (e.g., effect of special coaching); (e) temporary emotional states and strength of habits related to particular test stimuli (e.g., question calls to mind a recent bad dream); and (f) luck in the selection of answers by guessing.

Analogy for Validity and Reliability

Figure 2.1 helps to visualize the relationship between validity and reliability. Reliability is a necessary, but not sufficient condition for validity. That means that a higher degree of reliability must be present to be able to infer the results have validity. If not, the shots go off target (as in the first example)—the instrument is measuring *something* accurately, just not what the test was intending to measure. In the second case, the test results are valid but not reliable; a condition we know cannot exist in real life. That is, if something is not being measured accurately, then there is too much error and the test results are not reporting what we are claiming to measure. In the final case, the test results are both reliable and valid. The test results show that there is minimal error variance and higher true score variance, therefore measuring what we intend to with a higher degree of accuracy and dependability.

Fairness

Fairness, the reduction or elimination of undue bias, is also a special consideration in assessments (Kubiszyn & Borich, 1993). The aim is to reduce any introduction of bias that would artificially lower an individual's or a subgroup's scores because of inflammatory, biased, or specialized information. For example, assessments that refer to all individuals as "he" or stereotype the kinds of activities that certain ethnic or racial groups or genders might be involved in, may be seen as biased by individuals taking the assessment. When that happens, the emotional reactions from reading or hearing that information may cause the individual's score to be affected

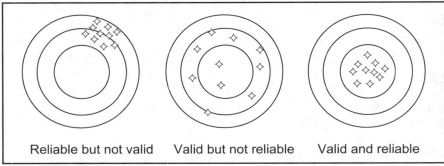

| Reliable but not valid | Valid but not reliable | Valid and reliable |

Figure 2.1
Analogy of Reliability and Validity

artificially. It is the duty of the assessment developer and user to screen for potentially biased and unfair items and content. For the test developer, such a review comes before the completion of the assessment. Asking other individuals who are sensitive to biased language or situations to review the assessment for fairness is a major step in reducing undue bias. This method does not necessarily involve statistics, but instead relies on the expert judgments of individuals familiar with bias and fairness (Ward & Murray-Ward, 1999). "When emotions are stimulated by gender-biased or racially biased items, those emotions can interfere with valid measurement, leaving us results that are less useful than they would be otherwise" (Kubiszyn & Borich, 1993, p. 99). Bias results in increased error variance.

Typical Fairness Questions

Fairness should be considered from as many perspectives as possible. Following is a partial list of questions that address fairness.
- How well are a variety of ethnic and racial backgrounds represented in the assessment examples?
- Are both genders represented nearly equally?
- How well are situations or examples given free of stereotypes and bias?
- To what degree is the language used free of bias and stereotypes?

Practicality and Usability

The final characteristics of tests and assessments to consider are practicality and usability. Ward and Murray-Ward (1999) indicated that *practicality* involves two aspects: whether the assessment (a) is "doable" and (b) serves the purpose for which it was intended in ways better than other available assessments. In the first case, there are some very practical considerations that become important, such as the user's time and level of expertise, and the costs in both monetary and human resource factors. In addition, considerations about the assessment itself such as the ease of administration, scoring, interpretation, and application or reporting, as well as the availability of accompanying documentation, protocols, and technical support become important.

The second aspect, the appropriateness of the assessment for the specific use, clearly depends on the potential user's answers to the previously mentioned factors. When the user evaluates the tool or procedure to make decisions about whether or not to adopt it, the basic question becomes: "Is this tool, given its validity, reliability, fairness, and practicality to my situation, better than any other tool on the market or that I could develop?" This is a very important question and must be answered with care.

Typical Usability/Practicality Questions

Following are some questions that may be considered when evaluating the practicality of an assessment tool. The answers to these questions are as important, and sometimes more important, than other criteria for evaluating an assessment.

- Is the instrument easily available and affordable to the user?
- How easy is the assessment to administer, score, interpret, and apply the results?
- How much time is required for administration, scoring, and interpretation?
- What is the availability of equivalent forms?
- What is the cost of each administration?
- How much time will it take to train staff to administer, score, and interpret the results of the instrument?
- How well is the assessment protocol described in the accompanying documentation?

Validation

Validation is the "process of gathering information about the appropriateness of inferences" or interpretations about a test or assessment (Salvia & Ysseldyke, 1998, p. 167). An assessment is validated through the systematic gathering of information that converges to inform the user whether or not the assessment is an appropriate, dependable, usable instrument for the intended purposes. The prior discussions about validity, reliability, fairness, and usability are important to understanding how a test can be validated and how a test can be evaluated for use.

There are three basic premises about test and assessment validation. First, evidence of reliability and validity increases the confidence that can be placed in the results of the instrument. If no information is given or the information or method used in incorrect or inconclusive, the user may reconsider whether the instrument is appropriate for his or her use. Second, the type of reliability and validity evidence that needs to be presented to the user depends on the type of instrument and how the results are to be used. For example, demonstrating evidence of criterion-related validity is appropriate only when the user is trying to predict a future or concurrent score from a present score. If there is no interest in this prediction, then evidence of criterion-related validity is not necessary. Third, multiple measures of validity and reliability increase the confidence in the results. That is, multiple measures or multiple trials help further establish evidence of reliability and validity. Conducting one test–retest is good; conducting two test–retests and calculating the internal consistency is better. The more evidence gathered the better to increase the confidence of the user.

Gronlund (1993) suggested a variety of ways to enhance validity and reliability while constructing a test or assessment. **Table 2.5** (p. 58) outlines some of these methods. More specific methods, in addition to these, are the topic of this section on validation.

The likelihood of developing a valid, reliable, fair, and usable assessment improves when following these steps:

1. Determine the purpose of the assessment
2. Develop the assessment specifications
3. Select and prepare appropriate item types
4. Validate items and the assessment

This section will focus on the first, second, and fourth steps; more information about the third step is detailed in Chapter 7.

Determine the Purpose of the Assessment

Two basic actions come under the heading of determining the purpose of the assessment. First, specify for which purpose the assessment is to be designed and used. Second, define the domain to be tested.

Specify the Purpose

The first step in developing and validating an assessment is to specify its purpose (Gronlund, 1993; Ward & Murray-Ward, 1999). For what purpose(s) will the assessment be used? For therapeutic recreation assessments, we can refer back to the purposes of client assessment presented in Table 1.1. These include:

- Individual client information
  - Initial baseline assessment (treatment planning/program placement)

Table 2.5
Ways to Enhance Validity and Reliability during Test Construction
(Adapted from Gronlund, 1993, p. 35)

Desired Features	Procedures to Follow
1. Clearly specified set of client outcomes.	1. State intended client outcomes in performance terms.
2. Assessment items are representative sample of clearly defined domain of client outcomes.	2. Prepare table of specifications or similar device for defining the domain and sample items.
3. Assessment items are relevant to the client outcomes to be measured.	3. Match the tasks tested with the specified task in the client outcomes.
4. Items are an appropriate level for effective assessment.	4. Match the intent of the assessment task with the client to be tested, as well as the use made of the results.
5. Items function effectively, distinguishing between those who need services and those who do not.	5. Follow general guidelines and specific rules for item writing and be alert for factors that distort the results.
6. Sufficient number of items to measure an adequate sample of attitudes, skills, or behaviors; provide dependable scores; and allow for a meaningful interpretation of scores.	6. Where the client's ages, limitations, or available assessment time constrict the number of items, test more frequently. When fewer than 10 items measure a task, use clusters of items and broader interpretation.
7. An assessment format that contributes to efficient assessment administration.	7. Write clear directions and arrange items for ease of responding, scoring, and interpretation.

- • Monitoring progress (formative information)
- • Summarizing progress (summative information)
- • Research on program efficacy and effectiveness
- • Communication within and among disciplines
- • Administrative requirements

As mentioned earlier, the most common use of client assessments in therapeutic recreation is placement of clients into intervention programs. Although other purposes are worthy, the following discussion will assume client placement into programs to be the primary concern.

Define the Domain

The next step involves defining the domain to be tested (Gronlund, 1993; Ward & Murray-Ward, 1999). What content should be on the assessment? As mentioned at the end of Chapter 1, this question has both a complex and a simple answer. Both rely on how the therapeutic recreation specialist has developed his or her overall therapeutic recreation program. On what theory or set of theories is the program designed? On the basis of what therapeutic recreation practice model was the therapeutic recreation program developed? How coherent is the program? How well does it address the overall needs of the clients? These questions and how they might be addressed within therapeutic recreation are presented in more depth in the next chapter. In the meantime, for the purposes of illustration, we'll use the Leisure Ability Model (Peterson & Stumbo, 2000) to define the domain of leisure lifestyle and therapeutic recreation practice.

The Leisure Ability Model uses three areas of service: (a) functional intervention, (b) leisure education, and (c) recreation participation. Leisure education contains: (a) leisure awareness, (b) leisure activity skills, (c) social interaction skills, and (d) leisure resources. The therapeutic recreation specialist is responsible for designing the comprehensive and specific programs that align with this model and meet the needs of clients. Say the specialist decides that the following areas are priorities, based on client need:

- • Leisure awareness
  - • Leisure barriers
  - • Leisure activity opportunities
- • Social skills
  - • Conversational skills
  - • Health and hygiene skills

- Leisure resources
  - Personal resources
  - Home resources

The specialist then has three tasks: (a) define the general outcomes to be achieved by clients in each area, (b) define those general outcomes in more specific terms, and (c) decide how to assess those outcomes. The general outcomes can be equated with client goals, or in systems language, *terminal performance objectives* (TPOs). The more detailed specifications are client objectives, or in systems terminology, *enabling objectives* (EOs) and *performance measures* (PMs). (See Peterson & Stumbo, 2000, for more information about systems design in therapeutic recreation programming.) The specialist must then begin to decide (although this may later be modified) how that information will be assessed—for example, through observation, interview, or self-administered assessments.

Following is an example of the domain to be tested, the general outcomes, the specific outcomes, and how those outcomes will be assessed.
Domain: Social Skills
General Outcome: To initiate conversation with new group of people
Specific Outcome:

1. After two weeks in the Social Skills program, the client will:
   a. Identify when interruption is appropriate
   b. Stand within two feet of group
   c. Make eye contact
   d. Listen to conversation of group without immediate interruption
   e. Say hello to known person(s)
   f. Make eye contact
   g. Use appropriate gestures in greeting
   h. Add to topic, ask questions, offer to help or otherwise contribute to conversation, while using appropriate gestures, and maintaining body space, as judged by the TRS

The next step is to develop an assessment blueprint or table of specifications.

Develop the Assessment Specifications

There are three steps in developing the assessment specifications: (a) selecting the client outcomes to be assessed, (b) outlining the content, and

(c) make a two-way chart that provides an overview of the outcomes and content (Gronlund, 1993; Gronlund & Linn, 1990; Kubiszyn & Borich, 1993; Salvia & Ysseldyke, 1998; Ward & Murray-Ward, 1999).

Select the Client Outcomes to be Tested

It is important to know the client outcomes expected from participation in the therapeutic recreation intervention programs as a starting point for building the client assessment. The specified client outcomes depend on the specific types of programs offered, the theory or model upon which the programs are based, the specific needs of the clients, and other factors that impact the types and range of programs offered. For example, what is the aim of each of the programs? To change attitudes? To teach certain knowledge and facts (perhaps about resources)? To teach specific skills or behaviors? These go in concert with the content of the programs and assessment.

Outline the Assessment Content

The content of the assessment must match the content of the programs offered. That means that the outline of the assessment content must be in alignment with the content outlined in the program design. In our previous example, we specified the following areas for the intervention program:
- Leisure awareness
  - Leisure barriers
  - Leisure activity opportunities
- Social skills
  - Conversational skills
  - Health and hygiene skills
- Leisure resources
  - Personal resources
  - Home resources

It follows that the assessment content must match this outline with leisure awareness, social skills, and leisure resources. Although some information about background and functional abilities may be included on the assessment, these are the primary areas that should be included. Information on an assessment should relate to being able to place the right client into the right program for participation.

Make The Two-Way Chart

The third step is to make a two-way chart or table of specifications for the assessment instrument. The purpose of this table of specifications is to ensure that the assessment is representative of the content of the programs and intended client outcomes. It involves taking both the client outcomes along one axis and the content along the other, to show that the assessment in being built according to the programs offered and the outcomes targeted. The designer must decide how much emphasis will be given to each area. This again depends on the program. If the social skills program is daily for 2 hours, and the leisure awareness program is once a week for 1 hour, the relative weights within the table should reflect that.

Table 2.6 outlines a possible table of specifications given the information from the above example. The numbers in the middle of the table reflect how many items are to be devoted on the assessment to that area. The numbers reflect the relative weights for each area at that particular agency. More emphasis in programming should translate to more items on the assessment. Gronlund (1993) outlined a number of questions to determine those relative weights:

- How important is each area in the total programming process?
- How much of the program is devoted to each area?
- Which outcomes have greater retention and transfer value?
- What relative importance does the therapeutic recreation specialist assign to each area?

Weights in each category should accurately represent the emphasis given during programming. In this example, social skills and leisure resources have a larger emphasis than leisure awareness. More detail may be necessary to actually build the assessment than given on this table.

Select and Prepare Appropriate Item Types

After the table of specifications has been developed and refined, the next step involves writing and improving questions to be included on the assessment. These tasks include: (a) selecting the types of items to use, (b) matching the items to the specific client outcomes, (c) improving the functioning content of the items, (d) selecting the proper item difficulty, and (e) determining the number of assessment items to use. These tasks are discussed in more detail in Chapter 7.

Validate Items and the Assessment

After the content and emphasis has been defined and the items written, the final, ongoing step is to collect evidence of validity and reliability of the assessment's results. The following provides a brief summary of the steps to be taken to provide evidence of validity and reliability.

A Few Measurement Reminders

- Every measurement instrument results in a score that possesses some degree of error. The mission of validation is to reduce the error as much as possible.
- Each score consists of a combination of a true score and error score. The error score or variance error is the part validation tries to reduce.

Table 2.6
Sample Table of Specifications

	Attitudes # of items	Knowledges # of items	Behaviors # of items	Total # items
Leisure awareness				
Leisure barriers	3	3	2	
Leisure activity opportunities	0	4	3	15
Social skills				
Conversa-tional skills	0	4	5	
Health and hygiene skills	2	4	5	20
Leisure resources				
Personal resources	2	3	4	
Home resources	2	3	4	18
Total	9	21	23	53

- Validity and reliability are a matter of degree—not automatic and not absolute. The confidence of an assessment's results can be improved by collecting as much evidence as possible about the assessment's validity and reliability.

- All reliability and most validity depend on reliability coefficients. The correlation coefficients range from -1.00 to +1.00. A -1.00 reliability means that as one score increases, the other decreases at the same rate (a direct negative relationship). A zero reliability means there is no direct relationship between the scores. A +1.00 score means that as one score increases, the other also increases at the same rate (a direct positive relationship). Usually correlation coefficients of .40 to .70 are considered acceptable, depending on the nature and purpose of the measurement.

Deciding What Type(s) of Validation Are Needed

Establishing the purpose of the assessment helps indicate what types of validation procedures need to be conducted. Consider the following examples:

- If the test user wishes to determine how an individual performs at present in a universe of situations that the test situation is claimed to represent, collect evidence of *content validity*.

- If the tester wishes to forecast an individual's future standing or to estimate an individual's present standing on some variable of particular significance that is different from the test, collect evidence of *criterion-related validity*.

- If the test user wishes to infer the degree to which the individual possesses some hypothetical trait or quality (construct) presumed to be reflected in the test performance, collect evidence of *construct validity*.

Gronlund (1993) reminds us:

For some interpretations of test scores only one or two types of evidence may be critical, but an *ideal* validation would include evidence from all three categories. We are most likely to draw valid inferences from test scores when we have a full understanding of: (1) the nature of the test content and the specifications that were used in developing the test, (2) the relation of the test scores to significant criterion measures, and (3) the nature of the psychological characteristic(s) or construct(s) being measured by the test. Although in many practical situations the evidence falls short of this ideal, we should gather as much relevant evidence as is feasible within the constraints of the situation. (p. 161)

The same holds true for reliability information. The type of instrument and its purpose determines which reliability test is most appropriate, and multiple instances of reliability information help increase the confidence in the assessment's results. Consider the following examples:

- If the tester wishes to establish that the test results remain stable over time, use the *test–retest method*.

- If the tester wishes to establish that two forms have "equal amounts" of reliability, use the *equivalent forms method*.

- If the tester wishes to establish that one form has reliability within itself, use the *internal consistency methods*.

Ways to collect evidence for validity will be reviewed first, and then ways to collect reliability evidence will be discussed.

Content Validity

Content validity is the extent to which a test or instrument measures a representative sample of the domain of tasks or content under consideration (e.g., Does assessment represent important aspects of program and independent leisure lifestyle?).

Ways to Establish Content Validity

- Define area to be measured and establish its relevance to the intended outcomes.

- Review professional literature, opinions of experts, or logical analysis of target program or behaviors.

- Create assessment blueprint (or table of specifications) that identifies major elements of content, then write items for each element. The finished assessment should be proportional to the specifications on the table.

Criterion-Related Validity

Criterion-related validity is the extent to which test performance is related to some other valued measure of performance. It is used when an estimate of "other" performance needs to be predicted, in the future or at the same time, from another score or instrument—the criterion). It is normally called *predictive validity* when one score is used to predict another in the future. It is called *concurrent validity* when the prediction is simultaneous.

Ways to Establish Criterion-Related Validity
- Use logical inference that criterion is acceptable and reasonable.
- Calculate validity correlations between instrument results and criterion results.

Construct Validity

Construct validity is the extent to which test performance can be interpreted in terms of certain psychological constructs. A *construct* is a psychological trait or quality that we assume exists to explain some aspect of behavior.

Ways to Establish Construct Validity
- Define concepts or constructs to be measured by conducting extensive literature review of the theoretical framework.
- Describe the development of the test, including any aspects of measurement that may affect the meaning and interpretation of scores.
- Collect evidence of content validity and criterion-related validity, if necessary.
- Calculate validity coefficients and determine patterns of relationships between the results of this measurement instrument and others that measure the same construct.
- Compare scores of this instrument and other related instruments by the scores of known groups.
- Compare the scores of the instrument before and after some targeted treatment or intervention.
- Perform factor analysis for subcomponents of instrument—see how items "load" on certain factors.
- Analyze mental processes used in responding to the items.

Reminder: General Threats to Evidence of Validity

- *Instrument*: unclear directions, unclear/ambiguous items, items too easy/too difficult, pattern of responses.

- *Administration*: varying directions or methods, environmental factors, insufficient time, interruptions.
- *Subjects*: attitudes, motivation, health, reluctance, response set, rapport, perceived credibility.
- *Reliability*: lack of reliability threatens validity.
- *Intended use*: constructed for one purpose but used for another, may not be valid.

Reliability

Reliability refers to the consistency of measurement—how consistent test scores or other evaluation results are from one measurement to another.

Ways of Estimating Reliability
- *Test–retest method* (measure of stability): Give the same test twice to the same group with a short time interval between tests. Compute a correlation coefficient to relate the scores of the first and second testing.
- *Equivalent forms method* (measure of equivalence): Give two forms of the test to one group. Compute a correlation coefficient to relate the scores of the two forms.
- *Test–retest with equivalent forms* (measure of stability and equivalence): Give two forms of the test to the same group with time interval between forms. Compute a correlation coefficient to relate the scores on the two forms.
- *Split-half method* (measure of internal consistency): Give test once. Score two equivalent halves of test (e.g., odd vs. even items); correct reliability coefficient to fit whole test by Spearman–Brown formula.
- *Kuder–Richardson* (measure of internal consistency): Give test once. Score total test and apply the appropriate Kuder–Richardson formula.
- *Alpha* (measure of internal consistency): Give test once. Score total test and apply formula to compute alpha.
- *Interrater reliability* (measure of rater consistency): Have more than one rater observe the same situation. Compute: (a) simple agreement, (b) point-to-point agreement, (c) percentage of agreement for the occurrence of target behaviors, and/or (d) kappa index.

Reminder: General Threats to Reliability

- *Length of test*: The longer the test, the higher the reliability; lessens chance factors such as guessing.

- *Spread of scores*: The larger the spread of scores, the higher the estimate of reliability.

- *Difficulty of items*: Problems with items if they are too easy or too difficult; because both easy and difficult tests result in a restricted set of scores. As noted earlier, the bigger the spread of scores, the greater the likelihood that the measured differences are reliable.

- *Objectivity*: The degree to which equally competent scorers obtain the same results.

- *Lasting and general characteristics of the individual*: Reading skills, general skills, comprehension, attitudes, habits.

- *Lasting and specific characteristics of the individual*: Knowledge/skill, attitudes, reactions to specific test questions.

- *Temporary and general characteristics of the individual*: Health, fatigue, motivation, rapport, testing conditions.

- *Temporary and specific characteristics of the individual*: Fluctuations in memory, motivation, attention.

Summary

This chapter covered the measurement properties of validity, reliability, fairness, and usability. Validity is a matter of degree. Test validation includes collecting evidence of content validity, criterion-related validity, and construct validity. Each of these concepts was defined and ways to increase their evidence was presented. Reliability is also an important measurement characteristic of assessment tools. It is also a matter of degree and addresses how consistent the assessment's results are over time, over occasions, or between people. Ways to estimate reliability were discussed. Fairness improves both the validity and reliability by treating all test takers equally. Usability is a nonmeasurement term concerned with the instrument's ease of use and cost. The next chapter infuses all these topics with therapeutic recreation programming and its relationship to client assessment.

References

Anastasi, A. (1968). *Psychological testing* (3rd ed.). London, UK: Macmillan Company.

Green, K. E. (1991). Reliability, validity, and test score interpretation. In K. E. Green (Ed.), *Educational testing: Issues and applications*. New York, NY: Garland Publishing.

Gronlund, N. E. (1993). *How to make achievement tests and assessments* (5th ed.). Boston, MA: Allyn & Bacon.

Gronlund, N. E. and Linn, R. L. (1990). *Measurement and evaluation in teaching* (6th ed.). New York, NY: Macmillan Publishing.

Hoy, C. and Gregg, N. (1994). *Assessment: The special educator's role*. Pacific Grove, CA: Brooks/Cole Publishing.

Kaplan, R. M. and Saccuzzo, D. P. (1982). *Psychological testing: Principles, applications, and issues*. Monterey, CA: Brooks/Cole Publishing.

Kubiszyn, T. and Borich, G. (1993). *Education testing and measurement: Classroom application and practice* (4th ed.). New York, NY: Harper Collins.

Peterson, C. A. and Stumbo, N. J. (2000). *Therapeutic recreation program design: Principles and procedures* (3rd ed.). Needham Heights, MA: Allyn & Bacon.

Salvia, J. and Ysseldyke, J. E. (1998). *Assessment* (7th ed.). Boston, MA: Houghton Mifflin.

Stumbo, N. J. (2001). Revisited: Issues and concerns in therapeutic recreation assessment. In N. J. Stumbo (Ed.), *Professional issues in therapeutic recreation: On competence and outcomes* (pp. 215–236). Champaign, IL: Sagamore Publishing.

Ward, A. W. and Murray-Ward, M. (1999). *Assessment in the classroom*. Belmont, CA: Wadsworth Publishing.

Witt, P. A. and Ellis, G. D. (1987). *The Leisure Diagnostic Battery users manual*. State College, PA: Venture Publishing, Inc.

Chapter 3
Therapeutic Recreation
Program Considerations

Client assessment intricately relates to therapeutic recreation intervention programming. When the aim is to produce meaningful, predictable, and targeted client outcomes, assessment cannot be separated from program design and delivery.

For many therapeutic recreation specialists, however, these relationships are not practiced and a disconnect exists between client assessment and program design and client outcomes. While most therapeutic recreation specialists excel at designing and delivering programs, the programs often have little connection to a solid assessment of client need, and therefore are not aimed at specific, measurable client outcomes. The importance of credible client assessment to intervention program delivery and client outcomes is not well-understood or practiced. However, output cannot be measured if the input is not known. Assessment has been neglected because it is "too hard," because it involves measurement (and therefore statistics), because worthless assessments have been marketed unscrupulously, and because professionals have been nonchalant. The state of affairs of client assessment in therapeutic recreation is less than desirable. See **Figure 3.1** (p. 72; adapted from Peterson & Stumbo, 2000, p. 62) for an illustration of the relationship between program design/activity analysis and client characteristics/assessment that produces intervention programs and client outcomes.

Although it might be unusual to have a chapter on programming in an assessment text, it is provided to reinforce the relationship between the two. **Table 3.1** (p. 73; adapted from Gronlund, 1993) illustrates the ways in which intervention and client assessment are similar. Both require that the client outcomes be clearly specified, and that the assessment closely parallel the intervention to be provided.

One of the first steps in making the connection is to determine which theories and model of service best fits the agency's purpose and clients' needs. Chapter 1 provided a brief overview of the need to establish theory-based practice and Caldwell (2001) provided an excellent and common sense approach to this issue. The selection of a practice model to provide the basic blueprint for services is also important (Peterson, 1989; Ross & Ashton-Shaeffer, 2001).

The Leisure Ability Model (Peterson & Stumbo, 2000) has been chosen within this text and others as the basis for program design and delivery. The choice of a model makes an impact on the types of assessments and interventions that will be appropriate. In referring to the practice of psychology, Palmer and McMahon (1997) made a similar point:

> It is important to appreciate that [the counselor's] particular model of counseling (that is the theoretical framework in which [he or she was] trained) will make assumptions about the nature of the human condition—about what it means to be human. These assumptions will fundamentally colour the counsellor's beliefs about the nature of the problems for which people seek help, the type of intervention which should be offered and the significance and meaning of the relationship between [the counselor] and the person [he or she] hope[s] to assist. (pp. 13–14)

This chapter provides basic background information on designing therapeutic recreation intervention programs as it relates to client assessment; however, the reader is referred to Peterson and Stumbo (2000) for a fuller description and explanation of comprehensive and specific program design. A solid understanding of the concepts and rationale underlying the provision of therapeutic recreation services is needed by all individuals who desire and profess to practice.

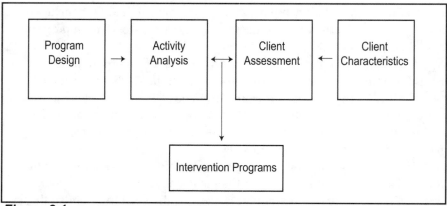

Figure 3.1
Input Considerations for Delivering Intervention Programs
(Peterson & Stumbo, 2000, p. 62)

Table 3.1
Relationship between Intervention and Client Assessment
(Adapted from Gronlund, 1993)

Intervention	Client Assessment
Intervention is most effective when:	*Client assessment is most effective when:*
1. It is directed toward a clearly defined set of intended client outcomes.	1. It is designed to measure a clearly defined set of intended client outcomes.
2. The methods and materials of intervention are congruent with the outcomes to be achieved.	2. The nature and function of the assessment items is congruent with the outcomes to be measured.
3. It is designed to fit the characteristics and needs of the clients.	3. The assessment items are designed to fit reading level and other relevant client characteristics.
4. Intervention decisions are based on meaningful, dependable, and relevant information.	4. The assessment results provide meaningful, dependable, and relevant information.
5. Clients are periodically informed concerning their progress.	5. Provision is made for giving the client early feedback of the assessment results.
6. Remediation is provided for clients not achieving their intended outcomes.	6. Individual assessment items or clusters of items reveal specific client weaknesses.
7. Intervention effectiveness is periodically reviewed and the intended client outcomes and intervention are modified as needed.	7. Assessment results provide information useful for evaluating the appropriateness of the objectives, methods, and materials of the intervention.

Foundational Concepts of Therapeutic Recreation Services

This section overviews several foundational concepts of therapeutic recreation services, including: (a) a leisure lifestyle, (b) a rationale for therapeutic recreation services, and (c) the Leisure Ability Model (Peterson & Stumbo, 2000).

Leisure Lifestyle

The rationale that follows has been established through a logical set of assumptions concerning typical adult leisure behavior. Primary to this discussion is the concept of *leisure lifestyle*. It has been defined as follows:

> Leisure lifestyle [is] the day-to-day behavioral expression of one's leisure-related attitudes, awareness, and activities revealed with the context and composite of the total life experience. (Peterson, 1981, p. 1)

Leisure lifestyle implies that an individual has sufficient skills, knowledges, attitudes, and abilities to participate successfully in and be satisfied with leisure and recreation experiences that are incorporated into his or her individual life pattern. An essential aspect of leisure lifestyle is the focus on day-to-day behavioral expression. This implies that leisure lifestyle is a routine engaged in as a part of the individual's daily schedule. The quality of and activities within one's leisure lifestyle may vary, but the fact remains that each person has one. Traditional and nontraditional leisure activities and expressions are an ongoing aspect of living. Daily actions thus can be used to describe and characterize the essence of an individual's unique leisure lifestyle. Additionally, the leisure lifestyle of a person cannot be viewed independently of all other actions. Other aspects of the person's behaviors and patterns (e.g., work, school, religion, family, friends, community, health) interface with the individual's leisure lifestyle. Likewise, the individual's leisure lifestyle is influenced by collective and accumulated life experiences. These participation and satisfaction levels ultimately speak to a person's quality of life and happiness.

As such the concept of leisure lifestyle becomes the both the alpha and omega of programming. It acts as the *input* (starting point) to guide program design decisions on what content should be included in the total therapeutic recreation intervention program. It also serves as the *outcome* (end point) of all therapeutic recreation intervention programs in that the therapeutic recreation specialist provides programs to assist clients in developing and living a satisfying leisure lifestyle. The savvy therapeutic recreation specialist considers the typical leisure lifestyles of the clients he or she serves prior to planning, implementing, or evaluating therapeutic recreation programs. Using leisure lifestyle as a basis, the therapeutic recreation services rationale can be promoted and discussed. A sound rationale can be used to explain and justify providing a specific set of programs and activities for clients to reach desired outcomes.

Rationale for Therapeutic Recreation Services

The first assumption underlying therapeutic recreation services is that every human being needs, wants, and deserves leisure. Leisure presents contexts to try new behaviors, experience mastery, learn new skills, meet new people, deepen existing relationships, and develop a clearer sense of self. Leisure provides the context in which people can learn, take risks, interact, express individualism, and self-actualize (Kelly, 1990). Leisure tends to have less serious boundaries and consequences, as opposed to other activities, such as work. The benefits of leisure are numerous, diverse, and defined by the individual. **Table 3.2** (p. 76) provides an abbreviated list of benefits of therapeutic recreation programs that have been derived from Coyle, Kinney, Riley, and Shank (1991) and Peterson and Stumbo (2000).

The second assumption is that many (if not most) individuals experience barriers to full and satisfying leisure. For example, some individuals may view leisure as wasteful; some may not know how to access information about leisure opportunities; some may lack skills in meeting new people or establishing meaningful relationships; some may have safety and welfare concerns that prevent them from entering leisure facilities; and some may feel they have inadequate discretionary money to spend on leisure. While many adults overcome these barriers or learn to compensate for their consequences, many are constrained from full and satisfying leisure experiences. While some individuals may seek help and guidance in negotiating these constraints, many individuals do not, and thus reduce their chances for fulfilling leisure and receiving full benefit. **Table 3.3** (p. 77) provides a list of common barriers to satisfying leisure involvement, adapted from Peterson and Stumbo, 2000 (p. 8).

It then follows that many individuals with disabilities and/or illnesses may experience more frequent, severe, or lasting barriers than their counterparts without disabilities, simply due to the presence of their disability and/or illness. For example, some individuals may experience difficulty with the lack of physical accessibility in recreation or tourist facilities;

some may be addicted to substances that challenge their sober participation; some may have reduced physical endurance, coordination, or strength; some may have few skills due to lack of exposure to typical recreation and leisure opportunities; some may have difficulty making friends due to

Table 3.2
Typical Benefits or Outcomes of Therapeutic Recreation Services
(Adapted from Coyle, Kinney, Riley & Shank, 1991 and Peterson & Stumbo, 2000)

- Increased emotional control
- Improved physical condition
- Decreased disruptive behavior in group situations
- Improved short-term and long-term memory
- Decreased confusion and disorientation
- Decreased symptoms of anxiety and depression
- Improved mobility in community environments and situations
- Improved health indicators, such as bone density, heart rate, and joint mobility
- Improved coping and adaptation skills
- Increased awareness of barriers to leisure
- Improved ability to prevent, manage, and cope with stress
- Improved adjustment to disability and illness
- Improved understanding of importance of leisure to balanced lifestyle
- Improved communication among family members
- Increased ability to use assertiveness skills in a variety of social situations
- Improved opportunities for planning, making choices, and taking responsibility
- Improved ability to locate leisure partners for activity involvement
- Improved knowledge of agencies and facilities that provide recreation services
- Improved knowledge of leisure opportunities in the community
- Increased life and leisure satisfaction
- Increased ability to develop and maintain social support networks
- Improved general psychological health

social isolation or societal attitudes; and some may be unaware of leisure opportunities available to someone with their disabling condition. For some individuals these barriers and constraints are quite limiting and ultimately affect their leisure lifestyle, quality of life, health, and overall happiness or satisfaction.

Because they are likely to experience greater difficulty in full and satisfying leisure participation, many individuals with disabilities and/or illnesses need the additional help of a therapeutic recreation specialist to eliminate, reduce, overcome, or compensate for their leisure barriers. A

Table 3.3
Typical Barriers to Adult Leisure Behavior
(Adapted from Peterson & Stumbo, 2000, p. 8)

- Attitude that leisure is not important
- Lack of planning time or skills devoted to leisure
- Inability to make leisure-related decisions
- Fear of entering new situations or facilities
- Lack of leisure and recreation skills
- Lack of motivation to seek new alternatives
- Inappropriate social skills
- Lack of internal locus of control
- Concepts of "acceptable" age-related adult leisure behavior
- Lack of knowledge of recreation facilities and events
- Lack of experience in seeking leisure information
- Refusal to take responsibility for personal leisure
- Perceived inability to affect personal change
- Lack of financial means
- Limited knowledge of leisure opportunities
- Inability to make decisions regarding use of leisure
- Lack of reliable transportation
- Lack of ability to establish leisure as a priority
- Lack of lifelong leisure skills
- Negative feelings associated with playing instead of working
- Too tired to play
- Lack of a sense of competence in relation to leisure
- Lack of spontaneity (overplanning)
- Decrease in time (real or perceived) available for leisure

therapeutic recreation specialist who utilizes the Leisure Ability Model as the basis for service delivery helps to reduce clients' barriers to leisure involvement through the provision of functional intervention (formerly called treatment services), leisure education, and recreation participation services. The reduction of these barriers or constraints allows the individual to participate more fully in leisure experiences of his or her choice. The ultimate outcome of therapeutic recreation services is the improved ability of the individual to make and act on rewarding and successful choices for leisure participation. That is, the ultimate outcome of therapeutic recreation services is the improved ability of the individual to engage in a successful, appropriate independent leisure lifestyle.

Table 3.4 provides a partial listing of the attitudes, knowledges, and skills necessary to have a satisfying leisure lifestyle. When the individual has adequate attitudes, knowledges, and skills, and can independently and successfully engage in leisure of his or her own choice, he or she has the chance to receive the psychological, physical, and social benefits mentioned earlier (see Table 3.2, p. 76), as well as the more global benefits of improved health, wellness, and quality of life.

Thus when the purpose of therapeutic recreation is stated as facilitating "the development, maintenance, and expression of an appropriate leisure lifestyle," it implies a significant contribution. The improvement of the quality of an individual's life through a focus on the leisure component is much more complex than the provision of enjoyable activity or the delivery of some segmented therapy utilizing activity as the medium. Therapeutic recreation calls for a thorough understanding of the leisure lifestyle concept and the design of appropriate and comprehensive services that can be used to intervene in the lives of people in an influential and positive way.

Leisure Ability Model

The therapeutic recreation specialist who adheres to the Leisure Ability Model for therapeutic recreation service provision provides programs that have as their ultimate outcome a meaningful and personally appropriate leisure lifestyle. Depending on client need, the specialist designs and provides services based on three areas of service: functional intervention, leisure education, and recreation participation.

- *Functional intervention*: improving functional physical, social, cognitive, and affective abilities prerequisite to participating fully in recreation and leisure activities

- *Leisure education*: acquiring and utilizing attitudes, skills, knowledges such as the following:
  - *Leisure awareness*: cognitive appreciation of leisure;
  - *Leisure skills*: traditional and nontraditional leisure skills appropriate to disability/illness and life condition
  - *Leisure resources*: types of and ways to access leisure services, opportunities, and facilities
  - *Social skills*: communication, relationship building, and self-presentation skills related to leisure involvement
- *Recreation participation*: organized leisure participation with supervision

The end result of participation in these three levels of therapeutic recreation service is improvement in the clients' abilities to create, live, and enjoy their own personal interpretation of a leisure lifestyle. The therapeutic

Table 3.4
Typical Attitudes, Knowledges, and Skills Necessary for Leisure Participation

- Physical abilities that allow leisure participation
- Appropriate emotional control and expression
- Social abilities for interaction with self and others
- Cognitive abilities for naming, reasoning, recalling, strategizing, and associating
- Valuing leisure as an important aspect of life
- Decision-making, planning, problem solving, and prioritizing abilities
- Financial planning in relation to leisure
- Communication and relationship-building skills
- Health and hygiene skills
- Awareness of personal abilities and attitudes
- Access to leisure resources in the home and community
- Typical and nontypical leisure activity skills
- Balance between being able to plan for and spontaneously participate in activities
- Ability to try new experiences and activities
- Taking personal responsibility for leisure
- Seeking and utilizing information about leisure opportunities
- Locating and securing transportation to leisure experiences

recreation specialist helps each client to move toward this end result of a satisfying and rewarding leisure lifestyle.

Therapeutic recreation is usually accomplished through complementary services with other health care providers on a treatment or service team. Each client is served individually, through an assessment of needs that leads to development of a treatment, care, or service plan that details action that will be taken for achieving the client's goals. Therapeutic recreation programs are typically provided to small groups of clients who share similar needs and characteristics, although they also can be provided on a one-to-one basis. Clients are monitored periodically and evaluated at the end of their participation to determine if their goals have been met and outcomes achieved. The overall outcome of therapeutic recreation service provision is to aid the client in achieving a leisure lifestyle that is personally meaningful, satisfying, and fits into other aspects of his or her life.

Unique aspects of therapeutic recreation services include that they:

- *Focus more on abilities than dysfunction or pathology.* Instead of focusing on the body part or bodily function that is not working, therapeutic recreation specialists instead concentrate on how that dysfunction may affect a person's overall health and lifestyle, and what can be done to minimize, erase, or compensate for the dysfunction.

- *Focus exclusively on leisure abilities as a major aspect of life functioning.* Other disciplines may narrow their focus on physical abilities or health indicators (e.g., blood pressure, body temperature), while therapeutic recreation specialists concentrate on the multifaceted attitudes, knowledges, skills, and abilities that affect and are affected by leisure functioning.

- *Focus on the use of skills in the community.* Therapeutic recreation services are best delivered when they represent the reality of the lives of clients. As such, they are likely to be provided in natural settings in the community, outside of institutional walls. In this way, skills learned by clients are most immediately transferable to real life situations.

- *Focus on a combination of cognitive understanding, physical abilities, and social and emotional skills.* Human beings are complex individuals who behave in complex ways. Therapeutic recreation views clients through a psycho/social/biological lens that acknowledges the complexity of most individuals' lives.

Some therapeutic recreation specialists view their programs as a the actual activity is not important, it is used because it provides some important tool to improve a functional ability. For example, the card game Concentration may be used to improve short-term memory skills. The specialist is not interested in the client learning the game necessarily but is using it because it serves as a tool to improve a functional deficit (e.g., problems with short-term memory).

Conversely some therapeutic recreation specialists view their programs as an *end*. They primarily use specific leisure activities so their clients learn the skills of the activity and can experience the feelings associated with leisure through participating in the activity. The activity itself is of primary concern. For example, the therapeutic recreation specialist may teach a group of clients soccer skills so that they can continue to play the game when they end participation in the therapeutic recreation program. The reader is referred to Mobily (1985a, 1985b) for a more comprehensive review of these concepts and their implications for practice.

Whether the specialist chooses a *means* approach or an *end* approach, a systematic process for designing and planning therapeutic recreation intervention programs is still needed. The next section provides an overview of therapeutic recreation programming.

Therapeutic Recreation Accountability Model

Accountability means being held responsible for taking action and producing the desired outcomes. Accountable therapeutic recreation services start with a sound conceptualization of all the decision points that need to be made in providing the client with the best possible services. The Therapeutic Recreation Accountability Model (TRAM) (Peterson & Stumbo, 2000; Stumbo, 1996) was designed to help therapeutic recreation specialists conceptualize the connections between different tasks in the delivery of services to clients. These conceptual connections are important. If each job task in the model is handled separately, and without regard to how it affects and is affected by other parts of the model, services are likely to be fragmented and without consistent purpose. However, when various parts of the model are seen as interrelated and interdependent, services are more likely to be of high quality and oriented toward producing client outcomes. These logical linkages are crucial to providing clients with goal-oriented, outcome-based interventions. This in turn allows the specialist to be more accountable for program delivery and to be able to justify inclusion on the health care treatment team.

Components of the Therapeutic Recreation Accountability Model

TRAM was created to help specialists visualize the interactive nature of documentation and decision points involved in the delivery, implementation, and evaluation of accountable programs. Expanding on the models and concepts documented originally by Peterson and Gunn (1984) and Carter, Van Andel, and Robb (1995), the TRAM attempts to depict the relationship between program input factors (such as activity analysis and assessment) and output factors (such as program outcomes and client outcomes).

The Therapeutic Recreation Accountability Model is presented in **Figure 3.2**. Although each component of the model will be discussed separately, in practice, these elements are highly interactive. Interactive arrows could be drawn between all components of TRAM; those with the strongest relationships are provided.

Comprehensive and Specific Program Design

Program design involves establishing the direction of the therapeutic recreation department, unit, or agency (Peterson & Stumbo, 2000). This process entails gathering data about those factors (e.g., the community, agency and/or department, clients and profession) that impact the program and its clients, and prioritizing and selecting those programs that best meet client needs. Implementation and evaluation plans are created to ensure that the right programs will be delivered and reviewed systematically. Details about carrying out this process are provided through the Peterson and Stumbo (2000) and Carter, Van Andel, and Robb (1995) therapeutic recreation program planning models. The direction taken by the therapeutic recreation department at this point is crucial to the success of its remaining operations. Comprehensive and specific program design will be discussed in more detail later in this chapter.

Activity Analysis, Selection, and Modification

Activity analysis is the process used to systematically review specific activities to determine whether they have the potential to help clients achieve targeted outcomes. Activity analysis reviews the characteristics and requirements of an activity for client participation, so that the best activity—that is, one that can most efficiently and effectively help clients reach their goals—can be selected, designed, and delivered. Activity analysis:

is a process that allows the therapeutic recreation specialist to understand an activity and its potential contributions to behavioral outcomes. Activity analysis provides a more exact method of

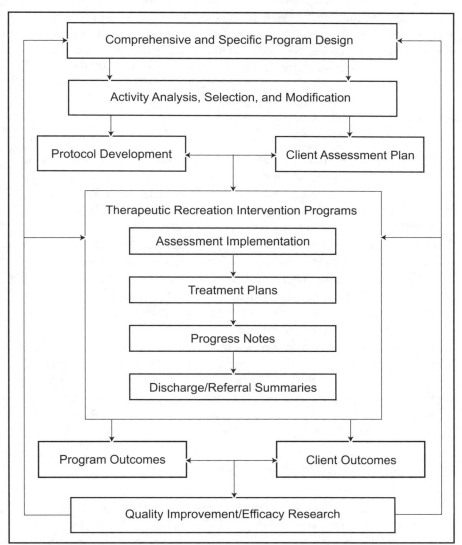

Figure 3.2
Therapeutic Recreation Accountability Model
(Peterson & Stumbo, 2000, p. 72)

selecting activities in that activity components are analyzed before utilization for the behavioral and interaction requirements. In activity analysis, different activities and their therapeutic or instructional value can be compared so that better programming decisions can be made. (Peterson & Stumbo, 2000, pp. 142–143)

An activity analysis helps the programmer to determine if any modifications need to be made to the selected activity so that clients will benefit most fully. Thorough activity analysis is a critical link to program planning because it helps ensure that the specialist is providing programs that meet clients' needs and abilities. Activity analysis is an additional accountability factor that helps the specialist know that the right services are being delivered.

Protocol Development

Protocols aid in the "standardization of interventions" (Knight & Johnson, 1991, p. 137). Protocols are "a group of strategies or actions initiated in response to a problem, an issue, or a symptom of a client. They are not programs or program descriptions, but are approaches or techniques that will lead to expected treatment outcomes" (Knight & Johnson, 1991, p. 137). Protocols provide a blueprint of treatment for a specific diagnosis or client problem. When validated through professional use and consensus they allow for program benchmarks to be set. Hood (2001) emphasized that protocols or "clinical practice guidelines" should provide enough detail and definition regarding intervention procedures to allow for both "best practices" and research for validation.

There are two kinds of protocols, diagnostic (based on client deficits) and treatment (based on specific programs). Both are useful for increasing the standardization of intervention programs within various service delivery agencies and departments across the country, primarily because they help define the input, process, and projected outcomes of well-designed intervention procedures (Ferguson, 1992).

Client Assessment Plan

Client assessment is the process used to place clients into therapeutic recreation programs based on their individual needs, strengths, and limitations. Without a valid and reliable assessment, a program has little chance of being an intervention and a client has little chance of attaining outcomes. That is, when clients are not assessed individually for their strengths, weaknesses, and program needs, and all participants are encouraged or invited to come to all programs, this signals that client outcomes will not be attained.

In this phase of the model, a plan for developing or selecting and implementing an assessment procedure is formed. Decisions about assessment content and implementation procedures are made. At least four major concepts are important to understanding this how these decisions are made: (a) the content of the assessment must reflect the content of the programs that have been selected for delivery to clients; (b) the match between the assessment content and the program content implies that the assessment must be valid for its intended use, primarily for placing clients into the most appropriate programs to address their needs; (c) in addition, the assessment process must be able to deliver reliable results, indicating that specialists need to have standardized procedures and tools; and (d) client assessments play an important role in determining the baseline of client needs, abilities, and limitations, and this baseline is crucial to proving (measuring) outcomes during or after the process of intervention. Later chapters expand on these concepts.

Intervention Programs and Client Documentation

Therapeutic recreation intervention programs are provided to clients based on need. It is common practice to group participants in programs based on their disability and/or illness characteristics that imply similar needs. For example, individuals with advanced Alzheimer's disease may demonstrate similar needs to reduce excessive wandering. Planning for intervention programs relies heavily on the programmer's knowledge of the disability and/or illness characteristics or expressed leisure-related needs of the participant group.

Shank and Kinney (1987) implied that the intervention process is one that requires thoughtful and directed planning. "The clinical or therapeutic use of activity implies a careful selection and manipulation of the activities in a prescriptive sense" (Shank & Kinney, 1987, p. 70). This means that *intervention programs must have the specific intention of modifying client behavior and be presented in a manner most likely to systematically produce these changes.*

The likelihood of program success is improved by the forethought given during planning. As mentioned previously, well-designed and systematic programs that include processes such as protocol development and activity analysis are much more likely to be planned as intervention and produce client behavioral changes.

The baseline for intervention is documented in a client assessment. Problems, strengths, and limitations are documented to determine the client's needs for services. As services are delivered, additional client documentation includes the client's individualized treatment or program plan, a periodic progress note(s), and a discharge/referral summary of services. The treatment or program plan outlines the goals and specific plan of action to be taken with a client (sometimes co-planned by the client). Progress notes are used to monitor progression toward or regression from the goals established in the treatment plan and to modify (if necessary) the original plan of action. Discharge and referral summaries are a compilation of the services received by the client, his or her reaction to the plan of action, as well as any future recommendations for leisure service involvement.

Program Evaluation/Program Outcomes

In specific program evaluation, the specialist must gather and analyze selected data in a systematic and logical manner to determine the quality, effectiveness, and/or outcomes of a program. It makes sense that the plan for program evaluation closely follows the plan for program implementation (Peterson & Stumbo, 2000). For example, program factors such as facilities, equipment, staff, budget, and advertisement/promotion can be evaluated as a function separately from individual client outcomes. Although they are undoubtedly interrelated, program documentation/evaluation focuses on program outcomes and client documentation/ evaluation focuses on client outcomes.

Program evaluation questions might include the following: Were there adequate staff to implement the program and supervise clients? Was the facility adequate for the purpose of the program? Was there enough space? Was the facility accessible? Was the equipment functioning properly? How effective and efficient was the program format in assisting the clients in achieving their outcomes? Evaluation helps to refine the focus of intervention programs and measure client outcomes.

Client Evaluation/Client Outcomes

Client evaluation implies that the focus will be on whether the client goals or outcomes targeted in the initial treatment plan have been accomplished. The focus will be on the end result of the intervention designed on behalf of the client, and is one part of patient care monitoring (Sheehan, 1992). For the most part, client evaluations will be conducted on an individual basis (e.g., as progress notes or discharge/referral summaries), although these individual evaluations may be synthesized later into grouped data that addresses larger program evaluation concerns. Again, the achievement of client outcomes may be highly interrelated to the achievement of program outcomes.

The targeted client outcomes vary based on the different client needs and varied purposes of the programs. In non-outcome-based programs, the focus of client evaluation may be the number of times the client attended a program or the level of client enjoyment. While these are sometimes important, when therapeutic recreation services are delivered as planned interventions, different client outcomes usually are expected. In intervention programs, the focus of service provision is client behavior or functional change as a direct, proven result of the program, and the focus of client evaluations becomes one of measuring and documenting those changes. "Outcome measurements become especially important if we view TR as an agent of change, as a means to modify behavior, attitudes or skills. This is important because the outcome measurements that we specify . . . will indicate what the client is expected to achieve during treatment" (Sheehan, 1992, p. 178). That is, specialists must target goals for client change that are expected to come about as a result of a well-planned and well-designed program. Typical questions concerning client outcomes include: Did the client achieve the targeted outcome within the planned program? If not, what prevented the client from achieving this end? Did the client learn a skill? gain new knowledge? change a behavior? change an attitude? Other specific questions may exist according to the treatment plan established for and with the client.

Client outcomes are dependent on well-designed programs in which clients are placed systematically, and in which interventions are delivered for a specific purpose. In essence, client outcomes, like program outcomes, rely on all previous parts of the Accountability Model being in place and being conceptually cohesive.

Quality Improvement and Efficacy Research

The most common method of evaluating therapeutic recreation services at the comprehensive program level is through quality assurance or quality improvement mechanisms (Huston, 1987; Wright, 1987). A parallel activity, that may or may not be a separate function, is efficacy research (Shank, Kinney & Coyle, 1993). Both of these activities provide useful data to document and improve the standard of care delivered to clients.

Quality assurance (now termed quality improvement, continuous quality improvement, or performance improvement) is defined as a "wide spectrum of activities ranging from determining an appropriate definition of care to establishment of actual standards of practice, that, if implemented, will result in acceptable levels of service" (Riley, 1991a, p. 54). Quality assessment is defined as a systematic process of collecting targeted data, analyzing and comparing data against predetermined standards, taking appropriate action if necessitated, and optimally managing the entire quality review operation (Riley, 1991a, p. 54; Wright, 1987; p. 56). Both of these functions focus on the quality and appropriateness of service delivery (Navar, 1991).

Quality improvement focuses on four areas: "good professional performance, efficient use of resources, reduction of risk, and patient/family satisfaction" (Navar, 1991, p. 6). These four areas can help the specialist to focus evaluative efforts and provide direction in defining the purpose of data collection. That is, they help establish the *content focus* of the evaluation process.

The quality improvement process, as outlined by the Joint Commission, involves 10 steps to be used by all health care providers in delivering and evaluating quality and appropriate services. These steps provide the *process* to be used in improving quality service delivery. The reader should be aware that other sources are available that explain in greater detail the application of quality improvement activities to therapeutic recreation services (cf. Riley, 1987a, 1987b, 1991b; Winslow & Halberg, 1992).

Efficacy research also focuses on the outcomes, benefits, or results of service delivery (Shank, Kinney & Coyle, 1993). It involves systematic data collection and analysis and aims to document service effectiveness, specifically client-based outcomes, for a particular group or groups of clients. While it does have distinct purposes and actions separate from quality improvement, it also shares some similar goals and professional benefits. In addition, it can be accomplished only through a careful and systematic analysis of program delivery factors. A particularly useful resource for more information about efficacy research is Shank, Kinney, and Coyle (1993).

The Therapeutic Recreation Accountability Model (TRAM) provides a visual representation of the totality of therapeutic recreation services. It helps to explain the relationship between program design and client assessment. A fuller explanation of TRAM is located in Peterson and Stumbo (2000).

Therapeutic Recreation Comprehensive Program Planning Model

The therapeutic recreation program design process includes both comprehensive and specific program design. The specialist first starts with the comprehensive process that allows an overall view of the factors (e.g., agency and staff) that impact the design, implementation, and evaluation of the program. Specific program design then follows and includes establishing the details of the content and process of delivering the program to clients.

Comprehensive Program Design

The Therapeutic Recreation Program Planning Model provides the basis for sound and logical program development. It helps the specialist examine the factors that most affect program development, and to develop programs, based on client need, in a systematic fashion. **Figure 3.3** (p. 90) displays the Therapeutic Recreation Program Planning Model from Peterson and Stumbo (2000, p. 82).

Analysis

A well-planned comprehensive program, which can appropriately address clients' leisure-related needs, must have a clear picture of its reason to exist. A statement of purpose and a set of goals provide this direction and definition. Prior to developing the statement of purpose and goals, a stage of analysis is required. The purpose of this analysis is to investigate thoroughly the clients and their leisure-related needs. In addition, it is necessary to study the various factors that influence the selection of the program direction, and, eventually, the operation of the total program. In essence, these areas are examined in the analysis stage to provide the background information necessary to write the mission statement and program goals in the conceptualization stage.

Four areas of analysis have been identified: the *community*, the *agency*, the *clients*, and the *therapeutic recreation department*. Within these four areas, there may be an overlap of some concerns and issues. However, if each of the four is addressed seriously and carefully, the program planner should have sufficient information for solid decision-making in the program development stages that come later. A detailed review of each of these four areas is essential to developing outcomes-based programs. Specific detail about the information needed in each of these four areas can be found in Peterson and Stumbo (2000).

Conceptualization

Mission Statement. The first major task of the conceptualization stage is to develop and write a statement of purpose. The statement of purpose is generally a one-sentence statement that concisely indicates the purpose of the comprehensive therapeutic recreation program. Once written this statement becomes the core from which the entire comprehensive program evolves. Following is an example for a mental health facility.

Example Mission Statement: Mental Health Facility
To provide clients with high quality, progressive, and innovative therapeutic recreation services that result in clients being able to function independently in their leisure upon discharge. These services include a wide range

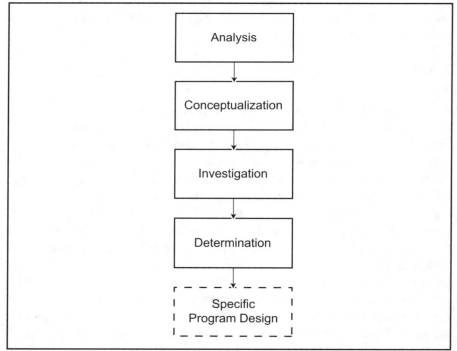

Figure 3.3
Therapeutic Recreation Comprehensive Program Planning Model
(Peterson & Stumbo, 2000, p. 82)

of programs that promote improvement in functional abilities and improvement in leisure-related skills and abilities.

Comprehensive Program Goals. Once a statement of purpose has been derived for a unit or agency, the next step is to develop comprehensive goals. Comprehensive program goals describe aspects of the statement of purpose in greater detail. They develop the comprehensive program's purpose. Usually goals are idealistic yet capable of being put into operation through program components. Goals are not directly measurable; they are statements of intent. The following continues the example of a mental health facility.

Example Comprehensive Program Goals: Mental Health Facility
1.0 To provide services targeted at improving the physical, social, emotional, and cognitive deficits of clients that hinder their leisure involvement. [functional intervention]
2.0 To provide programs that improve the clients' awareness of the need for leisure and its value in maintaining a healthy balance. [leisure awareness]
3.0 To provide services and programs that assist clients in improving their social interaction skills for use in a variety of settings and with a variety of people. [social interaction skills]
4.0 To provide skill improvement programs in both traditional and nontraditional leisure skills. [leisure activity skills]
5.0 To provide programs that teach clients about community leisure resources and how to use them as part of their overall leisure lifestyle. [leisure resources]
6.0 To provide programs that teach clients decision-making and planning skills in regard to utilizing their leisure time. [leisure decision-making and planning skills]

Investigation

After a statement of purpose and the comprehensive program goals are written, the next stage in comprehensive program planning is to investigate program components. Program components are the operational unit for implementation of the program. Each program component carries out some aspect of the statement of purpose and goals. The number of components depends on the resources available to the therapeutic recreation staff, as well as on the scope of the goals. Regardless of the number and type of components, it is essential that they flow from the goals that have been determined. Each component selected later will be refined and designed in detail. The term *specific program* is used to identify program components when they have been selected and are in the development process. The general term *program component* is used at the conceptualization, investigation, and determination stages to identify the programmatic idea that will be used to translate goals into operational units. The terms can be used interchangeably, if desired. Each component can be distinguished by its intended purpose, area of content, and interaction process. Each component is implemented and evaluated separately from the other components.

The process of converting goals into program components is a difficult and challenging one. It calls for experience, expertise, and creativity. A wide range of possibilities exists for transforming goals into program components. The planner is free to choose from existing program models or to create new delivery concepts. Familiarity with a large number of other programs and their implementation strategies is obviously useful to the planner, but more essential is the ability to conceptualize the components logically. The example of a mental health facility continues.

Example Program Components: Mental Health Facility

1.0 To provide services targeted at improving the physical, social, emotional, and cognitive deficits of clients that hinder their leisure involvement. [functional intervention]

Possible program components:

Physical Fitness, Concentration, Emotional Control, Orientation, Coordination, Social Tolerance, Anger Expression

2.0 To provide programs that improve the clients' awareness of the need for leisure and its value in maintaining a healthy balance. [leisure awareness]

Possible program components:

Importance of Leisure, Leisure Barriers, Leisure Attitudes, Leisure Values, Personal Responsibility, Current Leisure Lifestyle, Leisure Satisfaction, Balancing Leisure, Family Leisure

3.0 To provide services and programs that assist clients in improving their social interaction skills for use in a variety of settings and with a variety of people. [social interaction skills]

Possible program components:

Assertiveness Skills, Conversational Skills, Empathy Expression, Friendship Development, Developing Social Networks, Grooming and Dressing, Etiquette and Manners, Listening Skills

4.0 To provide skill improvement programs in both traditional and nontraditional leisure skills. [leisure activity skills]

Possible program components:
Expressive Activities, Physical Leisure Activities, Passive Involvement, Activities at Home, Solo or Dual Activities, Community Leadership, Pets and Plant Care, Travel Options, Relaxation, Low Cost Leisure Activities, Volunteer Opportunities

5.0 To provide programs that teach clients about community leisure resources and how to use them as part of their overall leisure lifestyle. [leisure resources]

Possible program components:
Home Resources, Facility Resources, Neighborhood Resources, Community Resources, Leisure Equipment, State Resources, Financial Aspects of Leisure, Leisure Activities, Personal Abilities, Family and Friends Resources

6.0 To provide programs that teach clients decision-making and planning skills in regard to utilizing their leisure time. [leisure decision-making and planning skills]

Possible program components:
Decision-Making Process, Leisure Planning Skills, Overcoming Leisure Barriers, Long-Term Coping Strategies, Leisure Options, Stress Reduction, Information Seeking, Self-Determination, Responsibility for Choices

These are just some options that may be available for program components to meet the intended comprehensive program goals. Selection of program components, again, depends on the nature of the agency, the clients, and the therapeutic recreation department. Note that the program components focus on the content and the intent of program goals. The next step is to determine which of the brainstormed program components are most likely to meet the most important needs of the clients.

Determination

The next stage in the comprehensive program planning process is the actual selection of program components that will operationalize the intent of the statement of purpose and goals. Many ideas and alternative program components were generated in the investigation stage. This information becomes the source for the determination process. The process starts by reviewing the possible program components and ascertaining their relationship to the established goals. Each alternative program component is studied for its strengths and weaknesses, its demands on resources, and its compatibility with other goals and program components. Eventually, after careful consideration, the specialist selects the most appropriate and desirable program components. A final check is made to ensure all goals are adequately addressed through the selected program components. The specialist then moves on to the actual development and specification of each program component.

Obviously, the determination stage uses the human decision-making process. If each of the previous stages has been completed carefully, the decisions required in the determination stage will be made utilizing good information and will allow the specialist to be as objective and logical as possible. The program components that are selected will be related directly to the statement of purpose and goals. These goals and purpose statements should represent adequately the leisure-related needs of clients. The end result is a systematically derived comprehensive program plan that is both internally consistent and externally justifiable.

An Example of Determination of Program Components. The mental health facility example illustrated in the conceptualization and investigation stages is used to show that not all brainstormed program components are selected for client participation. One of the major functions of the determination stage is to filter program components to determine the best ones to meet the intent of the statement of purpose and the comprehensive program goals. Social interaction skills, leisure resources, and decision-making and planning skills were designated as being the most important areas for this group of clients, and therefore, have the greatest emphasis. The program components will be translated later into specific program goals and specific programs.

Example Program Components: Mental Health Facility

1.0 To provide services targeted at improving the physical, social, emotional, and cognitive deficits of clients that hinder their leisure involvement. [functional intervention]

Chosen program components:

Physical Fitness, Emotional Control, Orientation, Social Tolerance, Anger Expression

2.0 To provide programs that improve the clients' awareness of the need for leisure and its value in maintaining a healthy balance. [leisure awareness]

Chosen program components:

Importance of Leisure, Leisure Barriers, Current Leisure Lifestyle, Leisure Values, Personal Responsibility

3.0 To provide services and programs that assist clients in improving their social interaction skills for use in a variety of settings and with a variety of people. [social interaction skills]

Chosen program components:

Assertiveness Skills, Conversational Skills, Friendship Development, Developing Social Networks, Hygiene, Grooming and Dressing, Etiquette and Manners, Listening Skills

4.0 To provide skill improvement programs in both traditional and non-traditional leisure skills. [leisure activity skills]

Chosen program components:

Expressive Activities, Physical Leisure Activities, Relaxation, Activities at Home, Solo or Dual Activities, Low Cost Leisure Activities

5.0 To provide programs that teach clients about community leisure resources and how to use them as part of their overall leisure lifestyle. [leisure resources]

Chosen program components:

Home Resources, Family and Friends Resources, Community Resources, Leisure Equipment, Financial Aspects of Leisure, Leisure Activities, Personal Abilities

6.0 To provide programs that teach clients decision-making and planning skills in regard to utilizing their leisure time. [leisure decision-making and planning skills]

Chosen program components:

Decision-Making Process, Leisure Planning Skills, Overcoming Leisure Barriers, Stress Reduction, Self-Determination, Responsibility for Choices

These first four steps of comprehensive program design set the stage for selecting and designing specific programs. Analysis, conceptualization, investigation, and determination all play a vital role in establishing a logical, defensible, and accountable system of programs. These four steps serve as the foundation to develop specific programs using a systems-designed approach. The result of such an approach is the increased likelihood of producing client outcomes that are of importance to the client and agency. The next section provides a brief overview of specific program design.

Specific Program Design

A *specific program* can be defined as:

A set of activities and their corresponding interactions that are designed to achieve predetermined goals selected for a given group of clients. The specific program is implemented and evaluated independently of all other specific programs. (Peterson & Stumbo, 2000, p. 106)

Aspects of this definition require further exploration. Implied in the definition is the concept that each specific program identifies and addresses some major aspect of functional intervention, leisure education, or recreation participation. One specific program usually cannot focus adequately on all of these areas of client need. Thus, specific programs are selected and developed that relate to different categories of client need. Some programs will address various functional intervention concerns; others will be developed to focus on the diverse aspects of leisure education; still others will center on recreation and leisure participation opportunities.

Once the general topic of a specific program is selected, objectives will be derived and stated. These objectives will be delineated for a given group of clients (usually a subgroup of the total population served by the agency). Activities then will be developed that relate directly to the identified objectives and are appropriate for the designated clients. *Activities* in this context does not mean just traditional recreation or leisure activities. It implies a broader category of actions or program content, which can include such areas as discussions, lectures, and written or cognitive exercises as well as traditional or nontraditional recreation activities. Thus, the term *activity* refers to the action, content, or media presented to the clients to address the objectives and, it is hoped, to achieve the desired outcomes.

Similarly, specific interactions will be designed to be used with those activities for that particular set of clients. The program is designed to be implemented for that particular set of clients, independently of other programs. Its objectives, activities, and interventions have their own timelines, staff, resource allocations, and designated evaluation mechanism. A given client is placed or referred to one or more specific programs based on the client's need and the program's designed ability to address that need. This method of programming enables the individual leisure-related needs of clients to be met. It also allows for specific programs to be added, deleted, or changed as clients' needs dictate. Because each specific program has its own focus (purpose and objectives), it can be evaluated based on its contribution to the overall mission of the therapeutic recreation unit, agency, or department. Likewise, the progress of an individual client can be carefully monitored, based on achievement and participation within each assigned or designated program.

Specific programs need to be developed and described so that they can be implemented by the specialist in a consistent manner. This description also allows the program to be repeated by the same implementer, or implemented by someone else. The thorough written description is also of value for the purpose of evaluation. Additionally, it allows the agency to maintain a high level of accountability in that all programs are documented before, during, and after implementation.

The total development of the specific program requires three stages of design:

1. *Program Plan*—includes statement of purpose, terminal program objectives (TPOs), enabling objectives (EOs), performance measures (PMs), and content and process descriptions (CPDs)

2. *Implementation Plan*—includes sequence sheet and implementation description

3. *Evaluation Plan*

Each of these three stages has sequential procedures and tasks. **Figure 3.4** (p. 98) presents an overview of the entire specific program design process. This particular chapter is not intended to detail all the information needed to design specific programs and the reader is referred to Peterson and Stumbo (2000) for more complete information.

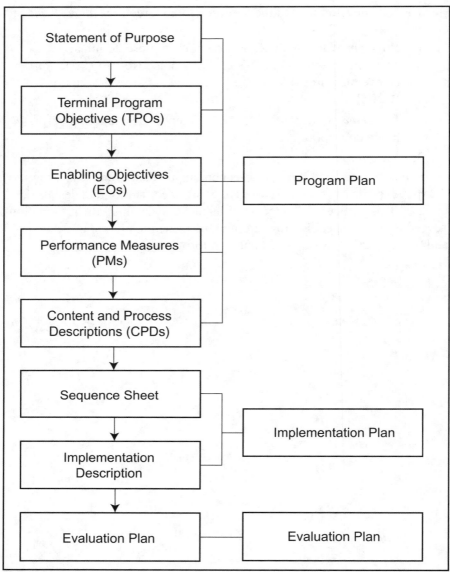

Figure 3.4
Development of the Specific Program
(Peterson & Stumbo, 2000, p. 108)

Summary

Therapeutic recreation has a unique combination of concepts related to its practice. The concept of a leisure lifestyle provides a foundation for understanding the *input* and *output* of therapeutic recreation programming. A rationale for understanding the basis of service provision is also important. Given these two pillars of support, the Leisure Ability Model of Therapeutic Recreation Service Delivery is adopted due to its *content* relevance and use in practice. The Therapeutic Recreation Accountability Model provides the *process* to augment the content within the Leisure Ability Model. This chapter also discussed both comprehensive and specific design to cement in the reader's mind their relationship to client assessment and client outcomes. Throughout the remainder of this text, the reader will use these basic concepts in understanding and using the assessment process.

References

Caldwell, L. (2001). The role of theory in therapeutic recreation: A practical approach. In N. J. Stumbo (Ed.), *Professional issues in therapeutic recreation: On competence and outcomes* (pp. 349–364) Champaign, IL: Sagamore Publishing.

Carter, M. J., Van Andel, G. E., and Robb, G. M. (1995). *Therapeutic recreation: A practical approach* (2nd ed.). Prospect Heights, IL: Waveland Press, Inc.

Coyle, C. P., Kinney, W. B., Riley, B., and Shank, J. W. (1991). *Benefits of therapeutic recreation: A consensus view*. Philadelphia, PA: Temple University.

Ferguson, D. (1992, July). *Recreation therapy protocols*. International Conference on Leisure and Mental Health, Salt Lake City, UT.

Gronlund, N. E. (1993). *How to make achievement tests and assessments* (5th ed.). Boston, MA: Allyn & Bacon.

Hood, C. D. (2001). Clinical practice guidelines: A decision making tool for best practice? In N. J. Stumbo (Ed.), *Professional issues in therapeutic recreation: On competence and outcomes* (pp. 189–214). Champaign, IL: Sagamore Publishing.

Huston, A. D. (1987). Clinical application of quality assurance in the therapeutic recreation setting. In B. Riley (Ed.), *Evaluation of therapeutic recreation through quality assurance* (pp. 67–96). State College, PA: Venture Publishing, Inc.

Kelly, J. R. (1990). *Leisure* (2nd ed.). Englewood Cliffs, NJ: Prentice Hall.

Knight, L. and Johnson, A. (1991). Therapeutic recreation protocols: Client problem centered approach. In B. Riley (Ed.), *Quality management: Applications for therapeutic recreation* (pp. 137–147). State College, PA: Venture Publishing, Inc.

Mobily, K. E. (1985a). A philosophical analysis of therapeutic recreation: What does it mean to say "We can be therapeutic"? Part I. *Therapeutic Recreation Journal, 19*(1), 14–26.

Mobily, K. E. (1985b). A philosophical analysis of therapeutic recreation: What does it mean to say "We can be therapeutic"? Part II. *Therapeutic Recreation Journal, 19*(2), 7–14.

Navar, N. (1991). Advancing therapeutic recreation through quality assurance: A perspective on the changing nature of quality in therapeutic recreation. In B. Riley (Ed.), *Quality management: Applications for therapeutic recreation* (pp. 3–20). State College, PA: Venture Publishing, Inc.

Palmer, S. and McMahon, G. (1997). *Client assessment*. Thousand Oaks, CA: Sage Publications.

Peterson, C. A. (1981). *Leisure lifestyle and disabled individuals*. Paper presented at Horizons West Therapeutic Recreation Symposium, San Francisco State University, San Francisco, CA.

Peterson, C. A. (1989). The dilemma of philosophy. In D. Compton (Ed.), *Issues in therapeutic recreation: A profession in transition* (pp. 21–34) Champaign, IL: Sagamore Publishing.

Peterson, C. A. and Gunn, S. L. (1984). *Therapeutic recreation program design: Principles and procedures* (2nd ed.). Englewood Cliffs, NJ: Prentice Hall.

Peterson, C. A. and Stumbo, N. J. (2000). *Therapeutic recreation program design: Principles and procedures* (3rd ed.). Needham Heights, MA: Allyn & Bacon.

Riley, B. (1987a). Conceptual basis of quality assurance: Application to therapeutic recreation service. In B. Riley (Ed.), *Evaluation of therapeutic recreation through quality assurance* (pp. 7–24). State College, PA: Venture Publishing, Inc.

Riley, B. (1987b). (Ed.). *Evaluation of therapeutic recreation through quality assurance*. State College, PA: Venture Publishing, Inc.

Riley, B. (1991a). Quality assessment: The use of outcome indicators. In B. Riley (Ed.), *Quality management: Applications for therapeutic recreation* (pp. 53–67). State College, PA: Venture Publishing, Inc.

Riley, B. (1991b). (Ed.). *Quality management: Applications for therapeutic recreation*. State College, PA: Venture Publishing, Inc.

Ross, J. and Ashton-Shaeffer, C. (2001). Therapeutic recreation practice models. In N. J. Stumbo (Ed.), *Professional issues in therapeutic recreation: On competence and outcomes* (pp. 159–189). Champaign, IL: Sagamore Publishing.

Shank, J. and Kinney, T. (1987). On the neglect of clinical practice. In C. Sylvester, J. L. Hemingway, R. Howe-Murphy, K. Mobily, and P. A. Shank (Eds.). *Philosophy of therapeutic recreation: Ideas and issues*. (pp. 65–75). Alexandria, VA: National Recreation and Park Association.

Shank, J. W., Kinney, W. B., and Coyle, C. P. (1993). Efficacy studies in therapeutic recreation research: The need, the state of the art, and future implications. In M. J. Malkin and C. Z. Howe (Eds.), *Research in therapeutic recreation: Concepts and methods* (pp. 301–335). State College, PA: Venture Publishing, Inc.

Sheehan, T. (1992). Outcome measurements in therapeutic recreation. In G. Hitzhusen, L. Jackson, and M. Birdsong (Eds.), *Expanding Horizons in Therapeutic Recreation XIV* (pp. 17–22). Columbia, MO: Curators University of Missouri.

Stumbo, N. J. (1996). A proposed therapeutic recreation accountability model. *Therapeutic Recreation Journal, 30*(4), 246–259.

Winslow, R. M. and Halberg, K. J. (1992). (Eds.). *The management of therapeutic recreation services*. Arlington, VA: National Recreation and Park Association.

Wright, S. (1987). Quality assessment: Practical approaches in therapeutic recreation. In B. Riley (Ed.), *Evaluation of therapeutic recreation through quality assurance* (pp. 55–66). State College, PA: Venture Publishing, Inc.

Chapter 4
The Assessment Process

Client assessment involves measurement of clients' needs, limitations, and abilities to place clients in programs designed to address those needs, limitations, and abilities. Assessment involves measurement, which means that the assessment must:

- Be selected or developed based on a specific purpose
- Be able to gather necessary information in a logical and straightforward way
- Meet the needs of the clients and intent of the agency
- Produce results that are valid and reliable to the greatest degree possible (Stumbo, 1991, 1997, 2001)

For therapeutic recreation specialists to do assessment well and with confidence, they must be familiar with a number of measurement terms and issues (see Chapter 2) and their application to the assessment planning and implementation processes. In the Therapeutic Recreation Accountability Model (introduced in Chapter 3) assessment planning is separated from assessment implementation. It is not that they are unrelated, but that thinking about the content and purpose of assessment should occur long before the actual implementation occurs. Much like recreation activities themselves, considerable effort needs to go into planning before the actual activity takes place.

Therefore, therapeutic recreation specialists must have an extensive understanding of measurement characteristics and the ability to apply those to the entire therapeutic recreation assessment process (Dunn, 1987; Stumbo, 1991, 1994/1995, 1997, 2001). Because there are so many decisions to be made surrounding client assessment, two models—the Assessment Planning Model and the Assessment Implementation Model (Peterson & Stumbo, 2000)—were created so that a greater level of detail can be presented. Both models follow the Therapeutic Recreation Accountability Model presented in Chapter 3. The two models have the following steps:

Assessment Planning

- Analyze the environment
- Define parameters
- Select or develop an assessment

- Establish assessment protocols
- Train staff and interns on the protocols

Assessment Implementation

- Review assessment protocols
- Prepare for assessment
- Administer assessment to client
- Analyze or score assessment results
- Interpret results for placement into programs
- Document results of assessment
- Reassess client as necessary/monitor progress

The decisions made during the Assessment Planning Model's steps are important because they affect the type of assessment selected or developed, as well as how it will be implemented for clients.

The Assessment Implementation Model addresses how the specialist interacts with the client while administering the assessment, as well as how results are used for decisions about client placement in programs. Although the decisions and actions taken during both the assessment planning and assessment implementation stages are interrelated, they are separated here so each step can be discussed more fully.

The Assessment Planning Process

From the very first considerations weighed by the specialist, client assessment decisions must be systematic, logical, and based on the measurement properties discussed in Chapter 2. Since assessment is highly related to program design, documentation, and client outcomes, the assessment planning process needs to relate closely to decisions in these areas.

The assessment planning process takes place during the initial conceptualization of a department or comprehensive program and is evaluated and updated periodically as the agency, clients, programs, or specialists change direction. The assessment planning process should provide a stable base of information from which decisions about the assessment implementation and client documentation phases are made (Stumbo & Rickards, 1986). **Figure 4.1** outlines the five basic steps to the assessment planning process.

Analyze the Environment

Agency Considerations

Similar to the analysis stage used in program design (see Chapter 3), the specialist must consider agency characteristics as the first step in assessment planning. Since each agency is unique in its mission, services delivered, and clients served, these factors among others, must be considered to select or develop and implement an assessment. Some sample questions about the agency that affect the client assessment choice might include:

- What is the mission of the agency? How does this mission differ from other local or regional facilities and agencies?

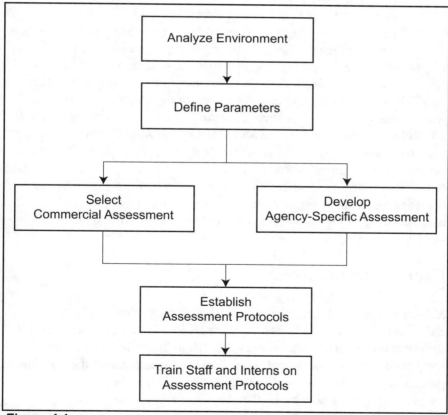

Figure 4.1
Therapeutic Recreation Assessment Planning Model
(Peterson & Stumbo, 2000, p. 214)

- What are new areas of program focus? How do they contribute to the continuing programs and services?
- What are the features or characteristics of the agency? How is it different (or similar) to other local and regional facilities and agencies?
- What national, state, and local standards impact the delivery of services at this agency?
- What client groups are served, and is this changing? What about length of stay? How is the clientele changing—for example, are they showing more severe illnesses or disabilities?
- What types of assessments are used by other disciplines in the agency? For each discipline, what is the primary focus of the items? How is the data collected?
- What types of resources are available for the purposes of client assessment?

The answers to these questions should assist the therapeutic recreation specialist in viewing the impact of the agency's characteristics on client assessment. For example, several agencies might serve individuals with substance abuse problems; however, they may differ greatly in whether they primarily deliver inpatient, outpatient, or day treatment programs; whether their intent is detoxification, individual counseling, or group peer counseling; or whether they are accredited by the Joint Commission. They also may differ greatly in the resources (e.g., time, money, staff) they dedicate to assessment processes. As such, the agency's characteristics will impact greatly the assessment procedure chosen by the therapeutic recreation specialist and other disciplines. The specialist must have a clear understanding of the nature, purpose, and operation of the sponsoring agency.

Client Considerations

Similar to agency characteristics, the specialist must review the typical characteristics of clients or participants served by the agency. Reviewing the client characteristics helps the specialist to know the level of content appropriate for the assessment, as well as how to implement the assessment procedure. Following are some sample questions that the professional should answer in beginning to plan the client assessment:

- What are the typical client needs of this population group? Why are they being admitted to or seen at this agency? How do their needs cluster?

- What are the typical limitations of this population group that would impact the assessment process? Describe their reading ability and comprehension level, their ability to make decisions regarding their treatment and their future, their level of independence, conversation ability, and honesty.

- Where will the clients be going after discharge or leaving the agency? How will their future impact their current services received, and, in turn, how will this affect the assessment?

These types of questions point to the need for the specialist to know his or her clients' characteristics well. Certainly, whether clients can read, respond to questions, be honest, value their treatment process, and the like all impact the decisions made by the specialist regarding the content and process of the assessment. If clients cannot read, then self-administered assessments are not likely to be used. If clients cannot focus for sufficient periods of time, then assessments must be shortened or administered in parts. It matters whether the client will be discharged to his or her own home or to another facility. The professional must have a firm understanding of generic client abilities and limitations, and their impact on the assessment process.

Therapeutic Recreation Program Considerations

One of the most important preliminary considerations is the types of programs offered within the therapeutic recreation department or agency. As discussed in Chapter 3, the basic program design is one of the first decision points in the entire accountability process. This also is conducted with client needs in mind and now is the time to determine the impact of those program decisions on client assessment (and perhaps client outcomes).

The specialist needs to consider both the content of the program (e.g., functional intervention, leisure education, recreation participation), the level of program (e.g., beginner, intermediate, advanced), as well as the purpose of the program (e.g., functional improvement, skill building, creative expression). These are important because they affect the types and depth of questions asked in the assessment. For example, if the program involves a sensory stimulation component for individuals with advanced Alzheimer's disease, the types and depth of information required on the assessment reflect this. For this example, due to the nature of the program, the assessment might involve observation (instead of interview), and several in-depth but short observational checklists leading to the best sensory technique for each individual (response to touch, smell, sight, hearing, taste). Because programs and assessment are so intimately linked, considerable attention must be paid to this area.

Sample questions regarding the therapeutic recreation program might include the following:

- What is the overall purpose of the comprehensive therapeutic recreation program?
- Which area(s) of the Leisure Ability Model do the therapeutic recreation programs represent?
- What specific content (e.g., functional intervention, social skills, assertiveness training, leisure education, community re-entry) is covered within the programs?
- At what level are the programs delivered? What is the intent of the program(s)?
- What client outcomes are expected as the result of participation in each of the therapeutic recreation programs? How are these outcomes related to client deficits and client goals?
- What type(s) of information are needed to determine whether or not a client could benefit from participation in the program? What is the minimal amount of information needed to do this?
- What standards affect therapeutic recreation programs that also may influence the client assessment tool or procedure?

As demonstrated in Table 1.6 (p. 13), the content of the assessment must match the content of the program. This means that the intent and delivery of the programs must be carefully outlined and considered so that this match may occur. This can be accomplished only when the programs and services to be provided to clients are specified in a significant degree of detail during comprehensive and specific program planning. Then, and only then, can the content of the assessment be determined.

Staff and Resource Considerations

The availability of staff and other resources plays a large part in the selection and implementation of client assessments. Staff becomes a consideration in that their talents, strengths, and weaknesses affect how well they conduct client assessments. How well they understand related concepts, such as validity, reliability, data collection, interpretation of scores, and documentation impact how they make assessment decisions. Continuing education and training focused on new developments in client assessment are important for staff on a regular basis, but their basic skill level does impact client assessment. Likewise, the amount and type of resources that the department or agency can devote to client assessment affects its quality and delivery.

However, this is not to say that lack of staff expertise or lack of resource commitment absolves the therapeutic recreation specialist from ultimate responsibility for the client assessment process. Just the opposite—it means that the resolve to become better or commit adequate resources to the assessment process must be strengthened.

Questions that address some of these resource concerns include:

- What talents, strengths, and weaknesses do staff bring to the assessment process?

- In what areas are additional staff education and training necessary to improve the overall process of client assessment?

- What is the department or agency budget for assessment, especially if commercial assessments are to be purchased?

- How much time can (or should) be allotted per assessment? per specialist? per client?

- In what environments can the assessment be conducted? Is there a quiet, safe, private space available to administer client assessments?

- How will assessment protocols be developed, and who will be responsible for ensuring that staff adheres to the protocols?

- Who will be responsible for ensuring that each therapeutic recreation staff and intern is properly trained in the assessment protocols? How often will this training occur?

All these factors point to the need for an honest appraisal of department and agency resources that can be devoted to the assessment process. If few resources are available, then the assessment must be tailored for this; if many resources are available, then a more comprehensive assessment might be appropriate. When making this appraisal, the decision makers will want to consider the importance of client assessment to proper program placement and the achievement of client outcomes. There is simply no way to produce client outcomes without properly designed and operating intervention programs and client assessments.

Define Parameters

After the agency, client, therapeutic recreation program, staff, and resource have been considered , the next step is to define more closely what the assessment is expected to do. Three basic areas need to be examined: (a) function, (b) content, and (c) implementation strategy.

Determining the Function of the Assessment

First, the specialist needs to decide what *function* the assessment will serve, from one of four options: (a) basic screening, (b) identifying the problem(s), (c) narrowing the problem(s), and/or (d) reassessing or monitoring client progress (Dunn, 1984; Peterson & Stumbo, 2000). To describe these four functions, let's use the example of physical functional abilities (functional intervention). In *initial screening*, the specialist may ask very basic questions, such as "Does the client have adequate physical skills to independently participate in leisure?" The answer (either yes or no) then primarily divides clients into two options: *yes*, the person has adequate skills and does not need physical skills training, or *no*, the person lacks adequate skills and does need physical skills training. The yes response means that the client is not placed into physical skills programs, and the no response means that the client may receive more intensive physical function evaluation and programs.

When *identifying problems*, the assessment may be used to determine a more detailed level of information about the client's abilities. For example, a question used to identify problems may be "Does the client have adequate flexibility?" If the answer is yes, then the client does not receive further programming in that area. If the answer is no, then the client receives further flexibility training. Obviously, several similar questions may be asked to address the entire physical domain, such as strength, endurance, coordination, and body composition.

In a similar vein, when further *defining problems*, more specific information is gathered. Using the same physical functioning situation, a narrowing question may be "If the client has difficulty with flexibility, where does the difficulty lie?" Answer options here might include (a) head and neck flexibility; (b) shoulder, arm, and hand flexibility; (c) trunk and hip flexibility; and (d) leg and foot flexibility. The specialist observes the client, and places him/her into programs that address the deficiencies as noted in the assessment (in this case physical flexibility). It is easy to address difficulties during a program when they have been adequately defined ahead of time with the assurance that they match the program content of the physical function program. The client with difficulties is placed into programs that address his or her needs or deficits and those specific needs are targeted during the program. For example, the client with flexibility problems may be placed in a flexibility class, where his individual goals focus on trunk and lower body flexibility.

The last function served by assessment is *reassessing* or *monitoring client progress*. In this capacity, an assessment that produces valid and reliable results can be used to reassess the changes that may have occurred in the client as a result of participation in the programs. Using the physical function example above, a similar question focuses on the current status of the client. The question might read, "What difficulties have been improved or remedied by participation in the physical function (flexibility) program?" Answers may include (a) head and neck flexibility; (b) shoulder, arm, and hand flexibility; (c) trunk and hip flexibility; and (d) leg and foot flexibility. When compared with the original, baseline assessment information, the reassessment information provides an analysis of the difference between preprogram and postprogram client skills. When adequately defined, reassessment should highlight which skills were improved as the result of program involvement, and which skills were not. **Table 4.1** provides an overview of these four functions.

Determining the Assessment Content

There is probably no more important step in the assessment planning process than to review closely the content of the assessment. As seen in

Table 4.1
Examples of Client Assessment Functions and Related Items
(Adapted from Peterson & Stumbo, 2000, p. 218)

Assessment Function	Purpose	Example of Items for Physical Function Programs
Basic Screening	Need for Services?	Does the client have adequate physical skills to participate independently in leisure?
Identifying Problem	Which Services?	Does the client have adequate flexibility? strength? coordination? endurance? body composition?
Defining Problem	Specific Training Needed?	If the client has difficulty with flexibility, where does the difficulty lie?
Reassessing or Monitoring	Progress Made toward Outcome?	What difficulties have been improved or remedied by participation in the physical function (flexibility) program?

Table 1.6 (p. 13), the content of the assessment must align with the content of the programs offered. This is crucial because if the assessment content is not aligned with the programs, the assessment will contain questions that do not lead to program placement. This does require, however, the specialist to conduct an in-depth analysis of therapeutic recreation program offerings. For example, if the major programs offered include functional intervention, leisure resources, and social skills, the assessment must ask the specific questions related to these content areas to know whether clients should or should not be placed in those programs. On the other hand, if these programs are offered and the assessment contains questions about leisure history, leisure interests, and leisure skills, then the information gained from the assessment will not be useful in placing the right clients in the right programs (Navar, 1991; Stumbo, 1992, 1993/1994).

In addition, the specialist must determine at what level the assessment questions should be asked. Leisure resources provides a clear example. If the leisure resource program teaches *utilization* of community leisure resources (i.e., teaching clients how to use resources instead of just basic knowledge), then the assessment also should focus on the utilization level of content (instead of knowledge). For example, a good leisure resource utilization question would be: "Describe how you would find out what time the art museum opens." The client is expected to explain the steps in finding out what time the art museum opens. (While asking the client to actually demonstrate the behavior would be even better, more time is involved.) A leisure resource *knowledge* question may be: "What time does the library open?" The knowledge question does not ask the client to explain or demonstrate the skill of utilizing the knowledge, and does not align with the program that teaches at the utilization level. The content and level of each assessment question should relate directly to some aspect of the therapeutic recreation programs offered. Again, it is important to match the content and intent of the assessment questions with the content and intent of the therapeutic recreation services.

Determining an Implementation Strategy

In addition to function and content, the third parameter that needs to be determined is the implementation strategy. There are four basic strategies for gaining client assessment information: (a) interviews, (b) observations, (c) self-administered questionnaires, and (d) records reviews. There is considerable interrelationship between the content of the assessment and the strategy for collecting the information. If the specialist desires in-depth information about the client's knowledge or perceptions, then interviews are appropriate. If the client's behavior is the focus, then observations are in order. If it may be necessary for the client to complete the assessment independently, or at another time, a self-administered questionnaire may be appropriate. Records reviews are important when the information needed is already stored elsewhere (e.g., in nursing's assessment), or the client is unavailable or incapable of completing an assessment interview, or as a confirmation of information gathered in an interview or observation.

In turn, the implementation strategy affects the way in which information is gathered and the types of questions asked. For example, one of the primary advantages to an interview is the ability to ask open-ended questions, probe for clarification, and interact with the client. Therefore, it is best to use open-ended questions (e.g., "Tell me about how you might spend a Saturday with no obligations."), use follow-up questions, and observe the client during the interview. The content and form of the questions should match the reason for selecting the implementation strategy.

Information gathered about the function and content of the assessment, as well as the implementation strategy, provides the basis for the remaining assessment selection decisions. Considerable attention needs to be paid to these three areas because they provide the foundation for decisions about whether to select a commercially available assessment or to develop an agency-specific assessment. Beyond the introduction provided in the next few sections, Chapter 5 focuses on assessment selection factors, Chapter 6 discusses commercially available assessments, and Chapter 7 outlines how to develop an agency-specific client assessment. The next two sections briefly cover the two fundamental selection decisions: buying an assessment or developing an agency-specific assessment.

Select a Commercial Assessment

After the assessment function, content, and implementation strategy have been determined, one option is to review and select a commercially available assessment for use. Several assessments have been developed and are available nationally for sale. Two examples are the Leisure Diagnostic Battery (Witt & Ellis, 1987) and the Leisure Competence Measure (Kloseck, Crilly, Ellis & Lammers, 1996). These assessments are examples of highly developed and tested assessments available from commercial vendors.

Caution is needed to make sure that the assessment selected for purchase fits the criteria mentioned previously and the criteria given in Chapter 5. While it may be tempting to purchase or use a commercial assessment because of its packaging, marketing, or availability, a systematic evaluation must occur to make sure that it fits the intended purpose and can produce reliable results for the clients on whom it will be used. The previous questions related to agency, clients, program, and resource considerations also apply to commercial assessments. These should be answered to the satisfaction of the therapeutic recreation specialist. Following are some additional questions to determine whether a commercial assessment is appropriate for use in a specific agency (see Dunn, 1989).

These are important factors to consider *prior* to purchase.

- Is the population on which it was validated the same as the clientele within the agency?

- Was the assessment developed upon a solid foundation of theory and therapeutic recreation content that would match the programs within the specific agency intended for use?

- How closely does the content of the assessment match the content of the programs offered at the specific agency?

- What evidence is given for validity (content, criterion-related, and/or construct) depending on the purpose of the test?

- What testing was done to make sure the assessment produces reliable results over time, between clients, and/or between administrations?

- How extensive is the protocol for administration of the assessment?

- How extensive is the protocol for analysis and scoring of the assessment?

- How extensive is the protocol for interpretation of scores?

- How will the scores produced enable placement of clients into the programs of interest?

- Do the time, money, and resources required to conduct the assessment with individual clients match with those available at the specific agency?

These questions and others need to be answered prior to the decision to purchase and use a commercial tool. Choosing a poorly developed tool or one that does not fit the agency's or clients' needs has no advantage over developing a quality agency-specific tool. The specialist needs to be very familiar with measurement characteristics to make a sound decision prior to purchase. More information about buying commercial assessments will be discussed in Chapter 5 and Chapter 6.

Develop an Agency-Specific Assessment

Similar to selecting an assessment that can be purchased, a client assessment can be developed by the therapeutic recreation specialist within a specific agency, given that adequate consideration and thought is given to its development and validation. In actual practice, more therapeutic recreation specialists rely on agency-specific assessments than on nationally available tests. One major reason may be that the content of commercial assessments rarely matches the content of the programs offered by specific agencies, and thus locally developed assessments, given adequate attention to development and testing, often are more closely aligned with the needs of the clients and types of programs delivered. This is similar to national standardized tests (e.g., ACT or SAT) versus the classroom test most often developed by the teacher. While the standardized tool has received repeated and advanced testing for validation purposes, it still does not meet the needs of the average classroom teacher because the content, purpose, and intended outcomes differ. So it is with therapeutic recreation assessments. This may continue to be the case until national treatment protocols are researched and utilized in all similar programs across the country. When this becomes the case, assessments to align with those programs will be developed and made readily available. Until that time, many therapeutic recreation specialists will continue to create their own assessments to use within their agencies. This means, however, that in order to have confidence in the ability of the results to place clients in the right programs, the specialist becomes responsible for reducing inadvertent error whenever possible. Development of an agency-specific assessment does not excuse the specialist from similar measurement and testing requirements as expected in national tests.

There are three basic steps in developing an agency-specific assessment: (a) planning the assessment, (b) item writing, and (c) item analysis and testing. In planning the assessment, agency, client, program, and resource factors must be noted, along with the assessment function, content, and implementation strategy as outlined previously. Item writing and analysis ensure that the results are as valid and reliable as possible. Of course, validation of the entire assessment procedure is of ultimate importance. Chapter 5 and Chapter 7 further discuss this information.

Establish Assessment Protocols

An assessment protocol provides information on the standardized procedures for preparing, administering, scoring, interpreting, and reporting assessment information. This documentation is necessary whether the assessment is commercially available or agency-developed. The best commercial assessments provide very detailed protocols to improve the specialist's ability to implement the assessment as it has been planned and tested. In the case of agency-specific assessments, the therapeutic recreation staff is responsible for developing and testing the assessment protocol. Dunn (1989) provided excellent guidelines for using or creating the necessary documentation to accompany assessments as shown in Figure 5.2 (p. 140).

A typical assessment protocol will include details concerning:

Preparation

- Environmental conditions under which the assessment is to take place (e.g., quiet, private location, minimal distractions, proper lighting, furniture arrangements)
- Needed resources (e.g., assessment kit, accessories, paper and pencil, score sheet, length of time required)

Administration

- Instructions for interviews (e.g., written script with introduction, transitions, explanations, acceptable probes, closing)
- Instructions for observations (e.g., written information on types of behaviors to be assessed, observation conditions)
- Exceptional conditions (e.g., procedures for when a person refuses to complete the interview or observation, fatigues quickly, or becomes disruptive)

Scoring

- How the answers to each question or item are to be scored (e.g., If a person responds to item 12 with "X" answer, how is this scored differently from the person who responds "Y" to the same item?)
- How the total assessment is scored (e.g., calculating sub-scores or total test scores)

Analysis and Interpretation

- How the answers to each question or item are to be analyzed and interpreted for program placement (e.g., In which programs does a person who scores a "5" belong?)

Reporting

- How the answers are to be recorded and reported to other disciplines, if appropriate (e.g., What is the standardized format for reporting assessment scores or results? How is program placement recorded?)

- Considerations of informed consent (e.g., clients' rights to confidentiality and privacy)

Train Staff and Interns on Assessment Protocol

Prior to implementation, each therapeutic recreation staff member and intern needs to receive complete training on the total assessment protocol—preparing for, administering, scoring, interpreting, and reporting assessment information. The purpose of this step is to ensure that all specialists are fully able to complete and adhere to the protocol as written. This will increase the likelihood that specialists deliver the assessment in a similar fashion, and will likely increase the reliability of the assessment results through consistency of efforts. Adherence to the assessment protocol will reduce unwanted error and increase confidence that can be placed in the results. Periodic training and evaluating adherence to the protocol is necessary to decrease discrepancies from specialist to specialist, and likely will be a vital part in the quality improvement process.

The Assessment Implementation Process

The five-step assessment planning process outlined in the last section occurs during the initial stages of overall program development, and is reviewed periodically as changing conditions warrant. On the other hand, the assessment implementation process as reviewed in this section takes place daily in the life of a practicing professional. The assessment implementation process occurs when the specialist actually gathers the information from the client for assessment purposes, transforms the information into a usable format, makes decisions on the information gathered, and reports it to other concerned professionals. This entire process is described within seven steps, as outlined in the Assessment Implementation Model found in **Figure 4.2** (p. 118). The seven steps include: (a) review the assessment protocol, (b) prepare for the assessment, (c) administer the assessment to the client, (d) analyze or score the assessment results, (e) interpret results for client placement into programs, (f) document results of the assessment, and (g) reassess the client as necessary to monitor progress.

Review Assessment Protocol

In this step, the specialist is responsible for initial preparation before beginning to administer a client assessment. The specialist also reviews (perhaps mentally) the standardized assessment protocol. When this is accomplished prior to assessment administration, the specialist is more likely to adhere to the protocol, which in turn is more likely to produce valid and reliable results. It is important that each specialist administer the assessment, according to the standardized protocol, to each client in the

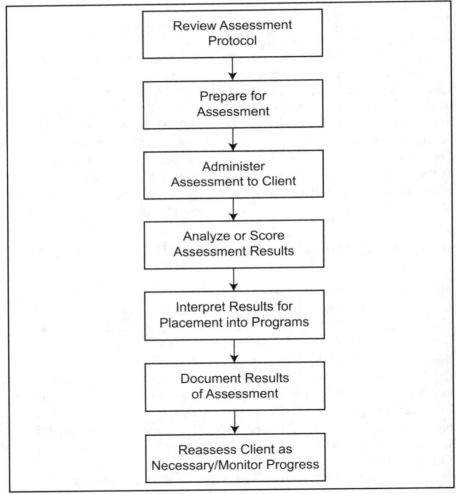

Figure 4.2
Therapeutic Recreation Assessment Implementation Model
(Peterson & Stumbo, 2000, p. 228)

same way every time. Deviations are likely to result in flawed results, translating into program placement errors and inability to produce and document client outcomes. Periodic staff training on this issue is beneficial to help specialists understand that adherence to assessment protocols is crucial to the entire process of placing clients into therapeutic recreation programs that will meet their needs.

Prepare for Assessment

This stage also is required prior to administration of an assessment. In this phase, the specialist is responsible for adhering to the protocol on preparation. For example, the staff member needs to gather any supplies or equipment needed for the administration of the assessment. The environment or place in which the assessment will occur needs to be secured and checked for availability, privacy, noise level, adequate seating (if necessary), adequate lighting, ventilation, and temperature. Whenever possible, the specialist should ensure that the environment remains the same from administration to administration. When the environment changes (e.g., loud noise levels, interruptions, distractions) the results of the assessment may be affected negatively.

Administer Assessment to Client

In this step the specialist implements the procedures for gathering the necessary information, usually from the client. Assessments in therapeutic recreation tend to be of four kinds: (a) interviews, (b) observations, (c) self-administered surveys, and (d) records reviews. Each type collects unique information and has its own advantages and disadvantages. These four types may be used in combination to strengthen the validity of the results.

Interviews

Interviews involve face-to-face contact with clients and/or their families. The primary reason for completing interviews is to allow the client to provide in-depth answers to open-ended questions while the specialist observes the client's behavior in an interview setting (Ferguson, 1983). Interviews are likely the primary way in which therapeutic recreation specialists gather information about clients. Interviews may be time-intensive and require great skill on the part of the specialist. Several principles apply to client assessment interviews:

- *Be consistent*. The protocol for administering an interview should include the words to be stated by the specialist. This includes establishing rapport, the introduction, transitions and probes during the body, and closure. Consistency increases reliability and reduces the chances for error in the assessment results due to the procedures used by the specialist.

- *Know the clients' characteristics*. Gathering information through client interviews may not be the most reasonable course of action for all client groups. Some individuals with cognitive deficits (e.g., acquired brain injury, cerebral vascular accident, mental retardation) or younger clients may not respond well to interview situations. The specialist often is responsible for gathering background information (perhaps from records reviews) about each client prior to interview situations.

- *Establish rapport/introduction*. It is important that the specialist establish rapport with the client (or family) by introducing himself or herself and the department, stating the purpose of the interview, explaining the basic structure of the interview and types of questions to be asked, and explaining how the information will be used for programming purposes. Issues of patient rights, confidentiality, privacy, and informed consent may be part of the interview's introduction. It is assumed that the environment is comfortable, quiet, private, and conducive to the interview process.

- *Ask open-ended questions*. Since the purpose of the interview is to gather in-depth information, it is a prime opportunity to ask open-ended questions to which the client may have an extended answer. (Reserve close-ended questions for self-administered surveys or observations.) Interview questions should contain content that parallels program content. Specialists should be aware that good open-ended questions are difficult to write, but worth the effort in terms of eliciting client responses.

- *Use probes and restatements for clarification*. The specialist should have specific questions ready for when clients are unclear or unsure of their answers.

- *Close the interview*. The interview closure summarizes the interview and the information that has surfaced. The specialist may reemphasize the results of the interview, how the results relate to program placement, and what goals or outcomes are to be expected or worked on. The closure also is a prime time to reiterate the services offered by the therapeutic recreation department, the schedule of programs, and how the specialist can be reached. The client should be thanked for his or her time and cooperation.

Chapter 8 further discusses the advantages, disadvantages, principles, and techniques related to interviewing clients for assessment purposes.

Observations

Observations involve the specialist viewing the client's behavior, either directly or indirectly. In some cases the client will know he or she is being observed, in other cases, he or she may not. The specialist should be aware of client autonomy and rights in conducting observations unknown to the client. The primary reason for conducting observations is to record the client's behavior (not perceptions of behavior as in interviews) in situations as real-life as possible. The specialist usually records observations of the client's behavior on score sheets that may include systems such as checklists, rating systems, and open-ended narratives (Stumbo, 1983). Typically, the specialist chooses to create close-ended rating systems to shorten the length of time spent recording the observations and to increase comparability across clients.

Principles that apply to observations include:

- *Be consistent.* Similar to interviews, the specialist needs to be consistent across observations. Protocols for administering observations should include the informed consent of the client, the environment or situation in which the client is to be observed, the scoring mechanism(s) for recording observations, and how scores result in treatment planning and program placement.

- *Determine which scoring system suits the purpose of the observation.* Several basic methods and techniques can be used to record client behavior. Each has its own advantages and disadvantages and should be selected with care.

- *Select behaviors that are clearly defined and observable within the available time period.* Behavioral rating systems are more easily created when the behaviors of interest are easily observable, and happen with enough regularity to occur within the observation time frame. For example, "interacting with other clients" is too vague to be usable and consistently recorded. Better examples of observable behavior might include: "greets other clients," "initiates conversation with peers," or "maintains eye contact."

- **Understand the limitations of observations**. Observations are excellent for recording client behaviors. They do not, however, explain the reasons or motives for the behavior. A specialist may observe a client sitting alone in a corner, but cannot draw conclusions about why this behavior is occurring simply from the observation itself. The specialist should always separate the description from the interpretation of that action or behavior.

Information regarding advantages, disadvantages, principles, and techniques related to observing clients for assessment purposes is located in Chapter 9.

Self-Administered Surveys

An option becoming more frequently used in therapeutic recreation assessments is self-administered surveys. Especially for individuals who are cognitively intact and can process information without the assistance of a specialist, self-administered surveys may provide a viable alternative. The primary purpose of survey assessment devices is to gather information quickly for the specialist. Since the client completes the survey without assistance and likely on his or her own time, this option frees the specialist of time spent on individual assessment. The major drawback would be the lack of rapport-building opportunities available in interview or observation situations.

For the most part, the questions on the survey should be close-ended (checklists, rating scales, or ranking) with open-ended response formats minimized. This reduces the burden on the client to provide lengthy, written responses whenever shorter, close-ended responses are a logical option.

Principles that apply to self-administered surveys include:

- **Be consistent**. The protocol for administering the self-administered survey should be consistent between specialists and between clients. Inconsistent instructions from "do whatever you can" to "take this very seriously" will change the nature of the client's responses, and will possibly add error to the results.

- **Provide complete written instructions**. Complete written instructions on the top of the survey help the client to finish the survey as accurately and as completely as possible. Written instructions at the end of the survey on how and to whom to return the survey are also important.

- *Ask only what is important to client placement into programs.* While this principle applies to all forms of assessment, it is especially important here to ask only what is important to client placement into programs. Since the self-administered assessment requires minimal specialist time, there is a tendency to ask many questions that have some curiosity factor, but are irrelevant to program placement. This can quickly become a privacy issue for clients.

Records Reviews

A fourth way to gain information about clients for placement into therapeutic recreation programs is to review some form of documentation kept by other disciplines or institutions. For example, instead of asking a client about his diagnosis during an interview, the specialist could locate this information on the main client chart prior to the interview. There are several reasons for conducting records reviews. First, it can give the specialist background about the client prior to other assessment forms, so the specialist can be informed and establish rapport more quickly. Second, it can be very repetitious to most clients to be asked for the same information from a variety of disciplines within a 1–3 day admission or intake period. Unnecessary duplication of information implies that the disciplines lack coordination in their treatment efforts. (The exception to this rule is to verify that a client is consistent in responding to set questions.) Third, the data from records reviews can help confirm any information gathered in other ways. If the client states active involvement in social events during an interview and similar information does not appear in other records, there may be need for further clarification from the client.

Principles that apply to records reviews include:

- *Information is only as good as its source.* The specialist should establish that the record is a credible source for gaining information about clients.

- *Check available written records prior to other assessment forms.* In almost all cases, having background information on the client, assuming it is correct, is helpful to other assessment gathering techniques.

- *Do not duplicate information that can found in documented records.* Unless there is a specific reason, clients should not be asked to repeat information already known and available elsewhere.

Regardless of information gathering technique(s) used, assessments need to be administered consistently. Each assessment technique needs a specific protocol consistent across (a) departments (if programs are similar), (b) specialists, (c) administrations by an individual specialist, (d) clients, and (e) assessment environments. Deviations from these consistencies lower the confidence that can be placed in the results and program placement decisions.

Table 4.2 provides a comparison of the advantages and disadvantages of the different methods of information gathering for assessment purposes. These comparisons are for illustrative purposes only; any method for collecting data can be improved by knowing the advantages and limitations of various methods.

Analyze or Score Assessment Results

Regardless of how the assessment gathers information (interview, observation, survey, records review), a scoring mechanism needs to be in place. Following the established protocol for scoring the assessment, the specialist summarizes the information collected through the assessment process in a clear and concise way. Also referred to as *data reduction*, this summary condenses quantitative data (numbers) and/or qualitative (words) data into an understandable and cohesive picture of the client.

Obviously it is easier and quicker to summarize and score assessment results that stem from close-ended or quantitative information. It usually takes longer to reduce and summarize qualitative data that result from open-ended questions. (However, it usually takes more effort and time to construct quality close-ended items than similar quality open-ended items.)

Unfortunately, the vast majority of therapeutic recreation assessments do not have adequate protocols for reliable scoring. Many assessments, because they rely on purely qualitative or open-ended data, are difficult to score due to the lack of an agreed-upon, congruent method of gathering and synthesizing information. For example, asking, "How do you spend your leisure time?" as an open-ended question with no established categories for marking an answer is likely to result in a diversity of difficult to categorize answers.

This step has been one of the most problematic for therapeutic recreation specialists. Because standardized scoring procedures are all but nonexistent (especially for agency-specific assessments), the specialist often is forced to rely on personal judgment for summarizing the results. This may fluctuate based on many superfluous reasons, such as mood, need to fill programs, or personal preference. That is, the specialist collects

Table 4.2
Comparison of Four Methods of Information Gathering for Assessment Purposes (Peterson & Stumbo, 2000, p. 233)

Interviews
Advantages
>   Opportunity to establish rapport with the client
>   Opportunity to explain department and programs to the client
>   Targets client's knowledge or perceptions of behavior

Disadvantages
>   Time consuming to administer for the specialist
>   Time consuming to score and interpret
>   Likely to be inconsistent between specialists, clients, and administrations

Observations
Advantages
>   Targets real behavior of clients
>   Can produce concrete data from which to compare clients' behaviors
>   Increased likelihood of being able to compare preprogram and postprogram behavior of individual clients

Disadvantages
>   Time consuming to develop and administer for the specialist
>   Does not get at reasons or motives for behavior
>   Difficult to view clients in similar, consistent situations

Self-Administered Surveys
Advantages
>   Time efficient for the specialist
>   May be time efficient for the client
>   Client can answer at own pace

Disadvantages
>   Client may not be the one completing the survey
>   Does not allow opportunity to establish rapport with the client
>   Limited opportunity to explain questions or meanings to the client

Records Reviews
Advantages
>   Time efficient for the specialist
>   In most settings data is readily accessible
>   Reduces redundancy for the client

Disadvantages
>   Information only as good as the source
>   Records may contain limited or dated information
>   Reduces personal contact with the client

assessment data (perhaps largely because of external or agency mandates), but then ignores any systematic procedure to score the results, and later places clients into programs based on personal preferences or the need to fill certain programs, or worse yet, every client is placed in every program. This inconsistent, unreliable "method" of program placement results in faulty decisions and the inability to produce client outcomes. As such, it jeopardizes the entire programming process and threatens the quality of therapeutic recreation program delivery.

Clearly, procedures for scoring are needed to make sense from the information given by the client, and to provide a consistent basis of program placement. Scoring can be simplified as long as it helps places the right clients into the right programs.

Interpret Results for Placement into Programs

After scores are calculated, the next step is to interpret what the scores mean for client placement into programs. The goal of this step is to make objective, consistent, and correct decisions for placing clients into therapeutic recreation programs. That is, the specialist wants to make correct Quadrant I and Quadrant IV decisions (see Table 1.7, p. 15). These placements should be based on the results of the assessment process obtained in the fourth step. If the results were obtained through a valid and reliable process, the interpretation of the results and placement decisions also are more likely to be valid and reliable. If two clients have similar scores or results on the assessment and they are placed in similar programs, as indicated as necessary from the assessment, then these "right" individuals are likely to be receiving the "right" service. On the other hand, if two clients have similar scores or results on the assessment, and they are placed in different programs, then the process is probably not producing valid or reliable results and is resulting in faulty interpretation and placement decisions. Some procedures, such as the Leisure Competence Measure, link scoring and interpretation quite closely. Some agencies develop local norms by accumulating client scores over time and looking for patterns.

Since consistency is a major issue in assessment, specialists aim to create standards from which to judge clients' scores for program placement. Scores either can be interpreted through norm-referenced or criterion-referenced means. These were discussed in Chapter 1 and will be reviewed here.

Norm-referenced scores provide benchmarks against which scores are judged according to how the client's peers score. For example, say the range of scores on a social skills assessment is from -10 to +10. A client's score is +5. One way to view this person's score is by *comparison with the scores of peers*. Where does a score of +5 stand in relative terms to all others admitted on the unit within the last 90 days? If everyone admitted in the last 90 days scored higher than this person, does that mean +5 is a low score, and the person should be placed in the Social Skills program? In norm-referenced situations like this one, how the group performs affects the interpretation of the individual's score and thus his or her placement into the program. For *criterion-referenced* scoring systems, each person is *measured against a set standard*. For example, if the standard is set so that anyone who scores below 0 is placed in the program, then a score of +5 means the person does not get placed into the Social Skills program. The individual's score is interpreted against a set, preestablished criterion. Whether the person qualifies depends on his or her individual score. It does not rely on others' scores—only whether or not the criterion was met. Every person can qualify or not qualify; each person is only judged against his or her own score, not in comparison with others.

Assessment scores can be interpreted in the same two ways. Individual scores can be compared against their peers, or against a certain measure or standard. The choice depends on what makes the most sense for program placement. Take the example of a social skills training program. Using a norm-referenced system, the specialist collects information and concludes that the clients who have the five lowest scores are the least socially skilled without some intervention programming. These individuals then would be targeted for the social skills training program for this time period. In a criterion-referenced system, the specialist collects data and finds that individuals who score below zero (criterion) need corrective programming. A client receiving a score below zero then would always be placed in the social skills training program, regardless of how other clients scored. Either method is effective depending on the intended outcome, and the selection decision should be based on the ability to improve the odds of correct program placement decisions.

It is clear that interpretation and use of assessment scores closely relates to how those scores are obtained and recorded. If data reduction or scoring is problematic, then interpretation of the data similarly will be problematic. Often specialists rely too heavily on personal judgment, and their placement of clients into programs is imprecise. This results in either clients not receiving necessary services (Quadrant II) or clients receiving unnecessary services (Quadrant III). The goal of quality client assessment is to make correct Quadrant I or Quadrant IV decisions the majority of the time.

Document Results of Assessment

This step is a vital checkpoint for the utility of the assessment results. One test of the entire assessment process is that the therapeutic recreation specialist is able to document unique, useful, and meaningful baseline information into the client's record. This information will help determine the action (course of treatment) taken with and for the client by the professionals involved in his or her care.

While the format of client records often is decided at the agency level, the department's staff, in consultation with other disciplines, usually decides the content that professionals enter into the record. The content to be reported from the results of the assessment is determined by the content of the programs, and in turn, the content of the assessment. Each contributing department has distinct areas of interest, usually parallel to their accepted scope of care within the agency.

One frustration, if the previous five steps have been done incorrectly or incompletely, is that the therapeutic recreation specialist has little valuable information to report. When prior assessment steps have not followed a logical, consistent, and justifiable sequence, or if programs are not based in a systematic analysis of client needs, the information provided by therapeutic recreation specialists may not differ greatly from other disciplines or may not contribute to the client's goals or treatment plan.

For example, a therapeutic recreation specialist may be providing valuable intervention programs with the content of (a) leisure awareness, (b) social interaction skills, and (c) community leisure resources. These are well-designed, outcome-oriented intervention programs that appear to be successful and complement the treatment programs of the other disciplines. However, the assessment content includes: (a) personal history, (b) past leisure interests, and (c) future leisure interests. How well does the content of the assessment match the content of the program? What can she say about client placement into programs? How will the "right" clients be placed systematically into the "right" programs? How will the link be translated in the client record?

The answer is that client placement into the correct programs is unlikely and the specialist will have little of value to report in the client record or to the treatment team. As a beginning, the specialist needs the assessment to reflect the program content of (a) leisure awareness, (b) social interaction skills, and (c) community leisure resources. Other information may have little value, and be regarded poorly by other members of the treatment team.

Reassess Client as Necessary/Monitor Progress

The final phase of reassessment was mentioned previously. Whenever the status of a client needs to be examined, conducting a reassessment using the same tool as the initial assessment appears logical. This reassessment may be necessary to write progress notes or discharge/referral summaries. If the original assessment tool produces results that are valid and reliable, then no better tool exists to determine the progression or regression of a particular client.

This does mean that the original assessment must have the precision (reliability) to determine sometimes small increments of movement. For example, if it is determined from the original assessment that a client lacks social interaction skills (and, therefore, the client is placed into a social skills program), the assessment must measure these skills with enough consistency to determine if change has been made during or at the completion of the program. If the assessment provides rough estimates of ability, then reassessment will be difficult, if not impossible. If this is the case, the specialist will have an extremely difficult time "proving" that the client achieved the intended outcomes of the therapeutic recreation program. This provides an additional reason why assessment items should be focused and yield concise results.

All seven steps point to the need for the assessment process and results to be both valid and reliable. This requires a great deal of specialist expertise, competence, and effort. Each step is intricately linked and poor decisions in one phase result in mistakes or poor execution in other phases. As the key information source for further involvement with the client, assessment plays a critical role in providing intervention to clients that can produce dependable outcomes.

Summary

Assessment planning and assessment implementation provide crucial links in the accountability chain. This chapter reiterated that a well-designed and comprehensive program of services is an essential foundation for that accountability. Assessment planning and assessment implementation rise from that foundation and illustrate the need to link assessment and programs. Assessment planning involves (a) analyzing the environment, (b) defining parameters, (c) selecting or developing an assessment, (d) establishing assessment protocols, and (e) training staff and interns on the assessment protocols. Assessment implementation includes: (a) reviewing the assessment protocols, (b) preparing for assessment, (c) administering the assessment, (d) analyzing or scoring the assessment results, and (e) interpreting results for placement into programs. Assessment planning and implementation are expanded in Chapters 5–9.

References

Dunn, J. (1984). Assessment. In C. A. Peterson and S. L. Gunn (Eds.), *Therapeutic recreation program design: Principles and procedures.* (2nd ed., pp. 267–320). Englewood Cliffs, NJ: Prentice-Hall.

Dunn, J. K. (1987). Establishing reliability and validity of evaluation instruments. *Journal of Park and Recreation Administration, 5*(4), 61–70.

Dunn, J. K. (1989). Guidelines for using published assessment procedures. *Therapeutic Recreation Journal, 23*(2), 59–69.

Ferguson, D. (1983). Assessment interviewing techniques: A useful tool in developing individual program plans. *Therapeutic Recreation Journal, 17*(2), 16–22.

Kloseck, M., Crilly, R. G., Ellis, G. D., and Lammers, E. (1996). Leisure Competence Measure: Development and reliability testing of a scale to measure functional outcomes in therapeutic recreation. *Therapeutic Recreation Journal, 30*(1), 13–26.

Navar, N. (1991). Advancing therapeutic recreation through quality assurance: A perspective on the changing nature of quality in therapeutic recreation. In B. Riley (Ed.), *Quality management: Applications for therapeutic recreation* (pp. 3–20). State College, PA: Venture Publishing, Inc.

Peterson, C. A. and Stumbo, N. J. (2000). *Therapeutic recreation program design: Principles and procedures* (3rd ed.). Needham Heights, MA: Allyn & Bacon.

Stumbo, N. J. (1983). Systematic observation as a research tool for assessing client behavior. *Therapeutic Recreation Journal, 17*(4), 53–63.

Stumbo, N. J. (1991). Selected assessment resources: A review of instruments and references. *Annual in Therapeutic Recreation, 2*(2), 8–24.

Stumbo, N. J. (1992). Re-thinking activity inventories. *Illinois Parks and Recreation Magazine, 23*(2), 17–21.

Stumbo, N. J. (1993/1994). The use of activity interest inventories in therapeutic recreation assessment. *Annual in Therapeutic Recreation, 4*, 11–20.

Stumbo, N. J. (1994/1995). Assessment of social skills for therapeutic recreation intervention. *Annual in Therapeutic Recreation, 5*, 68–82.

Stumbo, N. J. (1997). Issues and concerns in therapeutic recreation assessment. In D. Compton (Ed.), *Issues in therapeutic recreation: Toward the new millennium* (2nd ed., pp. 347–372). Champaign, IL: Sagamore Publishing.

Stumbo, N. J. (2001). Revisited: Issues and concerns in therapeutic recreation. In N. J. Stumbo (Ed.). *Professional issues in therapeutic recreation: On competence and outcomes* (pp. 215–236). Champaign, IL: Sagamore Publishing.

Stumbo, N. J. and Rickards, W. H. (1986). Selecting assessment instruments: Theory into practice. *Journal of Expanding Horizons in Therapeutic Recreation, 1*(1), 1–6.

Witt, P. A. and Ellis, G. D. (1987). *The Leisure Diagnostic Battery users manual*. State College, PA: Venture Publishing, Inc.

Chapter 5
Selection of Assessment
Instruments and Procedures

The previous chapters have discussed assessment concepts, measurement characteristics, programming considerations, and assessment planning and implementation processes. Inherent in all of these discussions is that selecting an assessment instrument or procedure is a crucial decision in the entire accountability process. Equally important as selecting and implementing the right *programs* for client involvement, selecting and implementing the right *assessment* for client placement into those programs stands as a monumental task for all therapeutic recreation specialists. This chapter expands on the information presented in the previous four chapters concerning the selection of assessment instruments and techniques. Assessment selection decisions need to be systematic, logical, and based on measurement properties (as discussed in Chapter 2).

Assessment Selection as Part of the Assessment Planning Process

Chapter 4 outlined the Assessment Planning Model and the Assessment Implementation Model (Peterson & Stumbo, 2000). These models were created to show the logical relationship between various decisions and actions before and during client assessment. They are significant parts of the entire Therapeutic Recreation Accountability Model. The steps in the two models include:

Assessment Planning Model
- Analyze the environment
- Define parameters
- Select or develop an assessment
- Establish assessment protocols
- Train staff and interns on the protocols

Assessment Implementation Model

- Review assessment protocols
- Prepare for assessment
- Administer the assessment to client
- Analyze or score assessment results
- Interpret results for placement into programs
- Document results of assessment
- Reassess client as necessary/monitor progress

This chapter will briefly review the first two steps of the Assessment Planning Model and then focus on the third step, *select or develop an assessment*. Understanding this information is important to the therapeutic recreation specialist who intends to provide intervention services that can produce predictable, meaningful, and desired client outcomes.

Analyzing the environment includes (a) agency considerations (e.g., mission, services delivered, other disciplines), (b) client considerations (e.g., typical needs, limitations, abilities, living environments), (c) therapeutic recreation program considerations (e.g., content, level, purpose of the program), and (d) staff and resource considerations (e.g., level of staff expertise, budget, time available for assessment, training). All four of these sources of information must be considered prior to evaluating the usability potential of client assessments.

Defining the parameters includes determining the function, content, and implementation strategy of the assessment. Functions of an assessment include (a) basic screening, (b) identifying the problem(s), (c) narrowing the problems(s), and/or (d) reassessing or monitoring client progress. The assessment content must match the therapeutic recreation program content, as Table 1.6 (p. 13) illustrates. Possible assessment implementation strategies include (a) interviews, (b) observations, (c) self-administered questionnaires, and (d) records reviews. Although none of these decisions are unchangeable, addressing these areas prior to selecting or developing an assessment instrument or procedure is fundamental.

Selecting or Developing an Assessment Instrument or Procedure

Once the environment has been explored and the parameters have been reviewed, the therapeutic recreation specialist must select a commercial assessment or develop an agency-specific assessment. Whether an assessment is purchased or created, the evaluation process is nearly the same:

The desired end result is an assessment that produces valid and reliable data that can be used with confidence and with minimal error to place clients into the right programs that address their needs and goals. The next two sections review some of the concepts behind purchasing an assessment or developing an agency-specific assessment. (These concepts are expanded in Chapter 6 and Chapter 7.)

Ward and Murray-Ward (1999, p. 217) identified 10 steps in selecting a commercially available test:

1. Identify the purposes of the testing
2. Select the committee
3. Establish the content and skills to be covered
4. Identify the technical requirements
5. Locate possibilities for tests and obtain copies
6. Locate sources of technical information for the tests and obtain copies
7. Evaluate the tests for coverage of content and skills and tentative selection
8. Evaluate the technical qualities of the selected test
9. Make the decision
10. Identify additional tests or information needed, if necessary

Gronlund and Linn (1990, pp. 321–324) simplified these into six steps. Questions suitable for clarifying each step are provided.

1. Define testing needs (What is the type of information to be sought? What are the objectives and outcomes of the program? How will the results be used?)
2. Narrow the choice (What are the selection criteria to be used for choosing the assessment? How do the agency, clients, program, and specialists affect this decision?)
3. Locate suitable tests (How many assessments are available for this purpose? for this group of clients?)
4. Obtain specimen sets (Most publishers provide specimen sets that can be examined by potential users.)
5. Review test materials (How well does the test manual describe: the uses of the test, qualifications needed to administer and score, evidence of validity and reliability, directions for administering and scoring, and the bases for interpreting scores?)
6. Use a test evaluation form (Examples follow in this chapter.)

Dunn (1984), specifically addressing therapeutic recreation client assessment, outlined a model to address assessment selection decisions. The following list is an adaptation of the steps she suggested.

1. Specify the purpose of the assessment

   The purpose is based on the types of decisions to be made from the assessment (similar to *function of the assessment*).

2. Specify the content of the assessment

   The content of the assessment depends on the program components and goals.

3. Identify selection criteria

   Criteria include:

   • Reliability, validity, and usability information

   • Whether the assessment (a) meets its intended purpose, (b) has the ability to gather the wanted information, (c) can gather the information accurately, (d) utilizes an appropriate method, (e) is appropriate for clients, agency, and situation, and (f) has adequate directions/manual.

4. Search Assessment Resources

   Assessment or measurement sources (e.g., *Mental Measurement Yearbook, Tests in Print, Journal of Educational Measurement, Journal of Counseling Psychology*), therapeutic recreation resources (e.g., *Therapeutic Recreation Journal, Annual in Therapeutic Recreation*), and continuing education opportunities at universities.

5. Compare Possible Procedures to Criteria

   Compare intended use and applicability to program, staff, clients, and agency with the assessments under consideration.

6. Select the Instrument

   Select the "best match" possible given the criteria and the resources available.

Dunn's (1984) selection process parallels the Assessment Planning Model's first three steps, which have the following principles in common:

1. Knowing the purpose of the assessment and how the results are to be used is important as a beginning foundation.

2. Tying the content of the assessment to the content of the programs will reduce error and increase confidence in client placement into programs as well as aid in the measurement of client outcomes.

3. Validity, reliability, fairness, and practicality are foremost considerations in choosing or developing client assessments for therapeutic recreation services.

4. Adequate information concerning development and directions for use, scoring, interpretation, and reporting is necessary, whether the assessment is to be purchased or developed.

5. A variety of assessments may need to be reviewed to select the best possible option.

6. An assessment manual should provide complete information about the development, validation, and projected use of the assessment so that an evaluation of its potential can be made.

7. Therapeutic recreation specialists should focus on selecting the *best* assessment after careful consideration of several options, regardless if they are purchased or developed.

These seven principles are the crux of selecting the best possible assessment for use with clients. Each therapeutic recreation specialist should concentrate on understanding these concepts and how they apply to client assessment. The next section contains four formal procedures to evaluate assessment instruments and procedures.

Four Tools for Evaluating and Selecting an Assessment Instrument

This section introduces four methods of formally selecting assessments for use with clients, including: (a) Assessment Selection Checklist (Stumbo & Rickards, 1986); (b) Guidelines for Using Published Assessment/Evaluation Instruments (Dunn, 1989); and (c) Test Evaluation Form (Gronlund & Linn, 1990); and (d) Evaluation of an Assessment Instrument (Anastasi, 1988).

Assessment Selection Checklist

Stumbo and Rickard's (1986) *Assessment Selection Checklist* (see **Table 5.1**, pp. 138–139) was constructed to aid therapeutic recreation profession- als in reviewing the validity and reliability information of an assessment without extreme technical knowledge on the part of the user. Areas include (a) facility/agency concerns, (b) program concerns, (c) population/client concerns, (d) staff concerns, and (e) administrative concerns. The Checklist requires the professional to answer several yes/no questions regarding the assessment he or she is evaluating. If the responses contain a significant number of "nos," the professional is encouraged to select a different assessment and begin the review process again. Primarily, the Checklist is intended for beginning users, without extensive background in measurement.

Table 5.1
Assessment Selection Checklist
(Adapted from Stumbo & Rickards, 1986)

Facility/Agency Concerns
Does the assessment instrument/procedure:

1. Align with the purpose of the agency? (e.g., treatment, referral)	Yes No NA
2. Align with the policies of the agency?	Yes No NA
3. Align with the resources available within the agency?	Yes No NA
4. Match the types of assessments currently used by the department/agency?	Yes No NA
5. Complement other facility assessments but emphasize TR and leisure involvement?	Yes No NA
6. Meet external accreditation requirements?	Yes No NA

Program Concerns
Does the assessment instrument/procedure:

1. Match the intent/goals/philosophy of the overall program?	Yes No NA
2. Match the intent/goals of specific programs?	Yes No NA
3. Align with the program documentation?	Yes No NA
4. Yield enough information to appropriately place clients into programs?	Yes No NA
5. Yield the right kinds of information to appropriately place clients into programs?	Yes No NA
6. Not repeat information gathered from other sources which is readily available to TR?	Yes No NA
7. Allow for information for both assessment and evaluation of the client at a later date?	Yes No NA
8. Yield information about clients in a consistent manner?	Yes No NA
9. Match the resources available within the therapeutic recreation department (e.g., cost, staff expertise, time for administration and scoring)?	Yes No NA
10. Meet professional standards?	Yes No NA

Population/Client Concerns
Does the assessment instrument/procedure:

1. Match the client's abilities? (if self-administered)

a. Can the client read the instrument?	Yes No NA
b. Can the client understand the questions?	Yes No NA
c. Can the client tabulate the results? (if appropriate)	Yes No NA

Guidelines for Using Published Assessment/ Evaluation Instruments

Dunn (1989) provided a set of Guidelines for Using Published Assessment/ Evaluation Instruments in the *Therapeutic Recreation Journal* (see **Table 5.2**, p. 140). These guidelines supply standardized evaluation criteria to use

Table 5.1 (continued)
Assessment Selection Checklist
(Adapted from Stumbo & Rickards, 1986)

2. Match the clients'	
a. Performance abilities?	Yes No NA
b. Needs	Yes No NA
c. Characteristics?	Yes No NA
3. Have validity for this population?	Yes No NA
4. Have reliability for this population?	Yes No NA
Staff Concerns	
Does the assessment instrument/procedure:	
1. Match the staff's abilities?	
a. Does the staff have expertise to administer and interpret instrument/procedures?	Yes No NA
b. Will they have time to administer the assessment?	Yes No NA
c. Will they have time to score and analyze the results?	Yes No NA
d. Can they interpret the results to place clients into appropriate activities?	Yes No NA
e. Will they have time to document the results?	Yes No NA
2. Match the training level of the staff?	Yes No NA
3. Require extensive scoring and analysis?	Yes No NA
4. Require extensive interpretation?	Yes No NA
5. Provide similar results/interpretation between individual staff?	Yes No NA
Administrative Concerns	
Does the assessment instrument/procedure:	
1. Have sufficient documentation on administration and interpretation methods?	Yes No NA
2. Have sufficient documentation about validity and reliability for similar populations and programs?	Yes No NA
3. Provide references for further reading about the instrument/ procedure?	Yes No NA
4. Have alternative forms or methods for administration?	Yes No NA
5. Fit within the budget allowed for assessment?	Yes No NA
6. Allow for public use?	Yes No NA
7. Allow for computer use in administration and scoring?	Yes No NA
8. Provide enough useful information to warrant its use?	Yes No NA
9. Combine readily with other assessments?	Yes No NA

Table 5.2
Guidelines for Using Published Assessment Procedures
(Adapted from Dunn, 1989)

Guidelines for Selection of Assessment Procedures
1. The assessment should provide evidence of validity.
    1.1 The assessment should be validated on a representative sample of sufficient size.
    1.2 The assessment should be valid for its intended use.
    1.3 There should be evidence of the relationship of subscores to total scores of those measures that produce subscores.
2. The assessment must provide evidence of reliability.
3. The manual and test materials should be complete and of appropriate quality.
4. A test user should demonstrate relevance for the assessment selection.
    4.1. The assessment should be relevant to the clients served by the agency.
    4.2 The assessment should be relevant to the decisions made based on assessment results.

Guidelines for Assessment Use
5. An assessment should be revalidated when any changes are made in procedures, materials, or when it is used for a purpose or with a population group for which it was not intended.
6. The assessment should be selected and used by qualified individuals.
7. The assessment should be utilized in the intended way.
8. Published assessments should be used in combination with other methods.

Guidelines for Administering, Scoring, and Reporting
9. The administration and scoring of an assessment should follow standardized procedures.
    9.1 During the administration of an assessment, care should be taken in providing a comfortable environment with minimal distractions.
    9.2 During the administration of assessments, the administrator should be aware of the importance and effect of rapport with the client.
10. It is the responsibility of the test user to protect the security of materials.

Guidelines for Protecting the Rights of Clients
11. Test results should not be released without informed consent.
12. Data regarding a patient's assessment results should be kept in a designated patient file.

concerning assessments and their related documentation. Assessment guidelines are provided for (a) selection; (b) use; (c) administering, scoring, and reporting; and (d) protecting the rights of clients. Users need to ensure that the assessment he or she is evaluating meets the criteria of the standards. The Guidelines can be used by the professional for selecting assessments through supplying descriptive, written evidence of how the assessment meets each standard. An assessment that does not sufficiently meet the standards can be discarded, and a new one evaluated. An understanding of measurement concepts is required prior to using the Guidelines, although information is given in the article.

Test Evaluation Form

Gronlund and Linn (1990) provided a test evaluation form within their chapter on test selection, administration, and use (see **Table 5.3**, p. 142). After the general description of the test, the form asks the user to indicate the technical features (e.g., validity, reliability, norms) and practical features (e.g., ease of administration, scoring, and interpretation, adequacy of test manual). The fourth and final section culminates in a general evaluation of the test for the purposes intended. The user needs considerable prior knowledge to provide adequate information within the categories.

Evaluation of an Assessment Instrument

Anastasi (1988) wrote several seminal texts on psychological testing. Her Evaluation of an Assessment Instrument format supplies specific topics for review and evaluation (see **Table 5.4**, p. 143). Although very similar to Gronlund and Linn's (1990) as well as Dunn's (1989), it is the most technically demanding; however, more information is provided on the actual form to guide the user. The topics covered on the evaluation form include (a) general information, (b) description of assessment instrument, (c) practical evaluation, (d) technical evaluation, and (e) summative evaluation. The user is to provide descriptive, written responses to items in each of the five areas listed.

Regardless of which of the four evaluation devices is used for the selection of assessment instruments, their use will improve the professional's decision. Even a cursory review of the elements provides the professional with the sense that there is more to selecting an assessment than lining up at a vendor's booth or buying from a product catalog. Each of these evaluation instruments leads the specialist in reviewing the essential properties of a quality assessment. It is only with these quality assessments that clients can be properly assessed and placed into the appropriate programs to meet their needs.

Table 5.3
Test Evaluation Form (Adapted from Gronlund & Linn, 1990)

Title	_____
Authors	_____
Publisher	_____
Publication date	_____
Purpose of test	_____
For grades (ages)	_____
Forms	_____
Scores available	_____
Administration time	_____

Technical Features
Validity: Nature of evidence (e.g., content-related, construct-related, criterion-related)
Reliability: Nature of evidence (e.g., stability, internal consistency, equivalence). Standard error of measurement (e.g., size, type)
Norms: Type, adequacy, and appropriateness to local situation
Criterion-referenced interpretation: Describe (if available)

Practical Features
Ease of administration (e.g., procedures and timing)
Ease of scoring and interpretation
Adequacy of test manual and accessory materials

General Evaluation
Comments of reviewers (see published reviews)
Summary of strengths
Summary of weaknesses
Recommendations concerning local use

Table 5.4
Evaluation of an Assessment Instrument
(Adapted from Anastasi, 1988)

A. General Information
1. Title of Assessment
2. Author(s)
3. Publisher, date of publication
4. Forms available
5. Type of assessment
6. Cost

B. Description of Assessment Instrument
1. General type of assessment (e.g., individual or group, performance, interest inventory)
2. Population for which it was designed (e.g., age range, characterisitics)
3. Nature of content (e.g., verbal, numerical, spatial, motor)
4. Subtests and separate scores
5. Type(s) of items

C. Practical Evaluation
1. Qualitative features (e.g., design of test booklet, editorial quality of content, ease of using, attractiveness, durability, appropriateness for examinees):
2. Ease of administration
3. Clarity of directions
4. Scoring procedures
5. Examiner qualifications and training
6. Face validity and examinee rapport

D. Technical Evaluation
1. Norms
   a. Type (e.g., percentiles, standard scores)
   b. Standardization sample (nature, size, representativeness, procedures followed in obtaining sample, availability of subgroup norms (e.g., age, gender, education, occupation, region)
2. Reliability
   a. Types and procedures (e.g., test–retest, parallel form, split–half, Kuder–Richardson), including size and nature of samples employed)
   b. Scorer reliability if applicable
   c. Equivalence of forms
   d. Long-term stability when available
3. Validity
   a. Appropriate types of validation procedures (content/construct/criterion)
   b. Specific procedures followed in assessing validity and results obtained
   c. Size and nature of samples employed

E. Summative Evaluation
1. Does the tool represent the Leisure Ability position of TR services? In what way?
2. Rate the objectivity/subjectivity of the tool: 1 (objective) to 5 (subjective)
3. Rate the strength of the tool as an individual evaluation instrument for TRS: 1 (very good) to 5 (very poor)
4. List the strengths and weaknesses of the tool
5. What would you suggest to improve the tool?
6. Is the assessment appropriate for use in your program?

Summary

In the assessment planning process, the therapeutic recreation specialist needs to be aware of the environment in which the assessment will be used and the function, content, and implementation strategy of the assessment prior to any decisions about buying or creating an assessment. Several authors have provided procedural lists of steps to be followed when selecting commercial assessments. These steps become very similar to the process used to develop and validate assessments. The next two chapters include more information about purchasing assessments for use in therapeutic recreation services as well as developing agency-specific assessments.

References

Anastasi, A. (1988). *Psychological testing*. New York, NY: Macmillan.

Dunn, J. K. (1984). Assessment. In C. A. Peterson and S. L. Gunn (Eds.), *Therapeutic recreation program design: Principles and procedures* (2nd ed., pp. 267–320). Englewood Cliff, NJ: Prentice Hall, Inc.

Dunn, J. K. (1989). Guidelines for using published assessment procedures. *Therapeutic Recreation Journal, 23*(2), 59–69.

Gronlund, N. E. and Linn, R. L. (1990). *Measurement and evaluation in teaching* (6th ed.). New York, NY: Macmillan Publishing.

Peterson, C. A. and Stumbo, N. J. (2000). *Therapeutic recreation program design: Principles and procedures* (3rd ed). Needham Heights, MA: Allyn & Bacon.

Stumbo, N. J. and Rickards, W. H. (1986). Selecting assessment instruments: Theory into practice. *Journal of Expanding Horizons in Therapeutic Recreation, 1*(1), 1–6.

Ward, A.W. and Murray-Ward, M. (1999). *Assessment in the classroom*. Belmont, CA: Wadsworth Publishing.

Chapter 6
Critiquing a Commercial
Assessment for Purchase

The previous chapter covered the important characteristics that should be inherent in all commercial assessments and provided several methods of selecting the most appropriate and highest quality assessments. Readers should be familiar with that information before beginning this chapter. This chapter will expand on the information in Chapter 5 and apply it to critiquing commercial assessments for use in therapeutic recreation intervention programs. The approach used in this chapter combines the criteria from the four evaluation tools illustrated in Tables 5. 1 (p. 138–139), 5.2 (p. 140), 5.3 (p. 142), and 5.4 (p. 143). These criteria will be discussed in four sections: (a) description of the assessment instrument, (b) practical evaluation, (c) technical evaluation, and (d) summative evaluation.

Description of the Assessment Instrument

One of the most basic steps in evaluating an assessment tool is to fully understand its content and procedures. In evaluating commercial assessments, it is important to get a clear idea of the:

- Content and purpose
- Population (client group)
- Design considerations
- Publication information

The *content and purpose* of the assessment is extremely important in deciding whether it's appropriate to use in a particular agency. The content of the assessment must match the content of the therapeutic recreation intervention program. In addition, the purpose (e.g., basic screening, identifying the problem(s), narrowing the problem(s), reassessing or monitoring) affects the focus of the assessment and changes the types of questions asked. Assessments that have as their purpose narrowing the problem(s) will ask more detailed questions than those whose purpose is basic screening.

The *client group* for which the assessment is intended should also be very clear in the assessment manual or information. For what disability or illness groups is the assessment intended? what age groups? any special considerations about the population (e.g., chronic illnesses vs. acute illnesses)? The client group for which the assessment is intended should be similar to the norm group on which the assessment was validated.

Design considerations may include how many forms are available, the types of items included on the assessment, how the assessment is administered, and time needed for administration, scoring, and interpretation. More discussion about these design factors will be included in the Practical Evaluation section.

Beyond the assessment's title and authors' names, *publication information* may include what company or individual publishes the assessment, how widely available it is, how many forms are available, what year was it developed, how many new versions have been developed or updated, and cost. Again, this publishing information may overlap with the practical evaluation, but some basic considerations need immediate attention prior to evaluating the more formal aspects of the assessment.

These four pieces of descriptive information (content and purpose, client group, design considerations, and publishing information) help the evaluator to distinguish between different assessments under consideration and to determine if further evaluation of the practical and more technical aspects of each assessment is warranted.

Practical Evaluation

The practical evaluation includes a variety of factors that make the assessment either attractive or prohibitive to the user. Most of the information should be included in a user's manual or other documentation purchased with the assessment. Practical aspects of the assessment include:

- Assessment documentation and materials—readability, ease of use, attractiveness, durability, appropriateness for clients (if necessary)
- Clarity and completeness of directions (protocols) for administration, scoring, interpretation, and reporting of results
- Environmental and timing considerations for administration of assessment
- Required specialist qualifications, expertise, and training
- Amount or nature of interaction required between the specialist and the client

Every commercial assessment should have an accompanying manual or set of materials that explain the development, validation, and intended use of the assessment. These materials should explain each of these factors in a clear, concise, and complete manner. The manual should be attractively packaged and durable for repeated use.

The assessment manual should also have complete and clear instructions or protocols for how the assessment is to be administered and scored. Information on the administration should include the type of environment in which the assessment should be given (e.g., free of distractions, private, comfortable). Scoring procedures should include full disclosure of how the assessment is to be scored, and whether this is done manually or through use of a computer. Scoring information also should include the meaning of the scores received by clients—that is, how the scores are to be interpreted and reported. The information should include whether the assessment is norm-referenced or criterion-referenced (see Chapter 1), and either the norms or criterions from which to judge an individual client's score. For example, is a score of +5 average for the norm group? Does a score of +10 mean the client reaches the threshold (criterion) for entry into a certain program? Do scores on subscales combine to form one final score? The information on scoring, interpretation, and reporting of the assessment results should be explicit, and provide the specialist with clear indications of what each assessment score means.

Any special considerations for the assessment environment also should be included in the documentation. Most assessments assume that the environment is to be private, free from distractions, and comfortable for both the client and the specialist. However, sometimes, special environments need to be created or considered. For example, if the assessment concentrates on physical motor ability, adequate physical space (e.g., gymnasium or open area) needs to be available. In addition, does the specialist need to provide special materials or situations? Some assessments need special materials, such as flash cards, while some depend on the specialist viewing the client during interactions with peers. The important point for the specialist to remember is that those special materials or circumstances are needed each and every time the assessment is administered to clients.

Specialist qualifications, expertise, or training are other considerations in the practical evaluation. Does the specialist need special qualifications? expertise? training? Does the specialist need special skill in interviewing? observations? scoring calculations? What is the typical therapeutic recreation specialist expected to know? Does the assessment under consideration require more than that? Does the assessment require training or expertise beyond these minimal competencies (see Chapter 1)?

The environment and specialist qualifications also combine to determine the quality and nature of the interaction between the specialist and the client. The manual should include specific information about the degree to which the specialist interacts with the client during the assessment. Should the specialist provide encouragement? praise? clarification? redirection? summarizing comments? If the specialist is conducting an observation, is interaction minimal? nonintrusive? direct? known? All of this information should be included in the materials that accompany the assessment.

The practical evaluation carries important considerations in choosing assessments. Without even getting to the technical aspects, the practical aspects may reveal whether an assessment is appropriate for use at a particular agency or with a particular group of clients. Whenever the practical aspects find that the assessment is inappropriate for the agency, program, or clients, it should no longer be considered, and another assessment should be selected for evaluation.

Technical Evaluation

Technical evaluation of an assessment is crucial to the decision of its acceptability. The assessment developer, in the provided assessment materials, should provide enough evidence about the development, validation, and intended use of the assessment to convince the potential user that this is the best possible assessment for purchase for this particular agency, program, and group of clients. This is accomplished by providing an abundance of information on: (a) the validation or norm group(s), (b) evidence of validity, and (c) estimates of reliability.

Norm Group(s)

Each assessment is designed with a particular group in mind—for example, individuals with physical disabilities, individuals with psychiatric difficulties, or individuals with mental retardation. Obviously, some assessments define their target group even more narrowly, such as individuals with mild mental retardation or individuals over 50. The nature and description of the norm group are important considerations in evaluating assessment tools.

Gronlund and Linn (1990) suggested five guidelines for determining if norm groups are adequate: (a) relevance to the intended user group, (b) representativeness to the user group, (c) recency of data, (d) comparability with client group, and (e) adequate description of norm group.

The norm group—or group on which the assessment has been tested—needs to be similar to the group for whom the specialist wants to use the assessment. If the assessment has been validated on children without disabilities under 15 and the intended user group is individuals over 60 in an assisted living program, the assessment should be discarded from consideration and another selected for evaluation. The assessment should be tested and validated on a representative sample of sufficient size (Dunn, 1989).

The description of the norm group should include the sampling procedure used to gather them (Random? Purposive? Convenience?), how representative or adequate the sample was (Large enough to increase confidence in the results? Too small or too confined of a sample?), and enough description to determine if they are similar to any particular local agency (Gender? Ages? Education? Occupation? Locale?). In particular to client assessments, the description also should include detailed information about the sample's disabilities and/or illnesses.

Assessments that have multiple norm groups or that have been tested in many groups with similar characteristics are usually seen as stronger. For example, if the assessment has been tested in agencies in Arizona, South Carolina, and Maine, this minimizes the regional differences that might have appeared if only testing one state or city . If the assessment is validated on individuals with strokes, spinal cord injuries, and arthritis, then we might have more confidence of its broader appeal. However, the sampling decision depends on the designed purpose of the test (i.e., some assessments are meant for a very select group). Again, if the evaluator finds that the norm group of the assessment in considerably different from the potential client group(s) to be served by the assessment, the assessment should be discarded and another selected for review.

These guidelines are helpful for both selecting norm groups for validation situations as well as evaluating the adequacy of norm groups to an intended user group. Determining that the norm group is relevant, comparable, and adequate is important to determining the technical aspects of the assessment.

Evidence of Validity

Chapter 2 provided an in-depth discussion of validity and its application to client assessments. In evaluating an assessment for use, it is important to consider this same information. Evidence of *content-related validity* is important for all assessments. Content-related validity shows that the items on the assessment are representative of the entire domain being tested. The results of the assessment are to be used to demonstrate how well an individual performs at present in a universe of situations that the test situation claims to represent. For example, an assessment measuring leisure barriers must show evidence of adequately representing all known leisure barriers for the group being tested. The question to be answered is: "How well does the content of this procedure constitute an adequate sample of the topic?" Evidence of content-related validity includes a definition of the domain or area being tested, a review of the professional literature, and a table of specifications for the assessment (see Chapter 2).

Evidence of *criterion-related validity* is appropriate for assessments that are used to predict concurrent or future results to another test or criterion. Criterion-related validity is important when the user wishes to forecast a client's future (predictive) or present (concurrent) standing on some variable of particular significance that is different from the assessment. The question to be answered is: "How well do the test's results predict the scores of the criterion test?" Besides making sure that the connection between the test and the criterion is logical, correlations are also calculated between the test results and the criterion results.

Evidence of *construct-related validity* is important for those assessments that measure some trait or attitude or psychological construct (e.g., leisure behavior, leisure attitudes, leisure satisfaction). In this case, the user wishes to infer the degree to which the client possesses some hypothetical trait or quality (construct) presumed to be reflected in the assessment results. The question to be answered is: "How well does this assessment measure the construct in question?" Evidence of construct validity is collected through multiple testing trials and includes correlations with other tests known to measure the same trait, factor analysis, convergent and discriminant analyses, and expert reviews of the test content.

For all types of evidence of validity, the reader is reminded that validity:

- Is a matter of degree, not an absolute
- Is dependent on many types of evidence
- Is inferred from available evidence but not directly measured
- Is specific to a particular use of the intended assessment
- Refers to the results, not the instrument itself
- Is a unitary concept

Estimates of Reliability

Chapter 2 covers the three basic types of reliability estimates: (a) stability, (b) equivalency, and (c) internal consistency. Because reliability is fundamental in its own right, as well as necessary for validity, assessment validation should show evidence of several reliability tests. For example, a single test–retest of an assessment would be inadequate to ensure the stability of the instrument's results.

Stability testing answers the question: "How stable is the assessment over time?" The usual period between initial test and the retest is 2 weeks, and the developer is hoping for approximately the same scores for each individual on both administrations. If the scores vary widely, the test is not seen as stable and dependable over time; that is, too much error is present in the results. Multiple stability tests help increase the confidence of the stability of the tool (given that the correlations are adequate). Stability is calculated with correlation coefficients between the two sets of scores.

Equivalent-form reliability is appropriate when there are two forms of the same test; for example, Form A and Form B. Equivalent-form reliability answers the question: "How similar is one set of scores to the other set of scores?" The two forms of the assessment are given to one group at the same time, or in a soon-to-follow administration. A reliability coefficient is calculated between the two sets of scores.

Internal consistency estimates are calculated when only one version of one test is given to a group. Internal consistency reliabilities answer the question: "How well do halves of this test represent the whole?" Internal consistency reliabilities split the test into two halves for calculation purposes. Different correlation coefficients do this splitting in different ways (see Chapter 2). Internal consistency coefficients are usually smaller than whole–test correlations.

In addition, for assessments that include observation, several kinds of *interrater reliability* indices exist. Four were mentioned in Chapter 2: (a) simple agreement, (b) point-to-point agreement, (c) percentage of agreement for the occurrence of target behaviors, and (d) kappa index. Each of these interrater reliability indices has advantages and disadvantages, and some acknowledge the difference between agreement and accuracy. Remember also that reliability:

- Refers to the results, not the test itself
- Refers to a particular type of consistency
- Explains what proportion of the test variance is nonerror variance
- Increases with the length of the test
- Increases with the spread of scores
- May vary at different levels of test performance
- Is a necessary but not sufficient condition for validity

Summative Evaluation

The final piece of the evaluation is to summarize all of this information to see if the assessment is suitable for use. That means reviewing each piece of information and comparing it to either to an ideal assessment or to a minimally acceptable assessment. Two major questions become crucial in this summative evaluation:

- What degree of error variance is likely to obtain in the results?
- What degree of confidence can be placed in the results?

A low degree of error variance and a high degree of confidence are the targets. Some additional questions to help summarize the evaluation include:

- What are the strengths of the tool or procedure?
- What are the weaknesses of the tool or procedure?
- What could be done to improve validity and reliability of the results?
- How objective is this tool or procedure in obtaining results?
- How well does this tool reflect the philosophy, theory, and/or service model adopted for the therapeutic recreation program in question?
- How well does this tool reflect the content of the therapeutic recreation program in question?
- How well does the validation group reflect the client group to whom it will be given?
- Given this information, is this tool recommended for use in this program and with these clients?

These four categories of evaluating or critiquing an assessment tool (description, practical evaluation, technical evaluation, and summative evaluation) can be completed on several assessments that the specialist is considering. Differences, strengths, and weaknesses can be compared and contrasted. In almost all cases, more than one assessment needs to be evaluated to select the one that reduces error and increases confidence as much as possible. The evaluation process gets much easier with practice.

The next section lists the most well-known commercially available assessments in therapeutic recreation based on the taxonomy provided in Chapter 1. The assessment instruments included represent a wide range of content and client groups.

Therapeutic Recreation Assessment Instruments

Given that theory and models, measurement properties, and the actual therapeutic recreation program all affect assessment selection and development decisions, the therapeutic recreation specialist must become knowledgeable about "what is" to know more about "what may become." There are approximately 50 to 60 client assessments that have been marketed or used for therapeutic recreation purposes (Burlingame & Blaschko, 1990; Howe, 1984; Stumbo, 1991, 1992; Stumbo & Thompson, 1986). Not surprisingly some are poorly developed or misused and some have considerable histories of impressive conceptual and statistical development.

Although this text will not review or evaluate individual assessments, the taxonomy given in Chapter 1 is used to sort the assessments by content. Some assessments may have content that falls into more than one category. The categories of the taxonomy include: (a) leisure attitudes and barriers, (b) functional abilities, (c) leisure activity skills, and (d) leisure interests and participation. Note that, for the most part, these tools are or have been nationally available; this list does not include agency-specific or locally developed assessment tools. References to locate more information about each of the assessments are listed in the **Appendix** (p. 301).

Leisure Attitudes and Barriers

- Brief Leisure Rating Scale (BLRS; Ellis & Niles, 1985)
- Comprehensive Leisure Rating Scale (CLRS; Card, Compton & Ellis, 1986)
- Leisure Attitude Scale (Beard & Ragheb, 1982)
- Leisure Diagnostic Battery (LDB; Witt & Ellis, 1982)
- Leisure Motivation Scale (LMS; Beard & Ragheb, 1983)
- Leisure Satisfaction Scale (LSS; Beard & Ragheb, 1980)
- Leisure Well-Being Inventory (McDowell, 1978)
- Life Satisfaction Scale (LSS; Lohmann, 1980)
- Over 50 (Edwards, 1988)
- Perceived Competence Scale for Children/Self-Perception Profile for Children (Harter, 1982/1983)
- What Am I Doing? (WAID; Neulinger, 1986)

Functional Abilities

- Activity Therapy Assessment (Pershbacher, 1988)
- Bond-Howard Assessment of Neglect in Recreation Therapy (BANRT; Bond-Howard, 1990)
- Bruninks-Oseretsky Test of Motor Proficiency (Bruninks & Oseretsky, 1972)
- Burlingame Software Scale (Burlingame, 1980)
- BUS Utilization Assessment (Burlingame, 1989)
- Communication Device Evaluation (Burlingame, 1990)
- Comprehensive Evaluation in Recreation Therapy: Physical Disabilities (CERT: PD; Parker, 1977)
- Comprehensive Evaluation in Recreation Therapy: Psychiatric/ Behavioral (CERT: PB; Parker, 1975)
- Fox Activity Therapy Social Skills Baseline (FOX; Patterson, 1977)
- Functional Assessment of Characteristics for Therapeutic Recreation (FACTR; Peterson, Dunn, & Carruthers, 1983)
- General Recreation Screening Tool (GRST; Burlingame, 1988)
- Idyll Arbor Reality Orientation Assessment (Idyll Arbor, 1989)
- Idyll Arbor Activity Assessment (Burlingame, 1989)
- Leisure Competence Measure (LCM; Kloseck, Crilly, Ellis & Lammers, 1996)
- Maladapted Social Functioning Scale for Therapeutic Recreation Programming (Idyll Arbor, 1988)
- Mundy Recreation Inventory for the Trainable Mentally Retarded (Mundy, 1966)
- Ohio Leisure Skills Scales on Normal Functioning (OLSSON; Olsson, 1988)
- Recreation Behavior Inventory (RBI; Berryman & Lefebvre, 1981)
- Recreation Early Development Screening Tool (REDS; Burlingame, 1988)
- Therapeutic Recreation Index (TRI; Faulkner, 1987)

Leisure Activity Skills

- Cross Country Skiing Assessment (Peterson, 1990)
- Downhill Skiing Assessment (Peterson, 1990)
- Functional Hiking Technique (Burlingame, 1979)

Leisure Interests and Participation

- Constructive Leisure Activity Survey #1 (CLAS #1; Edwards, 1980)
- Constructive Leisure Activity Survey #2 (CLAS #2; Edwards, 1980)
- Family Leisure Assessment Checklist (FLAC; Folkerth, 1978)
- Influential People Who Have Made an Imprint on My Life (Korb, Azok & Leutenberg, 1989)
- Joswiak's Leisure Counseling Assessment (Joswiak, 1979, 1989)
- Leisure Activities Blank (LAB; McKechnie, 1975)
- Leisure and Social Sexual Assessment (Coyne, 1980)
- Leisure Interest Survey 2.0 (Dixon, n.d.)
- Leisure Pref (Edwards, 1986)
- Leisurescope/Teenscope (Nall, 1983)
- Recreation Participation Data (RPD; Burlingame, 1987)
- State Technical Institute Assessment Process (STILAP; Navar, 1980)

Readers are encouraged to locate as many assessments within this taxonomy as possible and to review them according to the criteria outlined earlier in this chapter. Greater familiarity with available assessments increases the likelihood that one can be located that suits its intended purpose and client group.

Review of Important Points

Following is a summary list of important points to consider when critiquing a commercially available assessment in therapeutic recreation. Thorough familiarity with these concepts is helpful to properly critique an assessment.

Description

- What is the content covered by the assessment?
- What is the purpose of the assessment?
- What types and how many items are on the assessment?
- How many forms are available?
- How much time does the assessment take?
- Who publishes the assessment?
- How much does it cost?

Practical Evaluation

- How attractive, durable, and easy to use are the assessment materials?
- How extensive is the protocol for administration of the assessment?
- How extensive is the protocol for analysis and scoring of the assessment?
- How extensive is the protocol for interpretation of scores?
- How will the scores produced enable placement of clients into the programs of interest?
- What are the qualifications, expertise, and training required of the specialist?
- What is the nature of interaction between the specialist and the client?
- Does the time, money, and resources required to conduct the assessment with individual clients match with those available at the specific agency?

Technical Evaluation

- Is the population (norm group) on which it was validated the same as the clientele within the agency? For example, if the assessment was validated on nondisabled, cognitively intact adults, how does this compare to the population at the agency in question?

- Was the assessment developed upon a solid foundation of therapeutic recreation content that would match the programs within the specific agency intended for use? For example, if the specialist adheres to the Leisure Ability Model, does the assessment reflect that content?

- How closely does the content of the assessment match the content of the programs offered at the specific agency? For example, if the specialist drew a comparative chart (like Table 1.6, p. 13) how closely would the content of the assessment match the content of the programs?

- What evidence is given for validity (content-related, criterion-related, and/or construct-related) depending on the purpose of the test? All commercially available assessments should have extensive documentation covering their development and test statistics (and specialists should be knowledgeable enough to evaluate whether the validation process was/is appropriate). Were the correct statistics performed?

- What testing was done to make sure the assessment produces reliable results over time, between clients, and/or between administrations? What tests were conducted to demonstrate the instrument's stability, equivalence (if appropriate), and internal consistency? Were the correct statistics performed?

Summative Evaluation

- What degree of error variance is likely to be obtained in the results?

- What degree of confidence can be placed in the results?

- What are the strengths of the tool or procedure?

- What are the weaknesses of the tool or procedure?

- What could be done to improve validity and reliability of the results?

- How objective is this tool or procedure in obtaining results?

- How well does this tool reflect the philosophy, theory, and/or service model adopted for the therapeutic recreation program in question?

- How well does this tool reflect the content of the therapeutic recreation program in question?

- How well does the validation group reflect the client group to whom it will be given?
- Given this information, is this tool recommended for use in this program and with these clients?

This list of questions parallels the evaluation forms found in Chapter 5. All are concerned with the therapeutic recreation specialist making high quality judgments about the reviewed assessments. Part of this process is becoming a better consumer of what a well-designed assessment looks like and how it should perform. The therapeutic recreation specialist should make buying decisions only after careful review and reflection. These questions intend to aid in that process.

Summary

This chapter on critiquing a commercial assessment for purchase assumed a full understanding of the measurement and validation properties covered in Chapter 2. This chapter expanded on Chapter 5's overview of methods of evaluating the acceptability and usability of an assessment instrument for a particular use, including how this information can be used to critique available assessments instruments. The basic parts of this evaluation process include (a) a general description, (b) practical evaluation, (c) technical evaluation, and (d) summative evaluation. A list of the known available instruments in therapeutic recreation was given, with references for each assessment given in the appendix. The next chapter uses these same concepts in a discussion about developing agency-specific assessments.

References

Burlingame, J. and Blaschko, T. M. (1990). *Assessment tools for recreational therapy: Red book #1*. Ravensdale, WA: Idyll Arbor, Inc.

Dunn, J. K. (1989). Guidelines for using published assessment procedures. *Therapeutic Recreation Journal, 23*(2), 59–69.

Gronlund, N. E. and Linn, R. L. (1990). *Measurement and evaluation in teaching* (6th ed.). New York, NY: Macmillan Publishing.

Howe, C. (1984). Leisure assessment instrumentation in therapeutic recreation. *Therapeutic Recreation Journal, 18*(2), 14–24.

Stumbo, N. J. (1991). Selected assessment resources: A review of instruments and references. *Annual in Therapeutic Recreation, 2*, 8–24.

Stumbo, N. J. (1992). Re-thinking activity interest inventories. *Illinois Parks and Recreation, 23*(2), 17–21.

Stumbo, N. J. and Thompson, S. R. (1986). *Leisure education: A manual of activities and resources*. State College, PA: Venture Publishing, Inc.

Chapter 7
Developing an Agency-Specific Assessment

In Chapter 5, four methods of evaluating an assessment instrument or procedure were discussed and four evaluation tools were presented. In Chapter 6, these evaluation criteria were applied to critiquing commercially available assessments. In this chapter, those same evaluation criteria will be applied to those tools or procedures that are developed for use at a specific agency.

Many individuals feel that assessment development and validation is a complex enough process that it should not be advocated as a task for the typical therapeutic recreation specialist. Individuals with bachelor's degrees may not have the conceptual and statistical expertise for development and validation. Another view states that therapeutic recreation specialists are more likely to develop their own assessments (good or bad) than buy commercial assessments so instruction in correct methodology is important.

To align with the previous two chapters, the discussion about development will rely heavily on information about measurement and validation properties in Chapter 2, and will be divided into four sections:
- Description and development of the assessment instrument
- Practical development and evaluation
- Technical development and validation
- Summative evaluation

Instead of focusing on evaluation of information provided by commercial assessment materials, the focus will be on the decisions that the developer makes in creating and validating an assessment tool.

Description and Development of the Assessment Instrument

The initial step in developing an assessment involves getting a very clear idea of the content and purpose of the assessment, as well as the client group for which it is intended. In addition, the type of assessment (interview, observation, self-administered survey, or records review) and types of items are explored.

Selecting the Assessment Content

Selecting the content of the tool is one of the most important tasks of the developer. The most important piece of information comes from the content of the program. It is assumed that the therapeutic recreation specialist has developed a comprehensive therapeutic recreation intervention program from a logical set of theories and model(s) of practice (Caldwell, 2001; Peterson & Stumbo, 2000; Ross & Ashton-Shaeffer, 2001). For example, a therapeutic recreation intervention program might be based on self-efficacy or self-determination theories that help the client in (a) increasing the sense of personal causation and internal control, (b) increasing intrinsic motivation, (c) increasing the sense of personal choice and alternatives, and (d) achieving the state of optimal experience or "flow." In theory then, therapeutic recreation is provided to affect the total leisure behavior (leisure lifestyle) of individuals with disabilities and/or illnesses through decreasing learned helplessness, and increasing personal control, intrinsic motivation, and personal choice. This is accomplished through the specific provision of functional intervention, leisure education, and recreation participation services, which teach specific skills, knowledges, and abilities, and take into consideration the matching of client skill and activity challenge (Peterson & Stumbo, 2000, p. 11).

It is assumed that the program is based on the current literature (hopefully including research studies) about what is most needed by and most effective with the recipient client group. Evidence-based practice improves the accountability of the profession and provides a basis from which to design intervention programs. A solid programming foundation is a must for a solid assessment foundation.

Table 1.6 (p. 13) illustrated the effects of when programming and assessment content is parallel and when it is not. When the content of the assessment does not match the content of the program, it is very difficult, if not impossible, to place clients into intervention programs that are aimed at their presenting problems. Table 1.7 (p. 15) demonstrated that these assessment and placement decisions could either benefit or detract from the client's treatment.

The first step is to develop a list of content of the therapeutic recreation intervention programs designed for a particular client group within the agency (i.e., different units within an agency may need different assessments).

This content can presented in a list, such as the one found on Table 1.6. For example, using the programming model in Chapter 3, the therapeutic recreation specialist might decide that the following are important programming content areas for client involvement:

- Functional Intervention
  - Anger management
  - Physical conditioning
- Leisure Awareness
  - Leisure barriers
  - Self-awareness
- Social Skills
  - Relationship-building skills
  - Communication skills

This content also will need to be represented on the client assessment. The next tasks of the therapeutic recreation specialist is to: (a) define the general outcomes to be achieved by clients in each area, (b) define those general outcomes in more specific terms, and (c) decide how to assess these outcomes. As mentioned in Chapter 2, the general outcomes can be equated with client goals, or in systems language, terminal performance objectives or TPOs. The more detailed specifications are client objectives, or in systems terminology, enabling objectives (EOs) and performance measures (PMs) (see Peterson & Stumbo, 2000 for more information about systems design in therapeutic recreation programming). The specialist must then begin to decide (although this may later be modified) how that information will be assessed—for example, through observation, interview, or self-administered assessments.

Following is an example of the domain to be tested, the general outcomes, the specific outcomes, and how those outcomes will be assessed.
Domain: Social Skills
General Outcome: To initiate conversation with new group of people
Specific Outcome:

1. After two weeks in the social skills program, the client will:
   a. Identify when interruption is appropriate
   b. Stand within two feet of group
   c. Make eye contact
   d. Listen to conversation of group without immediate interruption
   e. Say hello to known person(s)
   f. Make eye contact

g. Use appropriate gestures in greeting

h. Add to topic, ask questions, offer to help or otherwise contribute to conversation, while using appropriate gestures, and maintaining body space, as judged by the TRS

Determine the Assessment Purpose

A tandem task is to determine the purpose of the assessment (Gronlund, 1993; Ward & Murray-Ward, 1999). For what purpose(s) will the assessment be used? For therapeutic recreation assessments, we can refer back to the purposes that were presented on Table 1.1 to describe the major purposes of client assessment. These are:

- Individual client information
  - Initial baseline assessment (treatment planning/program placement)
  - Monitoring progress (formative information)
  - Summarizing progress (summative information)
- Research on program efficacy and effectiveness
- Communication within and among disciplines
- Administrative requirements

The most common use of client assessments in therapeutic recreation is placement of clients into intervention programs. Although other purposes are worthy, the following discussion will assume that client placement into programs is the primary concern.

As mentioned in Chapter 4, the developer also has to specify the intended function of the assessment. If the assessment is to be used for client placement into programs, at what level of specificity is information needed? Four functions of client assessment in therapeutic recreation have been introduced: (a) basic screening, (b) identifying the problem(s), (c) narrowing the problem(s), and/or (d) reassessing or monitoring client progress (Dunn, 1984; Peterson & Stumbo, 2000). Each of these has a unique impact on the development of the assessment specifications.

Nature and Characteristics of the Client Group

Another important consideration in the development of an agency-specific assessment is the client group for which it is intended. The developer needs to have a reasonable understanding of the disability and/or illness mechanisms, the general social patterns, educational levels, and backgrounds of the clients, as well as any other types of information that impact the clients and how the therapeutic recreation intervention program is delivered to them. For example, a therapeutic recreation intervention program built for individuals with substance abuse problems is likely different than one designed for recently brain-injured individuals. A program for individuals in downtown Los Angeles may be very different than one in rural Wyoming. A basic rule of thumb is that the same client characteristics that affect the program design and delivery also affect the assessment content and delivery. The designer must be intimately familiar with these characteristics and their influences on the both programs and assessments.

Type of Assessment

The fourth beginning consideration is the type of assessment. Which is the most appropriate? Interviews? Observations? Self-Administered Surveys? Records reviews? Although this decision can later be modified or types of assessment combined, an initial idea of what type of assessment is appropriate for collecting information is important. Some information that may be reviewed include:

- How many clients are to be assessed every day? every week?
- How much staff time is available for client assessment (e.g., administration, scoring, interpreting, and reporting)?
- What resources can be devoted to assessment (e.g., facility space, photocopying)?
- What are the skills of the specialists within the department?
- What is typical of other disciplines in the agency?
- What are the advantages and disadvantages of each method?
- Which will yield the best information for client placement into programs?

Each of these four initial considerations (content, purpose, client group, and type of assessment) is foundational for additional steps in the development process. The next step involves developing a table of specifications for the assessment and writing assessment items according to that table.

Practical Development and Evaluation

After the basics have been determined, the next tasks involve providing details to those decisions. The therapeutic recreation specialist needs to provide more detail about program participation outcomes and how these will align with the assessment. When these have been specified on a table of specifications, items can then be written according to that plan.

Develop the Assessment Specifications

There are three steps in developing the assessment specifications: (a) selecting the client outcomes to be assessed, (b) outlining the assessment content, and (c) making a two-way chart that provides an overview of the outcomes and content (Gronlund, 1993; Gronlund & Linn, 1990; Kubiszyn & Borich, 1993; Salvia & Ysseldyke, 1998; Ward & Murray-Ward, 1999).

Select the Client Outcomes To Be Assessed

It is important to know the client outcomes expected from participation in the therapeutic recreation intervention programs as a starting point for building the client assessment. The specified client outcomes will depend on the specific types of programs offered, the theory or model upon which the programs are based, the specific needs of the clients, and other factors that impact the types and range of programs offered. For example: For what outcomes was each program built? What should the client be able to do as a result of participation in the therapeutic recreation intervention program? Does this involve attitude change? increase in certain knowledge? change in some behavior? learning of some skill? In what areas are these being taught? Functional intervention? Leisure education? Recreation participation? A well-designed and well-documented comprehensive program lends itself easily to specifying the client outcomes and assessment content.

Outline the Assessment Content

The content of the assessment must match the content of the programs offered. That means that the outline of the assessment content must be in alignment with whatever content was outlined in the program design. In our most recent example, the following areas were specified for the intervention program:

- Functional Intervention
  - Anger management
  - Physical conditioning
- Leisure Awareness

- Leisure barriers
- Self-awareness
- Social Skills
  - Relationship-building skills
  - Communication skills

It follows then that the assessment content must match this outline. Although some information about background and other information may be included on the assessment, these are the primary areas that should be included. Every piece of information on an assessment should relate to being able to place the right client into the right program for participation.

Make The Two-Way Chart

The third step is to make a two-way chart or table of specifications for the assessment instrument. The purpose of this table of specifications is to ensure that the assessment is representative of the content of the programs and intended client outcomes. It involves mapping the client outcomes along one axis and the content along the other, in an effort to show that the assessment in being built according to the programs offered and the outcomes targeted. Then the designer must decide how much emphasis will be given to each area. This again depends on the program. If the social skills program is daily for 2 hours, and the leisure awareness program is once a week for 1 hour, the relative weights within the table should reflect that.

Table 7.1 (p. 170) outlines a possible table of specifications given the information from the above example. The numbers in the middle of the table reflect how many items are to be devoted on the assessment to that area. The numbers reflect the relative weights for each area at that particular agency. More emphasis in programming should translate to more items on the assessment. Gronlund (1993) outlined a number of questions to determine those relative weights:

- How important is each area in the total programming process?
- How much of the program is devoted to each area?
- Which outcomes have greater retention and transfer value?
- What relative importance does the therapeutic recreation specialist assign to each area?

Weights in each category should accurately represent the emphasis given during programming. In this example, social skills and functional intervention have a larger emphasis than leisure awareness. More detail may be necessary to actually build the assessment than given on this table.

Select Appropriate Item Types

After the table of specifications has been developed and refined, the next step involves writing and improving questions to be included on the assessment. The tasks include (a) selecting the types of items to use, (b) matching the items to the specific client outcomes, and (c) making the final selection of items.

Select the Types of Items to Use

There are two basic types of assessment items: (a) closed-ended and (b) open-ended. Closed-ended items include yes/no, true/false, matching, multiple choice, rating, and ranking items. These items are considered categorical, are easy to tabulate, and provide quantitative data. Open-ended

Table 7.1
Sample Table of Specifications

	Attitudes # of items	Knowledges # of items	Behaviors # of items	Total # of items
Functional Intervention				
Anger Management	2	3	5	
Physical Conditioning	0	4	3	17
Leisure Awareness				
Leisure Barriers	3	3	2	
Self-Awareness	2	3	2	15
Social Skills				
Relationship-Building Skills	2	3	4	
Communication Skills	2	3	4	18
Total	**11**	**19**	**20**	**50**

items include fill-in-the-blank, short answer, and extended answer. These items allow free style responses, are more difficult to tabulate, and provide qualitative data. **Table 7.2** provides an overview of closed-ended and open-ended item types.

The assessment developer has to decide which type(s) of items are most appropriate for the kind of information needed from the client. Each type of question format (e.g., checklists, ratings, rankings, fill in the blank, short answer, extended answer) has specific benefits and drawbacks. Knowing the kind of answers each type of format yields is important in selection.

The choice between closed-ended and open-ended questions depends on several factors. First is the purpose of the assessment and instrument. Is the purpose to gather in-depth information? to place a person into categories (programs)? to assess attitudes, knowledge, or skills? Second is the client's level of information about the topic at hand. Giving an individual options to which he or she can respond ("Which of the following are leisure barriers for you?") requires a different kind of understanding than asking for a free response ("What stops you from participating in leisure as you wish?"). Third is the ease or difficulty with which the information can be communicated. For example, is there a common understanding of the

Table 7.2
Types of Assessment Items

Closed-Ended Questions
- Considered categorical (e.g. demographics)
- Easy to tabulate and calculate statistics
- Provide quantitative data

Types:
   1. Checklists/True-False/Yes-No
   2. Rating or Likert scale
   3. Ranking

Open-Ended Questions
- Invite free-styled responses (e.g., suggestions, input)
- Difficult to tabulate, usually summary narrative
- Provide qualitative data

Types:
   1. Fill in the blank
   2. Short answer
   3. Extended answer

word "leisure?" "Leisure barriers?" "Leisure lifestyle?" Fourth is the specialist's insight into the clients' situations and potential responses. For example, it is easier to construct closed ended questions when the typical responses of the clients are known ahead of time.

Regardless of whether the assessment contains closed-ended or open-ended items, special consideration needs to be given to the construction of each item. Each item should be written clearly and without wordiness or vagueness. Items should be straightforward and not mislead the client or be easily misinterpreted. **Table 7.3** provides a list of criteria for constructing assessment items.

Checklist and True/False or Yes/No Formats

Items that use a checklist format produce simplistic data and can be easily answered and scored. However, the assessment developer must be very familiar with all options that potential clients may want to answer. For example, if the checklist question focuses on leisure barriers, the developer must be familiar with all the potential leisure barriers possible. For check-

Table 7.3
Criteria for Constructing Assessment Items

Avoid • Wordiness and ambiguity • Questions that are leading/threatening/critical/embarrassing or place client in awkward situation • Biasing the client • Questions that can be misinterpreted • Lengthy questions that demand too much time • Very superficial questions that do not get at the intended content • Questions that are too narrow or limited in scope • Double-barreled questions (i.e., asking two things in one item) • Negative items (e.g., never, not, except for, all but one) • Items that force clients to respond in socially desirable ways • Asking what cannot be answered by the client **Aim for** • Items clear in meaning and intent • Objectivity, fairness, and lack of bias • Responses that are definite, but not mechanically forced • Producing results that are valid and reliable for each individual • Maintaining the client's interest in completing the assessment

lists to be used successfully, the client must be able to find the options applicable to his or her life situation. "Other" options, with writing space provided, can be included but require additional time in both responding and scoring, and generally defeat the purpose of using checklists. An additional requirement is that each response listed should be mutually exclusive—that is, provide unique options, especially if only one response should be checked. Checklist items, due to their overall convenience for respondents, are often suitable to begin the assessment so the client is put at ease.

True/false and yes/no items are further simplified forms of checklists. The client only has two options from which to choose. Again, these types of questions may be used for very basic information, but do not capture the range or degree of possibilities that may be experienced by clients. Their usefulness is usually limited in assessing the richness of individuals' leisure experiences or lifestyles. For that reason, most true/false or yes/no items are followed with an "explain more" probe, that signals an open-ended question was likely more suitable. **Table 7.4** (pp. 174–175) illustrates several styles of checklist and true/false or yes/no item formats.

Ratings Questions/Likert Scale Formats

Unlike checklists, rating questions are used when focusing on the range or degree of a characteristic. For example, "To what degree are you satisfied with your leisure?" is far different than "Are you satisfied with your leisure?" Rating or Likert scales tend to ask for more-opened information, yet categorize the responses along a continuum of provided responses. Each response ("anchor") corresponds to a number, which allows for easier tabulation and analysis of the answers. Anchor words should be concrete, descriptive, and consistent throughout an instrument. The anchor words of "4 times a week" are better than "frequently" since individuals may interpreted the latter differently. Interpretations based on poorly constructed items result in lowered reliability of the instrument's results.

An even number of responses—usually four to six—are used so that the individual is not overwhelmed with too many choices (such as 10) and fine gradations that do not exist (e.g., What is the difference between an 8 and a 9?). Although it is assumed that an equal "space" lies between anchors, this is not always the case. The individual may feel that Very Satisfied and Satisfied lie closer together than Dissatisfied and Very Dissatisfied. **Table 7.5** (p. 176) provides poor and better examples of rating and Likert type questions.

Ranking Formats

Most individuals find ranking items to be difficult. In these questions, individuals are asked to rank (e.g., from 1 to 10) a series of events, items of importance, values, or priorities. Again, the "space" between rankings is assumed to be equal, although this is not always the case. Sometimes the response labeled by the individual as "1" is very close to the response given a "2", which is far away from the "3" response. The directions should make clear which end of the ranking scale is "high" (e.g., "10" means the worst pain you've ever experienced).

Table 7.4
Checklist, True/False, and Yes/No Formats

Checklists

Considerations
- The item stem (question) must match the response format
- Yields very simplistic data
- May be good questions to start the assessment
- Each response category should be mutually exclusive (not overlap)
- Responses should be exhaustive (cover the full range of possible answers)
- Make sure this format is the best way to ask this particular content
- May need one or two "other" options so the client can supply personal answers
- Use closed-ended whenever possible, to save the client time and effort
- Can use any of the following formats:
  __ Yes __ No [ ] Yes [ ] No ( ) Yes ( ) No 1. Yes 2. No

Poor Example
Describe the barriers to your leisure.

| _____ Money | _____ Family |
| _____ Time | _____ School |

Better Example
Which of the following are barriers to your leisure? Check all that apply.

_____ Lack of money	_____ Cannot find leisure partners
_____ Lack of time	_____ Inconvenient program times
_____ Lack of leisure skills	_____ Too many family obligations
_____ Lack of transportation	_____ Too much stress in daily life
_____ Other: _____	

It should also be noted that ranking questions and rating questions mathematically produce the same results. For example, a ranking question ("Rank these leisure barriers from 1 to 6, with 6 being the most confining") will produce the same results as a rating question ("Rate each of these 6 leisure barriers, 6 = Extremely Confining, 5 = Confining, etc."). **Table 7.6** (p. 177) demonstrates a poor and better example of ranking questions concerning leisure barriers.

Table 7.4
Checklist, True/False, and Yes/No Formats (continued)

Poor Example
What are your favorite movie categories?

Better Example
Which of the following are your favorite movie categories? Check no more than three.
_____ Westerns   _____ Drama   _____ Comedy
_____ Science Fiction   _____ Action   _____ Other: _____

True/False or Yes/No

Poor Example
Are you willing to pay more money to join the program?
_____ yes _____no

Better Example
Are you currently involved in leisure activities in your community?
_____ Yes   _____ No

Poor Example
Do you feel satisfied with your leisure?
_____ Yes _____ No

Better Example
In the past month, have you experienced any problems with your leisure?
_____ Yes   _____ No

Open-Ended Formats

Open-ended items produce qualitative information. They allow the individual to use his or her own words to describe satisfaction, an experience, an attitude, a feeling, or a thought. Open-ended questions range from fill-in-the-blank items that require a one or two word response, to short answer

Table 7.5
Rating Questions/Likert Scale Format

Considerations
- Use any time there is a range of possible responses
- Usually put most positive response to the left
- Usually have even number of responses (often 4 or 6) so there is no "middle" answer
- Ask the question as more open-ended
- Every response number should have an "anchor" word
- Make anchor words as concrete as possible—minimize interpretation
- Use the same format/response options throughout the assessment, whenever possible

Poor Example
Are you satisfied with the program offering?

very satisfied				not satisfied
1	2	3	4	5

Better Example
How satisfied are you with the program offerings? Circle only one.

Very Satisfied	Satisfied	Dissatisfied	Very Dissatisfied
1	2	3	4

Poor Example
How often do you play tennis at our facility?

Often	Frequently	Seldom	Never
4	3	2	1

Better Example
How often do you play tennis at our facility?

Daily	Weekly	Monthly	Less than Monthly
1	2	3	4

that require a few words, to extended answer questions that require lengthy responses. Open-ended questions allow verbal individuals to provide personalized and idiosyncratic information, and as such may provide the most valid information about the individual. Rather than conforming to a yes/no format or anchors on a rating scale, individuals can respond at length, and provide more descriptive, in-depth information about a topic. However, this validity may be increased at the expense of the result's reliability. Because the answers are unique and difficult to categorize, the tasks of scoring, interpretation, and analysis become problematic. Far too many agency-specific assessments in therapeutic recreation rely on open-ended responses without a systematic method of scoring, interpretation, and analysis. Examples of open-ended questions are provided in **Table 7.7** (p. 178).

Table 7.6
Ranking Format

Considerations
- Mathematically, ends up the same as rating questions
- Limit the number of options to be ranked
- Make clear whether "1" is high or low

Poor Example
Please rank the barriers to your leisure.
_____ Lack of money
_____ Cannot find leisure partners
_____ Lack of transportation
_____ Lack of time
_____ Inconvenient program times
_____ Lack of leisure skills
_____ Too many family obligations
_____ Other: _____

Better Example
Please rank the barriers to your leisure, with "1" being the largest barrier and "7" being the smallest barrier.
_____ Lack of money
_____ Cannot find leisure partners
_____ Lack of transportation
_____ Lack of time
_____ Inconvenient program times
_____ Lack of leisure skills
_____ Too many family obligations

Table 7.7
Open-Ended Questions

Fill in the Blank
What's the single most important thing that prevents you from doing the leisure activities you'd like to do?

Short/Extended Answers
Tell me about what prevents you from doing the leisure activities you'd like to do.

Special Case Formats

Contingency and matrix questions are additional format types. Contingency questions are coupled—the first asking usually a yes/no question and the second asking for expansion on that answer. An example would be "Do you know how to locate the local zoo? (yes/no). If yes, please tell me how you'd find it." The first question asks for basic information, the second asks for clarification. Contingency questions are used when the basic information cannot be assumed, but additional information is needed thereafter.

When several questions consecutively use the same item response format, for example, rating scales, they often are called matrix questions. The answers display in almost a column-like effect and form a visual line. Op-scan scored tests, such as those used in university and standardized testing settings, often fall into the matrix response category. Examples of both contingency and matrix formats are demonstrated in **Table 7.8**.

To illustrate more clearly the similarities, differences, and types of responses stemming from each item types, **Table 7.9** (p. 180) displays yes/no checklist, ratings scale, ranking or Likert, fill in the blank, and an extended answer questions focusing on leisure barriers as the content. Compare the responses elicited by each format of item. Which produce more mechanical responses? Which are easier to score, interpret, and analyze? Which are harder to score, interpret, and analyze? Which are likely to provide the most valid results? the most reliable results? Which are more comparable across individuals? Which provide the best baseline data from which to develop client goals and treatment plans? It is clear the assessment designer must consider a variety of factors in selecting the best item type(s) for the purpose of the assessment. The assessment developer should develop more items than needed so the best may be chosen for inclusion on the assessment. Like other tasks in assessment, item development and analysis needs considerable practice and concentration. Table 7.9

provides an easy comparison of the different item types and how they can be formatted.

Match the Items to the Specific Client Outcomes

The table of specifications drawn up earlier becomes extremely important at this juncture. Now the therapeutic recreation specialist makes sure that each item is called for within the cells of the table of specifications. For each content area (e.g., conversational skills, leisure barriers), a set number of items is needed to match the emphasis of the assessment to the emphasis of the programs. As seen in the example on Table 7.1 (p. 170), a predetermined number of items was set for each area of content. The task at hand is to select those items from those just written. Each item is chosen because it matches the intended content and the intended client outcome. If the item does not match both the content and the outcome, the item is discarded and

Table 7.8
Contingency and Matrix Formats

Contingency Questions
1. Has anything prevented you from participating in the leisure activities you'd like to do?
_____ Yes (if yes, go to #2)   _____ No (if no, skip to #3)
2. If yes, how recently?
_____ in the past day   _____ in the past week
_____ in the past month   _____ in the past year
Matrix Questions
Besides the statements presented below, please indicate whether you:
Strongly Agree (SA), Agree (A), Disagree (D), Strongly Disagree (SD) or are Undecided (U).
1. I experience leisure barriers almost daily.
SA   A   D   SD   U
[ ]   [ ]   [ ]   [ ]   [ ]
2. I have more leisure barriers than most people I know.
SA   A   D   SD   U
[ ]   [ ]   [ ]   [ ]   [ ]
3. The barriers to my leisure are increasing.
SA   A   D   SD   U
[ ]   [ ]   [ ]   [ ]   [ ]

Table 7.9
Examples of Item Formats Using Leisure Barriers as the Content
(Peterson & Stumbo, 2000, p. 225)

Yes/No Checklist
Does the client have physical barriers to his or her leisure?
Yes   No   Don't Know
Does the client have cognitive barriers to his or her leisure?
Yes   No   Don't Know
Does the client have emotional barriers to his or her leisure?
Yes   No   Don't Know
Does the client have social barriers to his or her leisure?
Yes   No   Don't Know
     Or
Which of the following physical barriers does the client have in his or her leisure? Check all that apply.
_____ Lack of endurance_____ Lack of coordination _____ Lack of mobility
_____ Lack of flexibility _____ Physical disability _____ Other (explain)

Rating Scale
How often do any of the following physical barriers negatively affect your
leisure time?   Less Than
                        Daily   Weekly   Monthly   Monthly

Lack of endurance?   1   2   3   4
Lack of coordination?   1   2   3   4
Lack of mobility?   1   2   3   4
Lack of flexibility?   1   2   3   4
Physical disability?   1   2   3   4
(explain) _____
Other   1   2   3   4
(explain) _____

Ranking
From 1 being the greatest barrier, to 6 being the least barrier, rank the follow-
ing physical barriers that may negatively affect your leisure.
_____ Lack of endurance
_____ Lack of coordination
_____ Lack of mobility
_____ Lack of flexibility
_____ Physical disability
_____ Other (explain) _____

Fill in the Blank
Finish this sentence:
The physical barrier that most prevents me from participating in leisure is

_____ .

Short/Extended Answer
Explain the physical barriers that most prevent you from participating in leisure.

another is selected or written. This process continues until the number of assessment items matches the proportions given on the table of specifications, and the total number of finished items matches the total number required on the table.

Make the Final Selection of Items

Good assessment item construction takes patience and practice. Sometimes an individual item may appear to be a good one, until it is combined with other items on an instrument. At this point, the item may need refinement or may need to be discarded and another written. When the first draft of items is finished it might be helpful to ask the following set of questions about each item, before it is included in the assessment form for further testing. The following set of guidelines will help in distinguishing between poor and better items.

Content

- Is the question necessary? useful? related to the program content?
- Are several questions needed on the subject?
- Do the clients have the necessary information to answer the question?
- Does the question need to be more concrete, specific, or closely related to the clients' personal experience?
- Is the question content sufficiently general and free of unnecessary detail?
- Will the clients be able to give the information that is asked for?

Question Wording

- Can the item be misunderstood?
- Does it adequately express the information needed?
- Is the wording biased?
- Is the question wording likely to be objectionable in any way?
- Would more personalized or less personalized wording of the question produce better results?

Question and Response Formats

- If a checklist is used, does it cover adequately in a defensible order, all the significant alternatives without overlapping?
- Is the form of response easy, definite, uniform, and adequate?

- Is the answer to the question likely to be influenced by the content of the preceding question?
- Is the question introduced in a natural way?
- Does the question come too early or too late from the viewpoint of arousing interest and receiving sufficient attention and avoiding resistance?

Ethical Issues

Does the item/assessment:

- Deal with areas that are too personal or private?
- Seem likely to have adverse psychological reaction?
- Call for self-incrimination or self-admission?
- Seem excessively "psychiatric?"
- Seem to promote values which are highly immoral, controversial or contrary to public opinion?
- Request personal or confidential information about someone besides the client?
- Seem to favor one side or another of a controversial issue?
- Enter an area that is politically sensitive?

These questions will help the assessment developer ensure that the items are in the best possible format. Continued practice in writing good items will help improve the final product. **Table 7.10** (pp. 184–185) provides examples of assessment items that were found in use by therapeutic recreation departments. How might each item or set of items be improved using these criteria?

Although item development and refinement is major task during the practical development and evaluation phase, other steps need to be completed. After the assessment items have been compiled and the form polished and finalized, attention is turned to the accompanying documentation. The manual should be both attractively packaged and durable for repeated use. The major piece of documentation includes the assessment manual or protocol. This includes complete, clear, and comprehensive directions for administration, scoring, interpretation, and reporting of scores. Later, after testing, the manual will include information on the validation procedure including the testing group and evidence of validity and reliability.

The assessment manual should have complete and clear instructions or protocols for how the assessment is to be administered and scored. Information on the administration should include the type of environment in which the assessment should be given (e.g., free of distractions, private, comfortable). Scoring procedures should include full disclosure of how the assessment is to be scored, and whether this is done manually or through use of a computer. Scoring information also should include the meaning of the scores received by clients—that is, how the scores are to be interpreted and reported. The information should include whether the assessment is norm-referenced or criterion-referenced (see Chapter 1), and either the norms or criterions from which to judge an individual client's score. For example, is a score of +7 average for the norm group? Does a score of +1 mean the client reaches the threshold (criterion) for entry into a certain program? Do scores on subscales combine to form one final score? The information on scoring, interpretation, and reporting of the assessment results should be explicit, and provide the user with clear indications of what each assessment score means.

Any special considerations for the assessment environment also should be included in the documentation. Most assessments assume that the environment is to be private, free from distractions, and comfortable for both the client and the specialist. However, sometimes, special environments need to be created or considered. For example, if the assessment concentrates on physical motor ability, adequate physical space, such as a gymnasium or open area, needs to be available. In addition, does the specialist need to provide special equipment or situations? Some assessments need special materials, such as flash cards, while some depend on the specialist viewing the client during social exchanges with peers. The important point for the specialist to remember is that those special materials or circumstances are needed each and every time the assessment is administered to clients.

Specialist qualifications, expertise, or training are other considerations in the practical development and evaluation. Does the specialist using the assessment need special qualifications? expertise? training? Does the specialist need special skill in interviewing? observations? scoring calculations? What is the typical therapeutic recreation specialist expected to know? Can a therapeutic recreation intern student complete the assessment? What is the training regimen? Does the assessment under consideration require more than the typical therapeutic recreation specialist knows? Does the assessment require training or expertise beyond these minimal competencies (see Chapter 1)?

The environment and specialist qualifications also combine to determine the quality and nature of the interaction between the specialist and the client. The manual should include specific information about the degree to which the specialist interacts with the client during the assessment. Should the specialist provide encouragement? praise? clarification? redirection? summarizing comments? If the specialist is conducting an observation, is

Table 7.10
Examples of Poorly Written Assessments/Items
(Peterson & Stumbo, 2000, pp. 223–224)

Example #1

RECREATION THERAPY EVALUATION

DIAGNOSIS _____ AGE _____

COMMUNICATION
Receptive Skills (e.g. Reading, Auditory Comprehension):

Swallowing:

COGNITIVE FUNCTIONING (e.g. Attention Span/Distractability,
Judgement/Problem Solving, Memory):

PHYSICAL FUNCTIONING RELATIVE TO ACTIVITY INVOLVEMENT
(e.g. Upper Extremity Use, Transfers, Vision, Hearing, Visual Percep-
tion/Left Neglect): _____

SOCIAL BACKGROUND (e.g. Transportation, Current Living Arrangements, Family Relationships):

Example #2

ACTIVITY INTEREST SURVEY   Frequency   Comments

1. Creative Expression:

---

2. Outdoor Recreation:

---

3. Physical Activity:

---

4. Passive Activity:

---

5. Social Activity/Commuunity Organizations:

Table 7.10 (continued)
Examples of Poorly Written Assessments/Items
(Peterson & Stumbo, 2000, pp. 223–224)

Example #3

TIME MANAGEMENT   [ ] At Present   [ ] Prior to Disability

1. OBLIGATED TIME   [ ] Work [ ] School [ ] Therapy [ ] Self Care
                        [ ] Household Activity   [ ] Other
2. UNOBLIGATED TIME/LEISURE - RECREATION PARTICIPATION
    A. With whom does patient spend most of his/her leisure time?
    [ ] Alone   [ ] Immediate Family   [ ] Extended Family
    [ ] Peers   [ ] Others _____
    B. During what time of day does patient usually engage in leisure/
    recreation activity?
    [ ] Mornings [ ] Afternoon [ ] Evening [ ] Weekdays [ ] Weekends
    C. How does the patient describe his/her leisure/recreation experience?
    [ ] Active   [ ] Planned   [ ] Structured   [ ] Participant [ ] Other
    [ ] Passive [ ] Spontaneous   [ ] Unstructured [ ] Spectator

Example #4

SOCIAL FUNCTIONING

Prefers being alone:

_____

Prefers being in groups/friends:

_____

Prefers one to one contact:

_____

Communication issues:

_____

Independent:

_____

EMOTIONAL FUNCTIONING

Makes needs known:

_____

Expresses emotion:

_____

Style of communication (e.g. aggressive/assertive):

_____

Attitude toward Recreational Therapy:

_____

interaction minimal? hidden? nonintrusive? direct? known? All of this information should be included in the materials that accompany the assessment.

All of these factors help in later improving the assessment result's validity and reliability. If one administration greatly differs from another, the error variance in the scores may be due to unintentional influences, rather than real differences in the clients' scores. That would mean that clients may be arbitrarily placed into programs, instead of being placed based on their real needs. Programs would then not meet their needs and not help them get to the targeted client outcomes.

The manual or accompanying documentation may be later modified during or after the validation procedure. However, its initial development during the beginning phases is important for clarity on how the assessment is to be administered, scored, interpreted, and reported. **Table 7.11** provides some sample questions to help improve the content and format of the assessment. The next step, technical development and evaluation, help determine the overall credibility of the agency-specific assessment.

Technical Development and Validation

Technical evaluation of an assessment is just as crucial to an agency-specific assessment as it is to a commercial assessment. The scope of the

Table 7.11
Hints for Improving the Format and Content of Client Assessments

- Use the method of data collection that is most suitable to the purpose and group of clients.
- Pay attention to the format of the items and how they flow from one to another.
- Start with easier, nonthreatening questions.
- Have enough questions that the content is covered but the client's time is not wasted.
- Pay attention to the overall format, grammar, and look of the assessment.
- Consider the relevance of the assessment topics to the client and his or her motivation to complete it.
- Minimize professional jargon and words with unclear or multiple meanings.
- Ask only questions that pertain to placing the clients into the therapeutic recreation intervention programs.
- Make sure that the responses can cover the full range of clients' behaviors or thoughts.

testing may not be the same, but testing should be completed nonetheless. It is the assessment developer's job to provide enough information about the development, validation, and intended use of the assessment to prove that it is adequate for the task of assessing clients for placement into programs. The developer should attempt to show that it is the best possible assessment for this particular agency, program, and group of clients. This is accomplished by providing an abundance of information on: (a) the validation or norm group(s), (b) evidence of validity, and (c) estimates of reliability.

Norm Group(s)

Each assessment is designed with a particular group in mind—for example, individuals with physical disabilities, individuals with psychiatric difficulties, or individuals with mental retardation. The more closely this group can be defined, the better to ensure that the assessment fits that group. In therapeutic recreation departments where multiple client groups are served, perhaps on different units, it may be that different assessments or versions of the assessment are needed.

As mentioned in the previous chapter, Gronlund and Linn (1990) suggested five guidelines for determining if norm groups are adequate: (a) relevance to the intended user group, (b) representativeness to the user group, (c) recency of data, (d) comparability with client group, and (e) adequate description of norm group.

The assessment should be tested and validated on a representative sample of sufficient size (Dunn, 1989). The testing group can be selected in a number of ways; for example, random sampling from a list of all patient admissions within the last x days, or purposive sampling of all men over 40, or systematically selecting every *n*th admission. Almost any method of sampling is acceptable as long as the assessment developer understands the advantages and disadvantages of the method for gaining an adequate sample. The sample should be large enough to engender confidence in the results, but small enough for the developer to handle. The developer should describe the sampling technique in detail as well as the characteristics of the testing sample (e.g., Gender? Ages? Education? Occupation? Presenting disabilities and/or illnesses? Previous admissions)? The characteristics of the sample group should be compared to the overall client base seen by therapeutic recreation services to determine if the two groups are similar. If not, a different method of sampling and a new group may need to be selected.

These guidelines are helpful for both selecting norm groups for validation situations as well as evaluating the adequacy of norm groups to an intended user group.

Evidence of Validity

Chapter 2 provided an in-depth discussion of validity and its application to client assessments. In developing an assessment for use, it is important to consider this same information. Evidence of *content-related validity* is important for all assessments. Content-related validity shows that the items on the assessment are representative of the entire domain being tested. The results of the assessment are to be used to demonstrate how well an individual performs at present in a universe of situations that the test situation claims to represent. For example, an assessment measuring leisure barriers must show evidence of adequately representing all known leisure barriers for the group being tested. The question to be answered is: "How well does the content of this procedure constitute an adequate sample of the topic?" Evidence of content-related validity includes a definition of the domain or area being tested, a review of the professional literature, and a table of specifications for the assessment (see Chapter 2 for more details). Table 7.1 (p. 170) provided an example of a table of specifications for a therapeutic recreation client assessment.

Evidence of *criterion-related validity* is appropriate for assessments that are used to predict concurrent or future results to another test or criterion. Criterion-related validity is important when the user wishes to forecast a client's future (predictive) or present (concurrent) standing on some variable of particular significance that is different from the assessment. The question to be answered is: "How well do the test's results predict the scores of the criterion test?" Besides making sure that the connection between the test and the criterion is logical, validity correlations are also calculated between the test results and the criterion results.

Evidence of *construct-related validity* is important for those assessments that measure some trait or attitude or psychological construct (e.g., leisure behavior, leisure attitudes, leisure satisfaction). In this case, the user wishes to infer the degree to which the client possesses some hypothetical trait or quality (construct) presumed to be reflected in the assessment results. The question to be answered is: "How well does this assessment measure the construct in question?" Evidence of construct validity is collected through multiple testing trials and includes correlations with other tests known to measure the same trait, factor analysis, convergent and discriminant analyses, and expert reviews of the test content.

For all types of evidence of validity, the reader is reminded that validity:

- Is a matter of degree, not an absolute
- Is dependent on many types of evidence

- Is inferred from available evidence but not directly measured
- Is specific to a particular use of the intended assessment
- Refers to the results, not the instrument itself
- Is a unitary concept

Estimates of Reliability

Chapter 2 covers the three basic types of reliability estimates: (a) stability, (b) equivalency, and (c) internal consistency. Because reliability is fundamental in its own right, as well as necessary for validity, assessment validation should show evidence of several reliability tests. For example, a single test-retest of an assessment would be inadequate to ensure the stability of the instrument's results.

Stability testing answers the question: "How stable is the assessment over time?" The usual period between initial test and the retest is two weeks, and the developer is hoping for approximately the same scores for each individual on both administrations. If the scores vary widely, the test is not seen as stable and dependable over time; that is, too much error is present in the results. Multiple stability tests help increase the confidence of the stability of the tool (given that the correlations are adequate). Stability is calculated with correlation coefficients between the two sets of scores.

Equivalent-form reliability is appropriate when there are two forms of the same test; for example, Form A and Form B. Equivalent-form reliability answers the question: "How similar is one set of scores to the other set of scores?" The two forms of the assessment are given to one group at the same time, or in a soon-to-follow administration. A reliability coefficient is calculated between the two sets of scores.

Internal consistency estimates are calculated when only one version of one test is given to a group. Internal consistency reliabilities answer the question: "How well do halves of this test represent the whole?" Internal consistency reliabilities split the test into two halves for calculation purposes. Different correlation coefficients do this splitting in different ways (see Chapter 2). Internal consistency coefficients are usually smaller than whole–test correlations.

In addition, for assessments that include observation, several kinds of *interrater reliability* indices exist. Four were mentioned in Chapter 2: (a) simple agreement, (b) point-to-point agreement, (c) percentage of agreement for the occurrence of target behaviors, and (d) kappa index. Each of these interrater reliability indices has advantages and disadvantages, and some acknowledge the difference between agreement and accuracy. Remember also that reliability:

- Refers to the results, not the test itself
- Refers to a particular type of consistency
- Explains what proportion of the test variance is nonerror variance
- Increases with the length of the test
- Increases with the spread of scores
- May vary at different levels of test performance
- Is a necessary but not sufficient condition for validity

Chapter 2 as well as psychological and educational testing books, provide more detail on how to collect evidence of an assessment result's validity and reliability. Once completed the results of the validation testing should be included in the assessment manual.

Summative Evaluation

The final piece of the assessment development is to summarize all of the above information to see if the assessment is suitable for use. That means reviewing each piece of information and comparing it to either to an ideal assessment or to a minimally acceptable assessment. Two major questions become crucial in this summative evaluation:

- What degree of error variance is likely to be obtained in the results?
- What degree of confidence can be placed in the results?

A low degree of error variance and a high degree of confidence are the targets. Some additional questions to help summarize the evaluation include:

- What are the strengths of the tool or procedure for this agency, program, or group of clients?
- What are the weaknesses of the tool or procedure for this agency, program, or group of clients?
- What could be done to improve validity and reliability of the results?
- How objective is this tool or procedure in obtaining results?
- How well does this tool reflect the philosophy, theory, and/or service model adopted for the therapeutic recreation program in question?

- How well does this tool reflect the content of the therapeutic recreation program in question? How stable is the content of the program?

- How well does the validation group reflect the client group to whom it will be given?

- What type of training is needed for the therapeutic recreation staff and how often should it occur?

- What types of departmental resources are needed to implement the assessment on a continuous basis, and are these available?

- Given the above information, is this tool recommended for use in this program and with these clients?

These four categories of developing and evaluating an assessment tool (description, practical evaluation, technical evaluation, and summative evaluation) can be completed simultaneously. It is also helpful to bring in therapeutic recreation colleagues to review the assessment development process and final product.

Review of Important Points

Following is a summary list of important points to consider when developing an agency-specific assessment in therapeutic recreation. Thorough familiarity with these concepts is helpful to properly develop an assessment.

Description

- What is the content covered by the assessment?
- What is the purpose of the assessment?
- What types and how many items will be on the assessment?
- How many forms need to be available?
- How much time will the assessment take?

Practical Evaluation

- How will the assessment materials be made attractive, durable, and easy to use?
- How extensive and easy to understand is the protocol for administration of the assessment?

- How extensive and easy to understand is the protocol for analysis and scoring of the assessment?
- How extensive and easy to understand is the protocol for interpretation of scores?
- How will the scores produced enable placement of clients into the programs of interest?
- What are the qualifications, expertise, and training required of the specialist?
- What is the nature of interaction between the specialist and the client?
- Does the time, money, and resources required to conduct the assessment with individual clients match with those available at this agency?

Technical Evaluation

- Is the population (norm group) on which it was validated the same as the overall clientele served by the therapeutic recreation department?
- Was the assessment developed upon a solid foundation of therapeutic recreation content that matches the programs within this agency? For example, if the specialist adheres to the Leisure Ability Model, does the assessment reflect that content?
- How closely does the content of the assessment match the content of the programs offered at the specific agency? How well does the table of specification match content of the therapeutic recreation programs?
- What evidence was produced for validity (content-related, criterion-related, and/or construct-related) depending on the purpose of the test? Were the correct statistics performed?
- What testing was done to make sure the assessment produces reliable results over time, between clients, and/or between administrations? What tests were conducted to demonstrate the instrument's stability, equivalence (if appropriate), and internal consistency? Were the correct statistics performed?

Summative Evaluation

- What degree of error variance is likely to be obtained in the results?
- What degree of confidence can be placed in the results?
- What are the strengths of the tool or procedure?
- What are the weaknesses of the tool or procedure?
- What could be done to improve validity and reliability of the results?
- How objective is this tool or procedure in obtaining results?
- How well does this tool reflect the philosophy, theory, and/or service model adopted for the therapeutic recreation program in question?
- How well does this tool reflect the content of the therapeutic recreation program in question?
- How well does the validation group reflect the client group to whom it will be given?
- Given this information, is this tool recommended for use in this program and with these clients?

This list of questions parallels the evaluation forms found in Chapter 5. All are concerned with the therapeutic recreation specialist making good assessment decisions. It requires the therapeutic recreation specialist to be knowledgeable about validation procedures and how they can be used to improve assessment results.

Summary

A clear understanding of Chapter 2 and Chapter 5 is necessary to fully comprehend this chapter on developing an agency-specific assessment. At the heart of assessment development lie measurement properties and validation procedures. This chapter used that information as a springboard to outline how an agency-specific assessment might be developed from a well-designed comprehensive therapeutic recreation program. The four basic steps of (a) description and determination, (b) practical development, (c) technical development, and (d) summative evaluation were used to outline the steps of assessment development.

References

Caldwell, L. (2001). The role of theory in therapeutic recreation: A practical approach. In N. J. Stumbo (Ed.), *Professional issues in therapeutic recreation: On competence and outcomes* (pp. 349–364). Champaign, IL: Sagamore Publishing.

Dunn, J. K. (1984). Assessment. In C. A. Peterson and S. L. Gunn (Eds.), *Therapeutic recreation program design: Principles and procedures* (2nd ed., pp. 267–320). Englewood Cliff, NJ: Prentice Hall, Inc.

Dunn, J. K. (1989). Guidelines for using published assessment procedures. *Therapeutic Recreation Journal, 23*(2), 59–69.

Gronlund, N. E. (1993). *How to make achievement tests and assessments* (5th ed.). Boston, MA: Allyn & Bacon.

Gronlund, N. E. and Linn, R. L. (1990). *Measurement and evaluation in teaching* (6th ed.). New York, NY: Macmillan Publishing.

Kubiszyn, T. and Borich, G. (1993*). Education testing and measurement: Classroom application and practice* (4th ed.). New York, NY: Harper Collins.

Peterson, C. A. and Stumbo, N. J. (2000). *Therapeutic recreation program design: Principles and procedures* (3rd ed.). Needham Heights, MA: Allyn & Bacon.

Ross, J. and Ashton-Shaeffer, C. (2001). Therapeutic recreation practice models. In N. J. Stumbo (Ed.), *Professional issues in therapeutic recreation: On competence and outcomes* (pp. 159–188). Champaign, IL: Sagamore Publishing.

Salvia, J. and Ysseldyke, J. E. (1998). *Assessment* (7th ed.). Boston, MA: Houghton Mifflin Company.

Ward, A. W. and Murray-Ward, M. (1999). *Assessment in the classroom.* Belmont, CA: Wadsworth Publishing.

Chapter 8
Interviewing as an Assessment Procedure

Interviewing clients is a typical way for therapeutic recreation specialists to gather assessment data; however, interviewing to elicit valid and reliable results involves a great deal of skill, patience, and practice. Interviews range from casual conversations to highly structured information-seeking sessions with a predetermined sequence of specific questions (Horvat & Kalakian, 1996; Kaplan & Saccuzzo, 1982; Salvia & Ysseldyke, 1998). Interviews involve face-to-face contact with clients and/or their families. The primary reason for completing an interview is to allow the client to provide in-depth answers to open-ended questions, while the specialist observes the client's behavior in an interview setting (Ferguson, 1983). This chapter focuses on basic approaches to interviewing, considerations for structuring and conducting interviews, and phrasing of interview questions.

Purposes of Assessment Interviews

Ferguson (1983, p. 17) outlined several purposes of interviews as client assessment techniques, including:

- To assess client readiness for treatment, both physically and emotionally
- To assess degree of client rationality and appropriateness for participation in specific activities
- To identify client's leisure behavior patterns and possibilities
- To provide increased insight into self and personal leisure values
- To identify client's strength and number of family and social relationships
- To determine personal strengths and assets as well as weaknesses and liabilities
- To assess lifestyle modifications needed for healthy leisure functioning

- To identify available leisure support systems and resources in the community
- To examine economic factors influencing client's leisure participation and patterns

Each of these purposes is important to understanding the nature of interview process. The purposes impact the types of questions to be asked and the direction the interview might take.

Definition and Types of Interviews

Stewart and Cash (1988) defined interviewing as "a process of dyadic, relational communication with a predetermined and serious purpose designed to interchange behavior and involving the asking and answering of questions" (p. 3). This definition implies that the interview involves two people in a dynamic and consequential two-way exchange of information. Unlike other exchanges that have primarily social purposes, the interview has a very specific purpose and usually has a very specific direction (Kaplan & Saccuzzo, 1982). An interview is conducted to discover another person's thoughts, feelings, or perspective that cannot be observed. Seven different types of interviews are listed in **Table 8.1**:

1. Information giving
2. Information gathering
3. Selection
4. Problems with interviewee's behavior
5. Problems with interviewer's behavior
6. Problem solving
7. Persuasion

For the most part, interviewing for the purpose of client assessment in therapeutic recreation services is primarily a function of information gathering, although other types, such as problem solving, may be involved.

There are two general approaches to interviews: directive and non-directive. The *directive approach*, also sometimes called a standardized interview, involves a set series of questions targeted for a specific end result and is conducted in a systematic and consistent manner over time. A *non-directive* or *client-centered approach* has much less structure, and the content and timing are often left to the interviewee. **Table 8.2** (p. 201) provides a comparison between directive and non-directive approaches. Interviewing for client assessment most often involves a directive approach that yields specific information that helps place clients into therapeutic recreation intervention programs. A standardized, directive approach also produces results that usually have greater validity and reliability and less error variance.

Table 8.1
Types of Interviews (Stewart and Cash, 1988, p. 6)

Information Giving
    Orientation
    Training, instruction, coaching
    Job-related instructions
    Briefings
Information Gathering
    Survey, polls
    Exit interviews
    Research interviews
    Investigations: insurance, police
    Medical: psychological, case history, diagnostic, caseworker
    Journalistic
Selection
    Screening
    Determination
    Placement
Dealing with Problems with the Interviewee's Behavior
    Appraisal, evaluative, review
    Separation, firing
    Correction, discipline, reprimand
    Counseling
Dealing with Problems with the Interviewer's Behavior
    Receiving complaints
    Grievances
    Receiving suggestions
Problem Solving
    Discussing mutually shared problems
    Receiving suggestions for solutions
Persuasion
    Selling products
    Recruiting members
    Fundraising and development
    Changing the way a person feels, thinks, or acts

Considerations When Creating Interviews

Interviewing for client assessment purposes usually involves an information gathering, directive approach. To succeed in gaining the kinds of information needed to place clients into programs, several considerations need attention.

First, the interview designer needs to consider the commonalities and differences that he or she may have with the interviewees. Do they have similar backgrounds? use a common terminology in the same ways? have similar experiences? Stewart and Cash (1988) stated "You will be able to communicate more effectively with the other party if you expand the area of perceived similarities and reduce the area of perceived differences" (p. 13).

Second, the interview developer needs to consider the dimensions of the relationship with the interviewee. The degree of control and power exhibited by the interviewer is one consideration. How much power does the interviewee perceive the interviewer to possess? What degree of control does the interviewer have over the content, timing, and pace of the interview? What are subtle yet important nuances of power—for example, the position of the table or desk, the seating arrangement, or the formality of the interviewing environment? Another dimension is the degree of warmth or concern shown to the interviewee. What is done to establish trust? What is done to establish a meaningful and mutual exchange? What body language of the interviewer displays warmth and caring for the interviewee? Interview exchanges that help to equalize power and exude warmth produce better results than those that are lopsided and intimidating.

Third, consideration needs to be given to the perceptions of the individuals involved. This includes self-perceptions ("I can be successful at this interview" or "I know I won't give the right answers") as well as perceptions of the other person. Perceptions are colored by the purpose of the interview and the environment, as well as the dress and body language of both parties. Whether the interviewer wears a business suit or a sweat suit affects how the interviewee perceives that individual. The degree of formality and the explanations given during the initial minutes of the interview help create the mindset of the interviewee.

A fourth consideration is the expected level of exchange between the two parties. Stewart and Cash (1988) noted three levels of communication:

- Level 1: Relatively safe, nonthreatening areas of inquiry (superficial, socially acceptable answers, comfortable)
- Level 2: More intimate and controversial areas (behaviors, thoughts, attitudes, beliefs, feelings)

- Level 3: Highly intimate and controversial areas of inquiry, (fully disclose person's feelings, beliefs, attitudes, perceptions, rarely take place without high level of trust)

Of course the level of a particular interview depends on the purpose and the relationship between the two individuals. Almost all interviews begin with Level 1 to lay the groundwork and establish a level of trust before moving on to Level 2 or Level 3. Again, a major factor that sets the tone for the level of communication is both verbal and nonverbal interactions. Verbal cues come from the words used, inflections, and the emphasis

Table 8.2
Two Approaches to Interviewing

Directive Interview
Advantages
> Easy to learn
> Takes less time
> Provides quantifiable data
> Can supplement other methods of data collection (e.g., question-naires, observations)
> Replicated by controlling variables (e.g., voice, facial expressions, appearance)

Disadvantages
> Inflexible
> Limited in variety and depth of subject matter
> Limits the interviewer's range of techniques
> Often replaces more effective and efficient means of collecting data
> Sensitive to changes in variables (e.g., voice, facial expressions, appearance)

Non-Directive Interview
Advantages
> Allows interviewer to probe deeply into subject matter
> Gives interviewer greater flexibility
> Gives interviewee greater freedom to give lengthy answers, volunteer information
> Tends to generate more information
> Allows the interviewer to adapt to each interviewee

Disadvantages
> Time-consuming
> Requires acute psychological insight and sensitivity
> Often generates unneeded information
> Tends to generate excessive information
> Adaptation to each interviewee may reduce replicability

given certain words. Nonverbal cues come from posture, body language, and other subtle physical expressions that provide meanings to the words being spoken.

A fifth consideration is the skill level of both the interviewer and the interviewee. Skilled interviewing takes a tremendous amount of practice and hard work. The interviewer needs to be able to evaluate and give feedback by continually confirming that the message is being received, readjusting the message as necessary, and trying again when difficulties are encountered. A skilled interviewer also needs to listen well and openly. Stewart and Cash (1988) discussed three facets of listening: (a) for comprehension by clarifying, probing, and asking for more specific information, (b) with empathy and candor, being nonjudgmental, and (c) for evaluation, reserving judgments until all the facts are in and the interviewee has expressed himself or herself.

A sixth consideration is called social facilitation (Kaplan & Saccuzzo, 1982). Social facilitation means that one individual in an exchange mirrors or parrots the other individual—if the interviewer is tense, angry, and impatient, the interviewee will reflect the same behaviors. If the interviewer is relaxed, calm, and reassuring, the interviewee will respond in kind. "Thus, if the interviewer wishes to create conditions of openness, warmth, acceptance, comfort, calmness, and support, he or she must exhibit these qualities" (Kaplan & Saccuzzo, 1982, p. 202).

A seventh consideration is the collective experience. A number of factors influence the success of the interview, such as time of day, day of the week, events preceding or following the interview, location and environment, interviewer's familiarity and ease with interviewing, interviewer's appearance and demeanor, and the cumulative effect of nonverbal communication between the two parties. All of these factors and more influence the perceptions carried into the interview by both the interviewer and the interviewee. They can either positively or negatively influence the outcomes of an interview.

Malik, Ashton-Shaeffer, and Kleiber (1991) addressed a number of considerations when interviewing individuals with mental retardation. Each therapeutic recreation specialist who plans to develop and conduct client assessments with individuals with mental retardation should read their article.

Awareness of these many factors, such as communication levels, the effect of the environment, and skills needed by the interviewer, is important to improving the exchange process and getting results that reflect the true thoughts, feelings, and behaviors of the client. That in turn helps to ensure that the client is placed into the most appropriate programs and services to meet his or her needs.

The interview process depends on the questions asked during the interview. The next section covers the dimensions of interview questions. The reader is expected to be familiar with the types of questions discussed in Chapter 7.

Types of Interview Questions

Open-Ended and Closed-Ended Items

The broadest categorization of interview questions is open-ended and closed-ended. The two types can be seen as opposites on a continuum. Open-ended questions allow the interviewee a great deal of latitude in determining the amount and kind of information to give as a response; for example, "Tell me about the social contacts you have in a typical week." Closed-ended questions generate a smaller range of responses and give the interviewee fewer options; for example, "Which of the following leisure activities is of most interest to you?" (with four or five choices).

The major advantage to open-ended items is that they allow the interviewee considerable freedom in answering, so that he or she can decide the amount or nature of information shared. The individual, especially in highly open-ended interviews, determines the direction that the interview takes. On the other hand, because of this freedom and latitude, open-ended interviews and items can be very time-consuming and end up at dead ends. Open-ended items require skill on the part of the interviewer to be able to refocus or redirect the topic. In addition, the interviewer is required to record the interviewee's answers as accurately as possible. Because of the free range of responses, they are often difficult to score, tabulate, and interpret into meaningful information.

Examples of open-ended items include the following. Notice that even though the questions are all open-ended, the first items are highly open and the latter ones are less open.

- Tell me about your leisure.
- What do you do for fun?
- What leisure activities do you do on the weekends?
- In what activities does your whole family participate?
- What is your favorite leisure activity?

Interview questions should directly relate to the purpose of the interview—placing the client into the right programs to reach the targeted outcomes. Note that the questions following relate directly to an area of therapeutic recreation content, as opposed to questions that are much more general and lack focus on leisure ability.

- How satisfied are you with your leisure?
- What actions do you take to manage stress on a daily basis?
- Explain how you would find out what time the city bus ran to downtown.
- What stops or prevents you from fully enjoying your leisure?
- Explain how you would introduce yourself to a stranger at a community center.
- What items or equipment do you have in your room/home that are available for leisure?
- Given that they take equal amounts of time and money, how do you decide between two recreation activities in which you would like to participate?
- If you had a Sunday afternoon with no obligations, what would you do?
- How would you find information about a new park in town?

Closed-ended questions are more restrictive in nature and supply possible answers to the client. Like open-ended items, they can also range from more closed to less closed. The major advantage of closed-ended questions is that they allow the interviewer more control over the exchange by asking for specific information to be supplied by the interviewee; however, this can also be a disadvantage. More questions can be asked in less time and the responses are easier to score, tabulate, and analyze. They require less interviewing skill on the part of the interviewer, although they do require expertise in proper development. Another disadvantage is the interviewee does not usually have opportunity to expand on his or her answers so sometimes too little information is gathered. Since the interviewer tends to direct the exchange, the client may not be able to volunteer added information and he or she sometimes can provide an answer without knowing its full meaning.

Examples of closed-ended questions include multiple choice, yes/no or true/false, rating or Likert scale, and ranking items. Chapter 7 gave several examples of closed-ended items.

Primary and Secondary Questions

Another way to categorize items is by the content they ask, rather than the format they use. Primary questions introduce a topic or a new area within a topic, while secondary questions elicit further information, either following a primary question or another secondary question. An example of a primary question is: "What recreation facility in the community do you use most often?" An example of a secondary question would be "How close is this facility to your home?"

Primary questions can help improve the flow of the interview by indicating the direction or pace of the interview. Following are some examples of primary questions and introductions that help move an interview along.

- In this next section, let's talk about activities you do with your family. What two activities does your family do together most often?

- The second section of this interview covers your attitudes toward leisure or free time. How important do you feel leisure is to your overall well being?

- Let's end the interview with your own goals during treatment. What would you like to accomplish while you are here?

Secondary questions then can take on a variety of forms that help the interviewee to clarify his or her response to the original question.

- What do you mean when you say?

- Could you explain that in more detail?

- What I understand you to say is...

- How does _____ relate to _____?

- What else would you like to add here before we move on?

- To summarize your comments thus far...

Stewart and Cash (1988) listed eight types of secondary questions. An example of each follows.

1. *Nudges*. I see. Go on. And then? Yes? What happened next? Uh-Huh?

2. *Clearinghouse probe*. What else would you like to say about this? What have I not asked that might be of importance? Have I missed anything you can think of?

3. *Follow-up to superficial response*. Tell me more about... What happened after...? How did you react to...?

4. *Follow-up to vague response*. I'm not sure I understand your point. Please define "tentative" for me.

5. *Follow-up to feeling or attitude response*. Why did you feel that way? How did you feel about that?

6. *Follow-up to irrelevant response*. Let's go back to that last question. I'm not sure what you mean by that.

7. *Follow-up to inaccurate response.* You mean 1986, don't you? Was that crochet or croquet?

8. *Mirror or summary follow-up.* Have I got it right? Is that what you meant?

It is important to know that there is a range of secondary question types. The intention is to have the client clarify or expand his or her answer to the primary question.

Neutral and Leading Questions

Another way to classify items is by whether they are leading or neutral (Stewart & Cash, 1988). Leading questions call for an answer with direction or pressure from the interviewer and often the setting, tone, and manner in which the question is asked sets the tone for the client's expected response. Neutral questions are without pressure or direction. Leading and neutral questions can overlap with open-ended/closed-ended and primary/secondary questions.

Examples of neutral questions include the following:

- Tell me more about your home life.

- What do you do when you get off work?

- How are you feeling about your use of free time?

Examples of leading question include the following:

- Your home isn't very inviting, is it?

- How many bars do you go to after work?

- You liked our program, correct?

More often than not, client assessments will contain only neutral questions so that the individual feels freer to give responses that truly reflect his or her feelings, thoughts, and behaviors. Practicing neutral questions and neutral body language is important for the competent therapeutic recreation specialist.

Regardless of the overall type of question, attention also must be paid to the phrasing of questions. The next section examines some principles to ensure that items are written and asked in the best way possible.

Phrasing of Questions

How a question is worded and asked greatly influences how the client will respond. Consider the following questions:

- How satisfied are you with your leisure lifestyle?
- Do you enjoy your leisure?
- Do you have enough fun in your life?
- Do you and your family engage in leisure and recreation activities that are wholesome, physically active, and require teamwork?
- What would you most like to do?
- What did you do for fun Saturday night?
- Do you want to learn origami?

As you read through them, you probably had a similar reaction as would clients. Some are too vague, some are too convoluted, and some might require information the client does not have.

Stewart and Cash (1988) provided five factors to consider when constructing interview items. These include (a) language, (b) relevance, (c) information level, (d) complexity, and (e) accessibility. *Language* includes avoiding vague words, such as "most" or "frequently" or absolute words, such as "all" or "every time." Designers are encouraged to use the simplest words possible that still convey the intended meaning. Vague descriptions are not as good as more measurable and concise descriptions.

The *relevance* of each item to the client and to the assessment outcome is important. For example, asking about religion when it is not a factor in programs should be avoided. A client's *information level* is also considered. A rule of thumb is not assume clients have information when it is not likely they do. *Complexity* of the item intent or structure should be minimized and each item should focus on a single thought, event, or person. Double-barreled questions, those that ask about more than one thing at a time, are confusing for clients and yield unreliable answers. *Accessibility* is a final consideration in the phrasing of items. Items that require the most personal information should be near the end of an interview so the person feels more comfortable divulging this information.

The assessment developer should examine language, relevance, information level, complexity, and accessibility of each item on the interview form. Attention to these areas will aid the client in responding in the most honest and open manner possible.

Preparing for the Interview

Hoy and Gregg (1994) suggested several steps to preparing for an interview assessment procedure. The first step is to review the client's record.

Basic information such as name, date of birth, medical history, and place of residence usually can be obtained from the client chart or file. Collecting this information ahead of time serves three purposes: (a) it minimizes client's need to repeat the same information from one discipline interview to another, (b) it conveys a message of concern and preparedness, and (c) it informs the client that basic information is known by the specialists providing services.

The second step is to decide who is to be involved in the interview and what purpose they will serve. For example, in some settings parents or other family members might need to be interviewed if the client does not have the maturity or cognitive ability to participate in an interview. In these cases, the therapeutic recreation specialist must decide who is the best source of information and can best represent the client's views.

The third step in preparation is to review the assessment form. Even after repeated administrations the therapeutic recreation specialist will benefit from reviewing the assessment form prior to the start of every interview. The client will be more confident with specialists who are familiar with the assessment tool and procedure.

The fourth step is to schedule the time and place of the interview. Depending on the agency, a special room or designated time may exist for all client assessments. However, usually the therapeutic recreation staff must schedule the time and place.

The fifth step is to prepare the environment prior to the beginning of the interview. This step is crucial to the actual interview process. The environment should be quiet, comfortable, private, and conducive to open conversation.

Each of these steps affects the outcome of the assessment. The interview is often the primary source of information that will be used for program placement. As such, it is also important to structure the interview so that useful information can be gained as effectively and efficiently as possible. The next section covers the three main parts to an interview.

Structuring the Interview

Austin (1997) indicated that the assessment interview in therapeutic recreation serves three purposes: (a) to gain information from interviewing or observing the client, (b) to develop a relationship and build rapport with the client, and (c) to orient the client to the therapeutic recreation program or department. The assessment interview has three parts or phases that can be structured to meet these purposes: (a) opening, (b) body, and (c) closing.

Opening

The first few minutes are the most important for setting the tone and determining whether the interviewer will get beyond Level 1 (superficial) interactions. Creating goodwill and trust, and establishing a relaxing and comfortable atmosphere are starting points. The therapeutic recreation specialist should greet the client by name and ask him or her into the interview room. The specialist should introduce him or herself and explain his or her position.

It is then the responsibility of the professional to orient the client to the interview process. The purpose, time, and length of the interview should be discussed as well as how the information will be used for the client's benefit and treatment. At this point, the specialist also may wish to orient the client (or family member) to the therapeutic recreation program or department. Time should be allotted to answer any questions the client or family member might have. The overview should be brief, nontechnical, and focused on the benefits to and outcomes for the client. This information and how it should be introduced should be included in the assessment interview protocol. Issues of patient rights, confidentiality, privacy, and informed consent also may be part of the interview's introduction.

Body

The body of the interview is the major reason for the exchange and contains the most substance. The body should follow the interview guide or schedule and include the major topics, subtopics, questions, and transitions between sections. Again, interviews used for client assessment in therapeutic recreation services usually are highly structured and sequential. The specialist is responsible for monitoring the timing and pace of the interview (Hoy & Gregg, 1994).

Stewart and Cash (1988) provided five different ways to structure the body of an interview guide, including:

1. Topical sequence: Natural divisions of a topic
2. Time sequence: Chronological order
3. Space sequence: Left to right, top to bottom, physical arrangement
4. Cause-to-effect sequence: Problem and then causes of the problem
5. Problem–solution sequence: Problem and solutions to the problem

Typically therapeutic recreation assessments are arranged by topic, usually program content. For example, the interview guide may be divided into five major sections by program area, such as Background Information, Leisure Awareness, Social Skills, Stress Management, and Leisure Resources. The questions pertain to the specific content area addressed by the intervention programs and determine whether or not the client is in need of treatment.

The types of questions to be used in the body have been introduced earlier in this chapter. Open-ended, neutral questions are used along with transitional statements to elicit information from the client in a timely manner.

Closing

The closing of the interview is very important and needs to be done well. The purpose of the interview and how the information will be used is reiterated. This provides continuity to the interview and assures the client of the importance of the interview. Rapport and trust building continue in the closing.

A variety of ways to close the interview were offered by Stewart and Cash (1988), including:

- Offer to answer questions: "What other questions do you have at this time?"

- Use clearinghouse questions: "Is there anything else you'd like to add?"

- Declare the completion of a purpose or task: "We're done for today."

- Make personal inquiries: "Will you be able to get back to your room by yourself?"

- Signal the time is up: "We're out of time for this assessment."

- Explain the reason for the close: "This gives me the preliminary information I need to develop a treatment plan for you to look at."

- Express appreciation or satisfaction: "You've done a good job in answering these questions."

- Exhibit concern for welfare and future: "I'm sure we'll be able to get you involved in programs to help you."

- Plan for the next meeting: "We're scheduled for next Thursday."

- Summarize the interview: "You seem to enjoy more physical activities but are hindered by your disability. Our plan will include working together to adapt some former activities for you as well as learn some new ones."

The interview closure summarizes the interview and the information that has surfaced. The specialist may re-emphasize the results of the interview, how the results relate to program placement, and what goals or outcomes are to be expected or worked on. The closure also is a prime time to reiterate the services offered by the therapeutic recreation department, the schedule of programs, and how the specialist can be reached. The client should be thanked for his or her time and cooperation.

General Rules for Interviewing

As with any data gathering technique, with interviewing there is also concern about reducing error and increasing confidence in the results (Kaplan & Saccuzzo, 1982; Peterson & Stumbo, 2000). One major concern is the types of errors produced by misinterpreting the meaning of the information given by the client. Does the interview guide faithfully represent the therapeutic recreation program content and does the information gained during the interview adequately reflect the client's attitudes, thoughts, and behaviors? Does the therapeutic recreation specialist faithfully represent the client's responses while recording them? Does the summary of the client's statements reflect the person's true responses? These are concerns of validity. An additional major concern is that the results are as consistent and stable over time as possible. Would the person give the same or nearly the same results if asked next week? Are the client's answers consistent with what else is known about the client? These concerns must be addressed not only during the development of the procedure, but also during its administration, scoring, and reporting.

Following is a collection of general rules to follow for improving the validity and reliability of results while conducting interviews (Austin, 1997; Babbie, 1986; Kaplan & Saccuzzo, 1982; Peterson & Stumbo, 2000).

Appearance and Demeanor

- Dress similar to that of the individuals being interviewing.

- Ensure that apparel is professional, clean, neat, and modest.

- Have a pleasant, relaxed, friendly, and responsive demeanor.

Interviewing Protocols and Training

- Gain a clear understanding of the purpose of the assessment and details of the therapeutic recreation intervention program.

- Begin with discussion about general guidelines and procedures for interviews.
- Review each question, its meaning, and its purpose on the interview assessment form.
- Clarify any special situations, such as an individual with hearing or speech difficulties, if the interview session should be interrupted, or if the client tires before the end.
- Practice and rehearse typical or atypical interview situations. Suggestions and corrections should be given so each individual administers the interview in the same manner.
- Have each individual demonstrate competence and adherence to the protocol on two or three clients before he or she can independently interview clients.
- Refresh training every other month or so to ensure that specialists adhere to the established protocol.
- Review client records to ensure that each specialist is documenting information in an accurate, timely, and meaningful way.

Familiarity with Interview Form
- Study the interview form carefully, question by question, and follow administration protocol.
- Start and continue the interview without stopping to study the interview guide.
- Know the clients' characteristics. Gathering information through client interview may not be the most reasonable course of action for all client groups. Some individuals with cognitive deficits, such as acquired brain injury, cerebral vascular accident, or mental retardation, or younger clients, may not respond well to interview situations. The specialist often is responsible for gathering background information (perhaps from records reviews) about each client prior to interview situations.

During the Interview
- Use the interview guide wording exactly. Any change or variation in the wording can cause a different (invalid or unreliable) response from the client.
- Use a vocabulary on the same level as the client, neither too simplistic nor too difficult.
- Identify and follow neutral probes on the form, so that each client is treated the same way.
- Avoid biased, prejudiced, evaluative, or judgmental comments.

- Avoid questions posed in ways to get only socially acceptable answers.

- Interject as little as possible, yet keep the flow of interaction occurring.

- Use active and reflective listening skills throughout the interview. Don't assume to know where the client is headed.

- Observe nonverbal cues for discomfort and restlessness.

- Be consistent. The protocol for administering an interview should include the words to be stated by the specialist. This includes establishing rapport, the introduction, transitions, probes, and closure. Consistency increases reliability and reduces the chances for error in the assessment results due to the procedures used by the specialist.

Recording Responses

- Record answers as they are given, and do not summarize, paraphrase, or correct.

- Avoid adding interpretation to the client's responses.

- Make marginal comments about the client's body language or facial expression.

Summary

Client assessment in therapeutic recreation services often involves an interviewing process. Most likely, it involves a structured, sequenced set of questions that each client is expected to answer. In the best cases, the questions are well-developed; focus on determining the client's current patterns, strengths, and weaknesses; and allow the therapeutic recreation specialist to make decisions about treatment planning and program placement. Besides the content of the questions, the specialist also initiates a welcoming and relaxed atmosphere. Several ways to improve the validity and reliability of interviews and reduce error variance were reviewed in this chapter.

References

Austin, D. R. (1997). *Therapeutic recreation: Processes and techniques* (3rd ed.). Champaign, IL: Sagamore Publishing.

Babbie, E. (1986). *The practice of social research* (4th ed.). Belmont, CA: Wadsworth Publishing.

Ferguson, D. D. (1983). Assessment interviewing techniques: A useful tool for developing individual program plans. *Therapeutic Recreation Journal, 17*(2), 16–22.

Horvat, M. and Kalakian, L. (1996). *Assessment in adapted physical education and therapeutic recreation* (2nd ed.). Dubuque, IA: Brown and Benchmark.

Hoy, C. and Gregg, N. (1994). *Assessment: The special educator's role.* Pacific Grove, CA: Brooks/Cole Publishing.

Kaplan, R. M. and Saccuzzo, D. P. (1982). *Psychological testing: Principles, applications, and issues.* Monterey, CA: Brooks/Cole Publishing.

Malik, P. B., Ashton-Shaeffer, C., and Kleiber, D. A. (1991). Interviewing young adults with mental retardation: A seldom used research method. *Therapeutic Recreation Journal, 25*(1), 60–73.

Peterson, C. A. and Stumbo, N. J. (2000) *Therapeutic recreation program design: Principles and procedures* (3rd ed.). Needham Heights, MA: Allyn & Bacon.

Salvia, J. and Ysseldyke, J. E. (1998). *Assessment* (7th ed.). Boston, MA: Houghton Mifflin.

Stewart, C. J. and Cash, Jr., W. B. (1988). *Interviewing: Principles and practices* (5th ed.). Dubuque, IA: Wm. C. Brown Publishers.

Chapter 9
Observation as an Assessment Procedure

Observation involves the specialist viewing the client's behavior, either directly or indirectly. In some cases the client will know he or she is being observed, in other cases, he or she may not. The specialist should be aware of client autonomy and rights in conducting observations unknown to the client. The primary reason for conducting observations is to record the client's *behavior* (not *perceptions of behavior* as in interviews) in as real-life situations as possible. The specialist usually records observations of the client's behavior on score sheets that may include systems such as checklists, rating systems, and open-ended narratives (Stumbo, 1983). Typically the specialist chooses to create close-ended rating systems to shorten the time spent recording the observations and to increase comparability across clients.

Systematic observation is a method of standardizing the procedures by which information about client behavior is targeted, recorded, scored, and interpreted. Systematic observations differ from casual observations in at least four ways. Systematic observation: (a) has a specific purpose (e.g., to collect assessment data about clients), (b) targets certain behaviors (e.g., social skills), (c) records behaviors systematically, and (d) has validity and reliability as primary concerns (Bickman, 1976). Systematic observation of client behavior is appropriate whenever the specialist needs to (a) document typical client performance or behavior, (b) document unusual client performance or behavior, (c) confirm the results of another nonbehavioral assessment, and/or (d) compare one client's behavior with another client's behavior (Levy, 1982). These four situations assume that the data collection, recording, and interpretation are conducted in ways that enhance the validity and reliability of the assessment results. It is inappropriate to use observations when the specialist wants to assess client interests, attitudes, or knowledge, or evaluate the meaning of client behavior and actions. The client's underlying feelings, thoughts, or motives will not be revealed during an observation (Thorndike & Hagen, 1977).

Advantages and Disadvantages of Systematic Observation

There are many advantages in using systematic observation as a method of client assessment (Dunn, 1991; Kazdin, 1977; Navar, 1984; Stumbo, 1983), including:

- Recording of behavior that occurs naturally in the environment (not usually contrived)
- Recording of actual behavior, rather than the client's stated intentions or interests
- Ability to record as behavior occurs
- Generalizability of observed behavior (on the unit) to unobserved behavior (in the community)
- Usable with young children and others for whom verbal communication is difficult or who have mixed thought processes
- Comparative ease of development and use
- Comparative low cost

Systematic observations can yield powerful information about what clients do, instead of what they say they do or want to do. However, observations also have a number of disadvantages (Dunn, 1991; Kazdin, 1977; Navar, 1984; Stumbo, 1983), including:

- Long-term cost in staff time of making direct observations
- Fitting the observer unobtrusively into the setting (observer effect)
- Potential subjectivity and bias of the observer (potential lack of reliability)
- Determining a meaningful and productive set of behaviors to observe
- Behavior must be frequently occurring to obtain accurate data base
- Determining the significance of an isolated item of behavior
- External nature and character of observation (inability to determine meaning of behavior)
- Specialist apathy toward increasing observational skills
- Ethical issues, including those involved in unknown observations, qualifications of the observer, and being truthful about intent of observation

All methods of assessment data collection have advantages and disadvantages. The specialist must decide which method has the fewest liabilities and best potential for gathering useful and meaningful information.

Steps to Developing Systematic Observations

There are five basic steps in creating systematic observation instruments (LaFrance, 1981). The first step is to determine the sample of target behavior that will be important to observe. What is the least amount of behavior that needs to be observed to place clients into the right programs? What are the most important kinds of behaviors to observe? What assessment data is needed through the observation that cannot be collected in any other way? Do only certain answers to a set of interview questions warrant a follow-up through observation? Will observations include extensive observations of the few clients who are most in need of special attention? These questions and others need to be answered for the exact behavior to be determined.

The second step is to determine the procedures for collecting, organizing, and analyzing data (Anastasi, 1968; Gronlund, 1981; Marshall & Rossman, 1989; Patton, 1987). These include the parameters to ensure that the behavior being observed is representative of the client's total behavior: who, when, where, for how long, under what circumstances, and how many occasions. Observations must be organized, focused, and systematic if they are to yield dependable data and results. Timing is an important consideration, especially if any antecedents would trigger specific client behavior. In addition, the system for collecting and recording data should allow for behavior to be recorded as immediately as feasible to minimize dependence on memory and to preserve the significant details of the original behavior.

The third step is to consider under which conditions the behavior will be observed. For example, will the behavior be observed under natural circumstances (e.g., a community out-trip) or under contrived circumstances (e.g., in the facility)? Will the observer be obtrusive and known to the client or unobtrusive and unknown? Unobtrusive observations can even include collecting artifacts, such as what games are left off the shelves or what the person may have at his or her bedside table. **Figure 9.1** (p. 220) provides a matrix of direct/indirect and known/unknown observations. Will the behavior be observed by mechanical or human means? Will a human record the behavior or will data be collected via an audiotape or videotape? For the most part, the most naturalistic setting and conditions will yield the most naturalistic responses (Alberto & Troutman, 1982).

The fourth step is to determine the data collection instrument. The type of instrument and method for collecting information depends mostly on the type of behavior that is to be recorded. What is most important to know about the behavior? Frequency? Duration? Number of occurrences? How much detail is needed? Presence or absence of a behavior or degree of a behavior? Is a full description needed? A variety of observation methods and techniques exist. Like other measurement instruments, observation tools should be pilot tested to increase the validity and reliability of the results. Interobserver reliability tests to measure the accuracy and agreement between observers are important.

The fifth step is to train the staff as observers. Observers should be reminded to function as an objective recording instrument and to interfere as little as possible with the behavior as it occurs. Like interviews, the specialist becomes the recording device, and should be diligent about not affecting the outcome of the assessment. Protocols for conducting observations should be developed and followed. Periodic in-service training should focus on minimizing observer drift, which occurs when an observer becomes less accurate in recording answers.

All these decisions become a practical compromise between cost/effort/time and comprehensiveness, and between completeness (depth) and number of occasions (breadth). At times, the initial desired method of observation becomes unfeasible and another must be selected.

Potential Sources of Error in Observations

Knowing potential sources of error within observations is important to eliminating or reducing their negative effects on the assessment results

	Direct	Indirect
Known	Observer is present Client knows of observation	Observer is not present Client knows of observation
Unknown	Observer is present Client does not know of observation	Observer is not present Client does not know of observation

Figure 9.1
Matrix of Direct/Indirect and Known/Unknown Observations

(Kazdin, 1977). Sources of error are divided into the four main factors within an observation: (a) specialist, (b) client, (c) instrument, and (d) conditions. Typical errors in each category are listed below.

Specialist
- Bias may be shown to certain clients or categories of clients
- The specialist changes the way in which he or she records behavior over time (observer drift)
- The specialist deviates from the observation protocol

Client
- The client has a reactive effect from awareness of being observed and changes his or her typical behavior
- The client displays socially desirable behavior that he or she thinks the observer wants to see
- The client is influenced to behave in certain ways by the appearance or manner of the observer
- As the observation progresses, the client changes in his or her reactions to the observer

Instrument
- The instrument contains unclear or unreliable behavior categories
- Too few incidents of behavior are recorded to demonstrate validity of an individual's results
- Open-ended items allow for too much variance and interpretation from the specialist

Conditions
- Clients are being observed in unusual circumstances that change their typical behavior
- Client behavior fluctuates due to weather, day of week, time of day, and location of the observation

Improving Confidence in Observational Assessment Results

As mentioned in earlier chapters, reducing error and improving confidence in the use of results are important to therapeutic recreation assessments. The previous list of errors diminishes the degree of confidence in the results, although the therapeutic recreation specialist can minimize these errors. Stumbo (1983) listed several suggestions to improve the validity and reliability of the observation's results, including:

- When pilot testing the instrument, use two independent observers for administration, scoring, and analysis
- Conduct and repeat periodic training of observational and recording techniques for each therapeutic recreation specialist
- Improve each specialist's awareness of personal biases, perspectives, and personal attitudes that may surface during observations
- Use as many methods and observers as possible (triangulation) to observe and record a situation to increase validity and reliability
- Succinctly define and operationalize domains and categories of behavior(s) being observed
- Obtain and maintain observer (specialist) consensus as to what behaviors are recorded, what criterion will be used, and which domains/categories include specific behaviors
- Determine criteria for analysis of behavior
- Determine time limits and parameters for observation
- Decide whether observation will focus on frequency, severity, and/or duration of behaviors
- Remain flexible while adhering to the observation protocol
- Describe the situations/behaviors as objectively as possible
- Pay attention to the client's nonverbal cues such as posture and facial expressions
- Review the accumulation of observations on a client to reveal patterns of behavior and record on a summary sheet
- Record behaviors as immediately as possible
- Use naturalistic settings to the extent possible
- Ensure that directions for the instrument are clear and concise, and that time required for recording behaviors is minimal
- Minimize observer interference in the situation

Cautions about Interrater Reliability of Observations

As mentioned in Chapter 2, one of the major sources of error in observations is the individual(s) performing the observation. The therapeutic recreation specialist(s) can become a source of error because observations require the evaluation of the specialist on whether or not the behavior occurred or to what extent the behavior occurred. The more concise and descriptive the behavioral observation tool, the less opportunity for rater error (Gronlund, 1981; Kazdin, 1977).

Remember that there is a difference between agreement and accuracy of two raters' observations. Even though two or more scorers agree, their observations may not be accurate to what actually occurred. *Accuracy* refers to the extent to which observations scored by an observer match those of a predetermined standard for the same data. *Agreement* reflects the extent to which observers agree on scoring behavior. Usually there is no firm basis to conclude that the one observer's data should serve as the standard (i.e., is accurate).

In Chapter 2, Salvia and Ysseldyke's (1998) four different methods for calculating interrater reliability were discussed: (a) simple agreement, (b) point-to-point agreement, (c) percentage of agreement for the occurrence of target behaviors, and (d) kappa index. These calculations range from calculating how many times observers agree and disagree to calculating proportions of actual versus expected observations. Each of these calculations varies on its attention to the difference between agreement and accuracy.

Four major problems have been noted concerning this discrepancy between agreement and accuracy: (a) reactivity of the observers, (b) observer drift, (c) complexity of scoring systems and behaviors, and (d) observer expectancies and feedback. Each will be discussed in terms of the problems it presents and recommendations to reduce its effects. In many cases, awareness of these problems can help reduce their effects. Adequate training, information, and feedback can improve the validity and reliability of observation results.

Clients often react to being observed. Likewise, observers also react when they know they are being checked. They not only become more accurate in their observations, they also start to record more like those who evaluate their ratings. When reliability checks are conducted, it is recommended they be unobtrusive and covert, observers be told that all observations will be checked for accuracy, and that several different evaluators be used.

A second problem is observer drift—the tendency of observers to change the manner in which they apply the definitions of behavior over time (Patton, 1987). With multiple observers high levels of agreement can be maintained even when accuracy has declined. To counteract observer drift, it is recommended that all observers be trained simultaneously with periodic refresher courses and that observers not score their own observations.

A third problem is complexity of some scoring systems as well as the complexity of some behaviors being recorded. Complex rating systems may actually decrease reliability. In addition, the greater diversity of behavior scored within a single tool can lower interobserver agreement. Solutions include adding similar complex situations in the training and refresher sessions and paying attention to the complexity during calculations.

A fourth problem is observer expectancies (Thorndike & Hagen, 1977. In many cases, observers record what they expect to find and ignore those behaviors they did not anticipate. While this is difficult to counter, the best training includes reminders to enter observation situations with an open mind and to record behavior as it occurs.

Observational Recording Methods

There are three basic methods for recording observations: (a) checklists, (b) rating scales, and (c) anecdotal records or critical incident records. The appropriateness of the selected method depends upon the type of observation to be made, the purpose of making the observation, and the feasibility of the recording method for the situation at hand. *Checklists* provide a structured, standardized method of recording whether a characteristic is present or absent, or whether an action is taken or not taken. They are useful for assessing mastery of concrete learning tasks, performance skills, or finished products. *Rating scales* provide a structured, standardized observation form similar to checklists, but can indicate degree of the characteristic or action. *Anecdotal records* or *critical incident reports* provide narrative, factual descriptions of actual behavior. Sometimes these reports document typical behavior and sometimes they record atypical client behavior.

Checklists

Advantages

- Leaves little room for interpretation
- Easy to administer, score, and interpret if appropriate behaviors/actions are chosen for observation
- Interrater reliability tends to be high when concrete behaviors are observed

Disadvantages

- Difficult to define human behaviors in discrete categories
- Cannot be used when degree or frequency of occurrence is important
- Only a crude measure of total behavior, unless behaviors are consistently patterned

Rules for Effective Use

- Identify and clearly state each specific action desired in the total performance of the behavior
- Include those actions which represent common errors to be sure they are observed (e.g., following procedures)
- Arrange desired actions in appropriate order of occurrence, if possible
- Provide simple procedure for checking action as it occurs

Table 9.1
Example of Checklist

Activity: Quiltmaking Class Client: Velma Date: January 12		
Procedures		Followed? Yes/No
Traced template from pattern book onto plastic grid sheet		
Cut out plastic grid sheet template		
Traced around plastic template onto back of fabric with pencil		
Cut enough fabric pieces for one quilt block		
Threaded needle with 18" length of thread		

Rating Scales

Advantages
- Directs observation toward specific and clearly defined aspects of behavior
- Provides common frame of reference for comparing all clients on same set of characteristics
- Provides convenient method of recording judgments of the observers
- Easy to administer and score if well-constructed

Disadvantages
- More difficult to construct because of precision needed to reduce interpretations
- Difficult to use one form for all clients if desired behaviors differ
- Personal biases enters into rating (e.g., generosity error, severity error, central tendency error, halo effect, logical error)

Rules for Effective Use
- Characteristics should be significant to treatment outcomes
- Characteristics should be directly observable
- Characteristics and points in the scale should be clearly defined
- Four to six rating positions should be provided
- Raters should be permitted to omit ratings where they feel unqualified to judge
- Ratings from several observers should be compared wherever possible

Anecdotal Records

Advantages
- Provides snapshots of meaningful incidents and events in the lives of clients
- Allows for recording behaviors in a nonstandardized format
- Allows for recording of environment, antecedents, and consequences of behaviors

Disadvantages

- Amount of time required in maintaining adequate system of records
- Difficulty in being objective when observing and reporting behavior
- Obtaining an adequate sample of behavior
- Difficulty in deciding level of detail to record
- Inconsistent wording used in the anecdotal record
- Difficulty in collating and analyzing information

Table 9.2
Example of Rating Scales

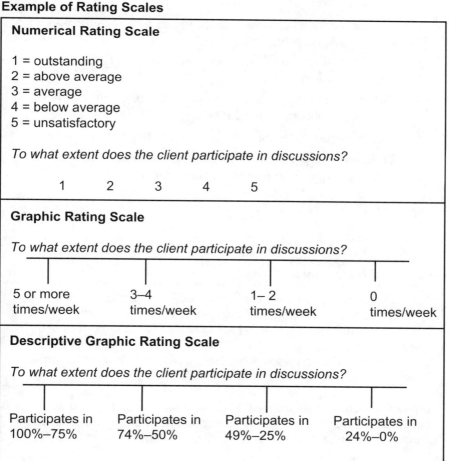

Numerical Rating Scale

1 = outstanding
2 = above average
3 = average
4 = below average
5 = unsatisfactory

To what extent does the client participate in discussions?

| 1 | 2 | 3 | 4 | 5 |

Graphic Rating Scale

To what extent does the client participate in discussions?

| 5 or more times/week | 3–4 times/week | 1– 2 times/week | 0 times/week |

Descriptive Graphic Rating Scale

To what extent does the client participate in discussions?

| Participates in 100%–75% | Participates in 74%–50% | Participates in 49%–25% | Participates in 24%–0% |

Rules for Effective Use

- Determine in advance what to observe, but be alert for unusual behavior
- Describe an event that is either representative of the typical behavior (anecdotal record) or significant because it is strikingly different from usual form of behavior (critical incident report)
- Observe and record enough accurate information about the situation to make the behavior meaningful (in relation to client problems or client goals)
- Make a record of the incident as soon after its occurrence as possible
- Limit the anecdote to a brief description of a single specific incident
- Carefully define behaviors related to incident, recording both positive and negative actions
- Clearly delineate the factual description of the incident separate from interpretations
- Collect a number of brief anecdotes on a client before drawing inferences concerning typical behavior
- Develop procedures for coding and recording behaviors
- Train observers, including practice sessions and in-services, to obtain practice in writing anecdotal records

Table 9.3
Example of Anecdotal Records

Factual: During the creative expression activity, Harold was very slow in starting work. He stopped his own work several times during the hour to wander around the room and look at what other clients were doing and tell them what was wrong with their work. Suzanne and Bill each told him to mind his own business. Harold did not complete his project during the hour, as did other clients.

Interpretation: Harold showed difficulty in staying on task. He was easily distracted, and frequently disturbed and criticized other clients during the session. His lack of concentration kept him from finishing his project during the hour.

Critical Incident Reports

Critical incident reports are similar to anecdotal records, but differ in two ways: (a) the situation recorded is unusual, and (b) recording antecedents, behavior, and consequences is required. Factual information is kept separate from interpretation.

Table 9.4
Example of Critical Incident Report

Antecedents: Sarah has stayed in her room during the evenings and talked of suicide during the past seven days. On Friday at 6:00 p.m., client's friends visited for 1 hour and Sarah went immediately to her room after they left.

Behavior: Friday at 8:00 p.m. Sarah was found sitting on floor of room closet smoking small amount of marijuana, and when approached by staff, stated "Why won't you people get off my back?"

Consequences: Sarah was escorted to treatment room by nursing staff for 1-hour observation. She cried and stated "Everybody's out to get me." Controlled Substance Report was filed by nursing staff.

Observational Recording Techniques

There are four observational recoding techniques that overlay on the three methods previously discussed. These four techniques include: (a) frequency or tally, (b) duration, (c) interval, and (d) instantaneous time sampling. The choice of a technique depends on what characteristic of the behavior is targeted (e.g., frequency, duration). The *frequency* or *tally* technique records the number of times a behavior occurs. *Duration* techniques are used when the length of the behavior is of concern. *Interval* techniques focus on both the occasions and durations of behaviors. *Instantaneous time sampling* techniques are used when an observer enters and exits the observation area periodically. The next section discusses the usefulness, rules for effective use, and examples of each of the four types of recording techniques.

Frequency or Tally Recording

Useful When
- Frequency of behavior (number of times behavior occurs) is to be recorded
- Behavior is very clearly defined
- Clients are to record their own behavior
- More than one individual is to be observed and recorded at one time
- Frequency needs to be converted into percentages or rate of occurrence

Rules for Effective Use
- Determine if behaviors are significant enough to warrant observation
- Minimize interpretation by establishing concrete and defined behaviors
- Results should be compared with results from other time spans, to show progression or regression
- If behavior occurs, mark is recorded; if no behavior occurs, no mark is recorded

Table 9.5
Example of Frequency or Tally Recording

Client: Jeanine	Activity: Tennis Skills	Time: Friday, 8:00 a.m. to 8:30 a.m.
Behavior		Frequency of Behavior
Stands in correct serving area of court		/////
Uses correct overhead serve		//
Serves ball over net in opponent's receiving area		///

Duration Recording

Useful When
- The length of occurrence of behavior is important
- Behavior is readily and easily observed

- Observer has significant time available to make observation
- Sweep second hand or stop watch can be used during observation
- Duration of behavior needs to be converted into percentages across time

Rules for Effective Use

- Limit the types of behaviors to be recorded, especially if they are likely to overlap, making recording difficult
- Behaviors must be clearly defined, observable and be of substantial duration
- Results should be compared with results from other time spans, to check progression or regression
- If behavior occurs, mark is recorded; if no behavior occurs, no mark is recorded; if behavior is carried over into other intervals, mark is recorded

Table 9.6
Example of Duration Recording

Client: Patricia	Activity: Community Out-Trip to YWCA			Time: Sunday, 9:15 to 10:15
Behavior	Duration (seconds)			Totals
On task (as appropriate to activity)	2	3	19	24
Appropriate conversations with peers	14	29		43
Walks around room, paces	112	143	157	412
Argues with leader	0			0
Argues with peers	43			43

Interval Recording

Useful When

- Need running account of occurrence or nonoccurrence of behavior (display of patterns)
- Need rough estimate of both frequency and duration
- Rate of behavior is low enough to count
- It is difficult to tell when behavior starts or stops without recording

Rules for Effective Use

- Determine size of intervals on basis of how often behavior occurs (large enough to allow observations, small enough for occurrences of behavior)
- Behavior must be clearly defined and observable
- Results should be compared with results from other time spans
- If behavior occurs, mark is recorded; if no behavior occurs, no mark is recorded; if behavior is carried over into other intervals, mark is recorded

Table 9.7
Example of Interval Recording

Target Behaviors	Codes	Subjects	Intervals
Biting other child	[<]	1. Tobias	15 seconds
Kicking other child	[/]	2. Mark	
Pinching other child	[X]	3. Janie	
Throwing toys at other child	[O]	4. Christina	

Intervals	1	2	3	4	5
Subjects	:00–:15	:20–:35	:40–:55	:60–:75	:80–:95
1. Tobias	< /		<< // O	OOO	//
2. Mark	<	//	XX		X
3. Janie	/	OO	/		/
4. Christina			X		

Instantaneous Time Sampling

Useful When

- Observer does not have ability to totally commit time to observations
- Behavior is infrequent
- Frequency and duration of behavior is not important variable
- Many individuals are to be observed at once

- Overall patterns are more important than frequency of individual behaviors

Rules for Effective Use

- Determine what behaviors or actions are to be observed
- Determine reasonable intervals for making observations
- Convert observations into percentages to make more generalized conclusions
- Construct form that allows for quick and unobtrusive check of absence or presence of behaviors

The therapeutic recreation specialist should be familiar with each of these methods and techniques of observational recording. Each has its own advantages and disadvantages, and is appropriate for certain situations. Familiarity and expertise with each of them ensures that the specialist can choose the one that best suits the circumstances and the clients. Practice is required to be an astute and accurate observer.

Table 9.8
Example of Instantaneous Time Sampling

Area: Large Activity Area	Date of Observation: February 14th, 12:00 to 1:00			
	12:00–12:15	12:15–12:30	12:30–12:45	12:45–1:00
Total number of clients in room	29	22	12	17
Clients playing cards	12	8	4	4
Clients watching television	9	12	7	13
Clients reading	8	2	1	0

Summary

This chapter covered several aspects of using observations as a client assessment technique, including advantages and disadvantages as well as steps to developing observational tools. Reducing errors and improving the confidence in the observation's results are important considerations when building and validating observational instruments. Observational methods (checklists, rating scales, anecdotal records, critical incident reports) as well as observational techniques (frequency or tally recording, duration recording, interval recording, and instantaneous time sampling) were discussed.

References

Alberto, P. A. and Troutman, A. C. (1982). *Applied behavior analysis for teachers* (2nd ed.). Columbus, OH: Merrill Publishing Company.

Anastasi, A. (1968). *Psychological testing* (3rd ed.). New York, NY: MacMillan Company.

Bickman, L. (1976). Observational methods. In C. Selltiz, L. Wrightsman, and S. Cook (Eds.), *Research methods in social relations*. New York, NY: Holt, Rinehart and Winston.

Dunn, J. K. (1991). *Integrating client assessment into therapeutic recreation practice*. Paper presented at the Assessment Workshop, St. Peters, MO.

Gronlund, N. E. (1981). *Measurement and evaluation in teaching* (4th ed.). New York, NY: MacMillan Company, Inc.

Kazdin, A. E. (1977). Artifact, bias, and complexity of assessment: The ABCs of reliability. *Journal of Applied Behavior Analysis, 10*(1), 141–150.

LaFrance, M. (1981). Observational and archival data. In L. H. Kidder (Ed.), *Selltiz, Wrightsman & Cook's research methods in social relations* (4th ed.). New York, NY: Holt, Rinehart and Winston.

Levy, J. (1982). Behavioral observation techniques in assessing change in therapeutic recreation/play settings. *Therapeutic Recreation Journal, 16*(1), 25–32.

Marshall, C. and Rossman, G. B. (1989). *Designing qualitative research*. Newbury Park, CA: Sage Publications.

Navar, N. (1984). Documentation in therapeutic recreation. In C. A. Peterson and S. L. Gunn, *Therapeutic recreation program design: Principles and procedures* (2nd ed., pp. 212–266). Prentice Hall, Inc.

Patton, M. Q. (1987). *How to use qualitative methods in evaluation*. Newbury Park, CA: Sage Publications.

Salvia, J. and Ysseldyke, J. E. (1998). *Assessment* (7th ed.). Boston, MA: Houghton Mifflin.

Stumbo, N. J. (1983). Systematic observation as a research tool for assessing client behavior. *Therapeutic Recreation Journal, 17*(4), 53–63.

Thorndike, R. L. and Hagen, E. P. (1977). *Measurement and evaluation in psychology and education* (4th ed.). New York, NY: John Wiley & Sons.

Chapter 10
Assessment Barriers and Issues

The purpose of this text is to fill a gap in the therapeutic recreation literature concerning client assessment. It aims to educate the reader about the
importance of client assessment, how assessment relates to treatment
planning and programming, and ways to improve the process of data
collection, analysis, interpretation, and reporting. It is clear that in the
profession's far and recent past, client assessment has traveled down a
rather rocky road.

> Over fifteen years ago, Witt, Connolly, and Compton (1980) called
> for an increased sophistication in therapeutic recreation assess-
> ment. "It seems improbable that any professional in the field would
> deny the importance of assessment within therapeutic recreation
> services. On the other hand, there appears to be some confusion
> over the purpose, approach and use of the assessment process in
> our services" (Witt, Connolly & Compton, 1980, p. 5). The call for
> sophistication of client assessment is as appropriate today as it was
> in 1980, since confusion and misuse remain as professional con-
> cerns. (Stumbo, 1997, p. 347)

This paragraph was the introduction to a chapter on client assessment
issues and concerns first written in 1995 for Compton's (1997) edited
volume *Issues in Therapeutic Recreation: Toward the New Millennium*. In
the 60-plus years since the origins of the profession, it seems sometimes
that little progress in therapeutic recreation assessment has been made. As
we enter the new century, the call for sophistication of client assessment
becomes increasingly urgent. On one hand, there is a national call for
achieving client outcomes while on the other hand, most therapeutic
recreation specialists are not receiving adequate training in the processes of
intervention, assessment, and outcome measurement (Stumbo, 2001).

This chapter explores some of the assessment concerns and issues that
are likely to occur when providing therapeutic recreation intervention.
These concerns and issues affect the quality of daily practice of therapeutic
recreation specialists.

Relationship between Intervention and Client Assessment

Client assessment is the initial step in establishing a meaningful baseline of the client's leisure-related interests, abilities, knowledge level, and/or attitudes. These baseline results provide the essential information for placing clients into the "right" intervention programs, and also provide the foundation for later determining the outcomes of therapeutic recreation intervention (Peterson & Stumbo, 2000; Stumbo, 1996). Horvat and Kalakian (1996, p. 9) stated: "Assessment is the critical link in the testing process that renders worthwhile the time spent gathering data. Assessment also provides the basis for what instruction should follow."

Client assessment and program design and delivery are linked strongly in those programs considered intervention. Perschbacher (1995, p. 1), in discussing the need for accurate and timely assessments in long term care, stated: "Resident assessments are the first step in understanding individuals. Assessments viewed as mere paperwork miss the point at which the activity program can make real differences in individual lives."

Intervention programs intend to bring about some behavioral change in the client as a direct result of participation and involvement. The focus of intervention programs is on producing client outcomes—that is, some specific predictable, measurable change in the client's behavior, skills, attitudes, and/or knowledge (Peterson & Stumbo, 2000). On the other hand, diversional (nonintervention) or purely recreational programs are designed and delivered with the intent of providing fun and entertainment for participants. Client assessment is crucial to intervention programs, and cursory to diversional or nonintervention programs. An important task for therapeutic recreation specialists is to determine the overall intent of their programs and the assessments used to place clients into programs.

As therapeutic recreation services move further toward intervention and away from diversion, the need for systematic and meaningful assessments increases. The connection between client assessment, intervention and client outcomes is a strong one and has been noted throughout the therapeutic recreation literature (Dunn, Sneegas & Carruthers, 1991; Navar, 1991; Olsson, 1992; Peterson & Stumbo, 2000; Riley, 1991; Sheehan, 1992; Stumbo, 1994/1995). Shank and Kinney (1991) noted that client outcomes are observable changes in the client's status as a direct result of the specialist's interventions and interactions. Riley (1991) discussed these as "measurable changes" and stated "the causal relationship between the process of care (intervention) and the outcomes of care (change in patient behavior) is crucial" (p. 59).

Both of these thoughts about the connection between intervention and outcomes assumes that a valid and reliable baseline of information is gathered to later "prove" the change in behavior or status. That is, the client assessment collects the baseline information on the needs, strengths, limitations, and current status of the client. This information provides the framework from which systematic intervention programs are prescribed and delivered for individual clients. An "end-of-services" summary (perhaps the assessment readministered as a posttest) may provide the evaluative data to determine whether the appropriate client outcomes have been achieved at the conclusion of the intervention or the client's length of stay. This evaluative measurement allows for conclusions about the achievement of client outcomes to be made. Thus the alliance between the assessment, the intervention, and the measurement of outcomes is of paramount importance.

Although these concepts are relatively simple to understand, they become difficult to put into practice when programs are not designed to produce specific outcomes and client assessments are not designed to align specifically with those programs. Only with these basic but necessary building blocks to achieving predictable and meaningful client outcomes will accountability for therapeutic recreation programs become a reality.

Issues in Implementing the Assessment Process

Issues and concerns in therapeutic recreation client assessment will be discussed through the lens of the Therapeutic Recreation Assessment Planning Model and the Therapeutic Recreation Implementation Model presented in Chapter 3. The models have been simplified into five topics: (a) assessment resources and specialist knowledge, (b) measuring desired characteristics or behaviors, (c) implementing assessments correctly, (d) scoring and analyzing assessments correctly, and (e) documenting results and reassessing for outcomes. This framework will be used, not necessarily to address how this process works, but the issues that must be considered while implementing it.

Assessment Resources and Specialist Knowledge

To perform exemplary assessment duties, the profession must have adequate resources and the professional must have adequate expertise. Both of these areas are concerns for client assessment in therapeutic recreation.

Not only is there a limited number of client assessments, there is a clear lack of appropriate and standardized assessments and available information about them. Therefore, it is not surprising that therapeutic recreation specialists often enter their jobs with less than adequate competence and continue to experience difficulties in the client assessment process throughout their careers. This section will discuss four issues: (a) lack of an adequate number of therapeutic recreation assessments, (b) lack of high quality therapeutic recreation assessments, (c) lack of assessment resources, and (d) specialist competence.

Lack of an Adequate Number of Assessments

For a profession as large and diverse as therapeutic recreation, there are few quality instruments commercially available for use. There simply are not enough instruments to meet the demands of the diverse programming of therapeutic recreation professionals. Not enough commercial instruments have the content to reflect the content of programs offered within therapeutic recreation services—meaning that most of the instruments available are not valid for the programs with which specialists would like to use them. Sylvester, Voelkl, and Ellis (2001) noted that therapeutic recreation assessments also lack multicultural sensitivity to the extent that validity and reliability may be jeopardized.

So what's a therapist to do? First, the specialist may buy instruments that are not appropriate (valid, reliable, or usable) for the purpose for which she or he would like to use them. The specialist then encounters the problem of not being able to make proper programming placement decisions, resulting in incorrect Quadrants II and III decisions (see Table 1.7, p. 15). This happens frequently when the specialist buys a popular assessment as the "magic bullet" and discovers that it provides no more useful results that any previous instrument the therapist had used.

Second, the specialist may borrow an assessment from a related field, such as adapted physical education. This may seem fairly attractive, and some therapeutic recreation textbooks advocate this approach. However, if the content of the assessment does not match the content of the therapeutic recreation program, the results will likely lead to random program placement, again resulting in faulty program placement decisions and lack of client outcomes. The same scenario is repeated: An assessment is selected and used, but the results do not help place the right clients into the right program, and the specialist is left with faulty Quadrant II and III decisions once again.

Third, the specialist may develop an assessment specifically for use within his or her agency. Unless the therapeutic recreation specialist is quite familiar with and complies with accepted assessment development and validation methodologies discussed in Chapter 2 and Chapter 7, this option can be problematic (Dunn, 1984; Kinney, 1980; Peterson & Stumbo, 2000; Stumbo, 1991; Touchstone, 1975). To counteract these pitfalls, the specialist needs to develop considerable expertise in assessment including competence in ensuring a reasonable degree of validity and reliability of the results. This text is a starting point for developing the necessary competence.

Lack of High Quality Assessments

There are two difficulties. One is that some assessments have not been validated in an appropriate manner. This may include those that use faulty validation techniques and those that have never been tested for the purpose of client assessment.

Both commercial and agency-specific assessments can have validation problems. "The available assessment instruments that are nonagency-specific are still sketchy, still evolutionary, and still conceptually cloudy" (Howe, 1989, pp. 217–218). For example, one assessment publisher reported reliability results on a four-point observation scale to within one point either way. So if one rater scored the client a 2 on some specific behavior, the other rater got counted for the *same score* if she or he had rated the same behavior a 1, or 2, or 3. Not surprisingly, raters averaged a 91% agreement using this method. In cases like this, the buyer needs to be aware that just because something is in print, it is not necessarily true or good or usable. Buyer beware!

Another problem is the use of measurement instruments for client assessment when they were not built or validated as client assessment instruments. For example, some instruments on the market were developed for research purposes to describe leisure attitudes, motivations, and satisfaction within a certain research population. They may have excellent statistics reflecting that purpose and for those populations for which they were intended. But to assume those statistics mean anything for client assessment is erroneous. For example, even though the National Council for Therapeutic Recreation Certification's test might be excellent, would it be appropriate for physical therapist licensure? Of course not. A test does not have goodness for all purposes; it is only as good as the statistics dictate for that specific purpose and population. Clearly this presents a case where specialists must be educated consumers before buying products that have no value for their programs or clients.

A third problem exists with activity interest inventories:

The tension between the applied and theoretical dimensions of the assessment process continues, especially with the continual proliferation of agency-specific assessment devices that are little more than interest inventories but are incorrectly used and touted for purposes way beyond those of such inventories. (Howe, 1989, pp. 217–218)

The problems specifically associated with activity interest inventories and similar instruments have been outlined elsewhere in the literature (Peterson & Stumbo, 2000; Stumbo, 1992a, 1992b, 1993/1994), and these problems remain in practice today. Stumbo (1991) stated that since activity interest inventories and other similar tools contain a relatively narrow *activity* definition of services, they miss the mark in helping understanding the broader *leisure behavior* and *functional independence* focus of most therapeutic recreation programs. As such they may provide little help in understanding client behavior. "A frustrating outcome of this misguided use of assessment as measurement is the realization that the results derived from an irrelevant assessment instrument are of little informative value in providing program direction and may totally misdirect program decisions" (Witt, Connolly & Compton, 1980, p. 6). In other words, without adequate standardization and validation of client assessment tools, improper program placement decisions (Quadrants II and III) will be made.

Lack of Assessment Resources

Another area for concern with therapeutic recreation assessment is the difficulty that most specialists have in locating information about available and usable assessments. Keeping abreast of current information about assessments and related issues is essential, although largely a difficult and fragmented enterprise. This area has improved but warrants continued attention.

Specialists must take responsibility to expend (sometimes great) effort to locate, read, and understand the published assessment literature. Authors need to continue to write and publish quality articles and books on assessment that are of high value to practice. Professional organizations and publishers need to continue to create avenues to provide easy access to the newest information. Educators need to ensure that the latest techniques and tools are an integral part of therapeutic recreation curricula. Only as each group continues to take responsibility for their part of the information chain, will better and more timely assessment information be widely available to all who desire it.

Specialist Competence

Sneegas (1989) and others identified the need for specialists to be better trained in assessment, research methods and leisure behavior, and called for better communication between "investigators and practitioners" to conduct needed research on client assessments (p. 233). This requires give-and-take between specialists and researchers, and between programming knowledge and measurement expertise. A balance is necessary for competence and for working relationships to be successful.

The assessment competencies suggested by the National Council for Therapeutic Recreation Certification, the American Therapeutic Recreation Association, and the National Therapeutic Recreation Society were outlined in Chapter 1. In addition, Horvat and Kalakian (1996) identified several qualifications for professionals conducting assessments, including:

- Knowledge of measurement principles, including validity, reliability, and objectivity
- Knowledge of potentials and limitations of test interpretations
- Competence in the administration and interpretation of specific tests
- Competence in assessment validation procedures
- Knowledge of procedures to avoid undue discrimination, such as age, gender, or cultural biases

These competencies require that education about assessments become a life-long process for the specialist, who needs to continue to learn about improving client assessment procedures throughout his or her career. Howe (1989, p. 219) in summarizing her book chapter on assessment stated:

But, what [this chapter] cannot give is the thorough and complete education needed to use assessment instruments or procedures well, mindful of both their strengths and their weaknesses. That training requires either formal degree work or continuing professional education. It takes time and study to gain the insight and skills to validate instruments, let alone to practice one's skills at assessment design, quantitative and qualitative data collection and analysis, and the interpretation and application of results. So, in that sense, any assessment is only as good as the TRS [Therapeutic Recreation Specialist] conducting it. [clarification added]

Measuring Desired Characteristics or Behaviors

An additional problem for the field of therapeutic recreation is that leisure behavior and independent functioning (two intended outcomes of therapeutic recreation programming) are such a challenge to define and then measure.

Complexities of Measurement

Citing work completed by Dunn (1984), Howe (1984), and Stumbo and Thompson (1986), Sneegas (1989, p. 226) noted that "there are few instruments designed to obtain assessment information related to leisure behavior which demonstrate adequate reliability, validity, and practical utility." Leisure behavior and functional independence are complex entities and their measurement is fraught with measurement dangers.

> The measurement of leisure behavior in individuals with disabilities and in special populations is not as simple as it might appear on the surface. The current state of the art for assessing leisure behavior is relatively undeveloped because obtaining valid and reliable measures of the leisure behavior of anyone (not even considering any additional problems presented by disability) is a complex process. (Sneegas, 1989, p. 224)

For instance, Sneegas (1989) discussed problems with how leisure is defined (time, activity, or state of mind), and therefore, measured through assessments. Sneegas (1989) warned against simplistic or univariate studies, and those that lack richness or contextual/qualitative information. In addition, this contribution to the literature examined some of these difficulties in light of assessing individuals with disabilities and special needs. For example, Katsinas (1992) made the case that most therapeutic recreation assessment tools are not refined enough to measure low levels of functioning or regressed behavior, and are not sensitive enough to measure small increments of behavioral change. Howe (1989, p. 217) noted that most therapeutic recreation assessments lacked the ability to measure "richness" and "complexity" of the individual client.

The lack of ability to measure the complexities of human behavior—especially for individuals with disabilities, illnesses, and/or special needs—is a major concern for therapeutic recreation assessment. The field needs more and better research describing and measuring the leisure behavior of clients. This in turn will improve the ability to standardize and validate tools to measure baseline and subsequent information.

Students and specialists alike must make the commitment to learn as much as possible about intervention programming, measurement qualities, and client assessment as they coalesce on one of the most powerful decision points in the therapeutic recreation intervention process—that of describing an adequate baseline of client behavior. As knowledge and use of assessments improve, so too will the quality of intervention programs and the success of therapeutic recreation within the health care arena.

Implementing Assessments Correctly

Assessment Planning

Assessment planning includes (a) analysis of the environment, (b) defining the parameters, (c) selecting or developing assessments, (d) establishing and following protocol, and (e) training staff and interns on the assessment protocols (Peterson & Stumbo, 2000, p. 214). These five steps establish the foundation for knowing what to assess and establishing the proper procedure to ensure the assessment will collect the best possible results. These first steps often are overlooked or taken for granted, which sometimes results in an assessment procedure that does not align with the agency's mission and overall targeted client outcomes.

Analysis of the Environment

While in the planning stage, specialists should take time to gather information about the agency's view on assessment.

> For example, several agencies might serve individuals with substance abuse problems. However, they may differ greatly in whether they primarily deliver inpatient, outpatient, or day treatment programs; whether their intent is detoxification, individual counseling, or group peer counseling; or whether they are accredited by the Joint Commission...As such the agency's characteristics will impact greatly the assessment chosen by the therapeutic recreation specialist and other disciplines. (Peterson & Stumbo, 2000, p. 215)

Likewise the client characteristics (e.g., gender, age, recidivism, home environment) and program characteristics (e.g., targeted client outcomes, program content, professional standards) affect the assessment plan.

Defining the Parameters

The function, content, and implementation strategy also become issues. Client assessment generally serves four functions: (a) screening, (b) identifying the problem(s), (c) narrowing the problem(s), and (d) reassessing or monitoring progress. These were discussed in Chapter 1. Each of these functions requires different types of questions, which impact on the validation process.

A significant issue is the content of the assessment. One point made repeatedly throughout this text is that the content of the assessment must match the content of the therapeutic recreation intervention program.

> While assessment clearly provides the foundation for individual program planning, its relationship to the program's conceptual foundation is as critical. The theory or philosophy that drives the program should be reflected in the assessment procedures. If the program seeks to build a client's repertoire of leisure skills in certain areas then an appropriate skill or activity-oriented inventory is needed. If the intent of the program is to increase the client's perceived competence or effectiveness in leisure, an instrument that measures levels of learned helplessness...or perceived leisure competence...may be needed. (Stumbo & Rickards, 1986, p. 3)

In addition, each chosen implementation strategy (e.g., interviews, observations, self-administered questionnaires, records reviews) also has implications because their purposes, methods, and outcomes differ fairly significantly. The decision of which data collection technique to use should be made with care.

Selecting or Developing Assessments

Regardless of whether the assessment tool or procedure is developed for a specific agency by the therapeutic recreation staff or purchased from a commercial vendor, the same basic measurement requirements apply. According to Dunn (1983, p. 63), it should be expected that assessments used in therapeutic recreation:

- Fulfill their intended purpose
- Have the ability to gather specified information
- Gather that information accurately
- Utilize an appropriate method
- Are appropriate for clients
- Are appropriate for the agency and the situation

Specialists must consider both the purpose and content, as well as other factors, before selecting or developing an assessment procedure. If a commercially available assessment can be located that meets the purpose and content needed in the assessment, then purchase is logical. However, this is relatively rare in that therapeutic recreation programs are based on unique factors such as community resources, agency mission, client characteristics, and agency resources (Peterson & Stumbo, 2000), and are not uniform across the country or across a particular state. Many professionals, then, must rely on developing assessments to meet their department's needs.

The major concern, regardless of whether the assessment is purchased or developed, is that professionals often fail to consider the purpose or function of the assessment and the necessity to match the content of the assessment with the content of the program. This match requires that the professional use comprehensive program design to create programs and that these areas be translated into assessment content. Failure to consider the link between program placement and assessment data results in poor decisions in Quadrant II and Quadrant III. This means that the link between the assessment results and the placement into programs is likely to be faulty and lack validity. If this link is not established, the content of the assessment will tend to be haphazard and not lead to appropriate program placement decisions. This is a major concern in therapeutic recreation assessment and program delivery.

Establishing and Following Protocols

In this step, the specialist prepares to administer a client assessment. All assessments, whether commercially sold or self-developed should be accompanied by adequate documentation that includes information on the development of the tool as well as standardized procedures for its use, analysis, and interpretation. For example, documentation should include the conceptual development of the tool, the validity and reliability statistics of validation studies and pilot tests, and resources needed to perform all steps of the assessment. Additionally, documentation should include standardized procedures for training (both staff and interns); preparing the assessment environment (including supplies); and administering, scoring, and interpreting the procedure. Dunn (1987, 1989) provided excellent guidelines for using or creating the necessary documentation to accompany assessments.

The major concern of this step is that both commercially available and self-developed assessments rarely have adequate accompanying documentation.

This lack of documentation decreases the opportunities for standardized (and hopefully, valid and reliable) procedures across staff and units. This means that results will interpreted and reported based on the fluctuating perceptions of individual staff members. The lack of uniform implementation of assessments, even within a single department, reduces the likelihood of correct and consistent placement decisions. For example, when personal interviews with clients are used as the primary data-gathering technique (see Chapter 8), the specialist becomes the instrument. Any fluctuation of the environment, body language, use of probes, length of interview, and the like can produce results that are more affected by the specialist than the client. Therefore, the results may not be valid for that client, and subsequent program placement may be in error. This lack of precision weakens the assessment process and increases the likelihood of incorrect program placement decisions—another important concern for the profession.

Training Staff and Interns on the Assessment Protocol

The most typical training that a new therapist or student intern receives on the assessment tool or procedure involves watching an experienced specialist conduct two or three assessments, and then independently administering assessments on his or her own. Shadow training is inadequate to teach the new employee or intern about the validation and development of the tool or the procedures with which the tool was validated. What are the procedures for a person unable to communicate? What are the standardized probes to the interview questions? How are uncooperative clients handled? What happens if the client becomes too fatigued to continue? What if the therapist detects the answers being given are not truthful? All these situations and more should be documented and handled in a similar manner by each therapist and intern. Protocols should include the frequency of intertherapist checks to make sure each therapist is administering the assessment to clients in a consistent manner. The accuracy and dependability of the assessment results are influenced greatly by the thoroughness and detail included in the protocol. The ability to be confident in the assessment results is a direct factor of these details.

Administering Assessments

In this step the specialist implements the procedures outlined and reviewed in the last stage. Assessments in therapeutic recreation include (a) interviews with clients and/or their families (see Ferguson, 1983, and Chapter 8), (b) observations (see Stumbo, 1983, and Chapter 9), (c) self-administered surveys, and (d) record reviews. Each type collects unique information and has its own advantages and disadvantages. Types may be used in combination to strengthen the validity of the results. Table 4.2 (p. 125) illustrated the relative advantages of each type of information-gathering assessment technique.

The primary concern with administration is that because there is no documented protocol, it is often inconsistent between departments (no two departments administer the assessment in the identical way), between specialists (no two specialists administer the assessment in the identical way) and within specialists (each specialist is not consistent from one administration to the next). These inconsistencies greatly affect the outcome of the assessment, thus affecting the placement of clients into programs. Incorrect decisions may be made, jeopardizing the likelihood that clients will receive needed treatment and will achieve the desired or intended outcomes. Adequate and uniform documentation, training, and guidelines would assist in alleviating this weakness.

An additional concern is the differing abilities of clients on singular or multiple units. Since administration needs to be consistent, when client abilities differ greatly (e.g., some clients who cannot read, some with cognitive disabilities, some with visual or hearing impairments), then the assessment(s) must be designed to meet these varying needs, be validated on these groups, and be administered as consistently as possible when these conditions are present.

In summary, the major issue regardless of technique chosen is that acceptable protocols are established and followed.

> Assessments need to be administered consistently to the fullest extent possible. That means that the assessment needs a specific protocol that is consistent across: (a) departments (if programs are similar), (b) specialists, (c) administrations by an individual specialist, (d) clients, and (e) assessment environments. Deviations from these consistencies lower the confidence that can be placed in the results and program placement decisions. (Peterson & Stumbo, 2000, p. 233)

Scoring and Interpreting Assessments Correctly

Following the established protocol for scoring the assessment, in this step the specialist summarizes the assessment results in a clear and concise manner. This summary (often referred to as data reduction) condenses quantitative data (numbers) and/or qualitative (words) data into an understandable and cohesive picture of the client. This summary communicates the results of the assessment and provides the basis for the development of a treatment plan.

Like previous steps, the major concern here is one of dependability and consistency. The overwhelming majority of therapeutic recreation assessments lacks adequate protocols for reliable and efficient scoring. Because many rely on purely qualitative or open-ended data, they are difficult to score due to the lack of an agreed-upon, congruent method of gathering and synthesizing information. For example, asking "How do you spend your leisure time?" as an open-ended question with no established categories for marking an answer, is likely to result in a diversity of answers that are difficult to categorize after the fact.

This diversity of answers and difficulty in categorization lead to one of the most problematic areas in assessment for therapeutic recreation specialists. Because standardized scoring procedures are all but nonexistent (especially for agency-specific assessments), the specialist often is forced to rely on personal judgment for summarizing the results. Without protocols, the interpretation of results can be influenced by mood, need to fill programs, and personal preference. In these cases, the specialist collects assessment data (perhaps largely because of external or agency mandates), but then is left without any systematic procedure to score the results. The therapist then has no choice but to place clients into programs based on personal preferences or the need to fill certain programs, or worse yet, every client is placed in every program.

This inconsistent, unreliable method of program placement results in faulty decisions and the inability to produce client outcomes. As such, it jeopardizes the entire programming process and threatens the quality of therapeutic recreation program delivery. (Peterson & Stumbo, 2000, p. 234)

Documenting Results and Reassessing for Outcomes

The goal of the final step is to make objective, consistent, and correct decisions for placing clients into therapeutic recreation programs. Program placements should be based on the results of the assessment process (not personal whims or agency pressures), so scoring, interpretation, and program placement are highly interrelated. If the results were obtained through a valid and reliable process, the interpretation of the results and placement decisions also are more likely to be valid and reliable. If data reduction is problematic, then interpretation of the data similarly will be problematic. Consider the following example. If two clients have similar scores or results on the assessment and they are placed in similar programs, as indicated as necessary from the assessment, then these "right" individuals are likely to be receiving the "right" service. On the other hand, if two clients have similar scores or results on the assessment, and they are placed in dissimilar programs, then the process is probably not producing valid or reliable results and is resulting in faulty interpretation and placement decisions. This results in either clients not receiving necessary services (Quadrant II) or clients receiving unnecessary services (Quadrant III).

Documenting the Placement/Treatment Plan in the Client Record

While the format of client records often are decided at the agency level, the content that professionals enter into the record usually is decided by the department's staff, in consultation with other disciplines. The content to be reported from the results of the assessment is determined by the content of the programs, and in turn, the content of the assessment.

One of the frustrations, if the previous five steps have been done incorrectly or incompletely, is that the specialist has little valuable or unique information to report. When prior assessment steps have not followed a logical, consistent, and justifiable sequence, or if programs are not based in a systematic analysis of client needs, the information provided by therapeutic recreation specialist may not differ greatly from other disciplines or may not contribute to the client goals.

For example, a therapeutic recreation specialist may be providing valuable intervention programs with the *content* of (a) decision making, (b) lifetime activity skills, (c) leisure resources, and (d) community reintegration skills. These are well-designed, outcome-oriented intervention programs that appear to be successful and complement the treatment programs of the other disciplines. However, her *assessment content* includes (a) personal history, (b) past leisure interests, and (c) future leisure interests. How well does the content of the assessment match the content of the program? What can she say about client placement into programs? What connection can be made between assessment "scores" and placement into programs? How will the "right" clients be placed systematically into the "right" programs? How will she know in which Quadrant her placement decisions are? How will assessment results be used for development of a client's treatment plan?

The answer is that client placement into the correct programs is unlikely and the specialist will have little of value to report in the client record or to the treatment team. As a beginning, the specialist needs the assessment to reflect the program content of (a) decision making, (b) lifetime activity skills, (c) leisure resources, and (c) community reintegration skills. Unless the program-to-assessment connection is made clear, other information may have little value and may be regarded poorly by other members of the treatment team.

Reassessing as Necessary to Show Progression or Regression

Documenting client outcomes relies on the ability of the specialist to measure change in the client's knowledge, attitudes, and/or skills. It was noted previously that one of the many difficulties in therapeutic recreation client assessment is that the results of assessment tools often lack validity and reliability and are imprecise. This compounds, then, the difficulty in being able to document client changes. However, when the assessment results are obtained using an instrument and protocol that yields valid and reliable data, this enhances the opportunity to measure client change.

If the chosen assessment instrument produces valid and reliable results, then no better tool exists to determine the progression or regression of a particular client. The specialist conducts the assessment, implements the intervention program, and administers the assessment again to measure client outcomes. This does mean that the original assessment must have the precision (reliability) to determine sometimes small increments of movement. For example, if it is determined from the original assessment that a client lacks social interaction skills (and, therefore, the client is placed into a social skills program), the assessment must measure these skills with enough accuracy to determine if change has been made during or at the completion of the program. If the assessment provides rough or crude estimates of ability, then re-assessment will be difficult, if not impossible. If this is the case, the specialist will have an extremely difficult time proving that the client achieved the intended outcomes of the therapeutic recreation intervention program.

This last phase is made more difficult by the fact that specialists often start the entire assessment process with weak, vague, or misdirected instruments. This brings to mind the computer phrase of "GIGO" or "garbage in, garbage out." One cannot end at the correct destination if the map is faulty.

Every step in the assessment process is intricately linked. Poor analysis of the client need or selection of a weak commercial tool are examples of faulty starting points that have significant impact on the remainder of the assessment process. The entire process requires a considerable amount of specialist expertise, competence, and effort to ensure that better decisions are made regarding each client's treatment. Without proper assessment, even the best intervention program will have little meaning in the lives of clients.

The Challenge

Therapeutic recreation assessment will advance rapidly and issues will be minimized greatly only when each student and specialist meets the challenge of improving the future state of the art in assessment. To meet this end, the reader is challenged to answer the following questions:

- What specific actions will you take to improve your personal knowledge of validity, reliability, and usability as measurement characteristics that affect the quality of therapeutic recreation assessments? What articles or books will you read?

- What specific actions will you take to better understand the crucial link between program design and client assessment in therapeutic recreation intervention? How will you improve your practice?

- What specific actions will you take to improve your ability to implement assessments through observations, interviews, self-administered surveys, or record reviews? Will this include practice sessions under peer review?

- What specific actions will you take to remain informed about new developments and literature concerning therapeutic recreation assessments? Does this plan include reading periodicals, journals, and books? Attending conferences and workshops? Developing assessments through research and cooperative partnerships?

- What specific actions will you take to come a better consumer of the therapeutic recreation literature? By what standards will you judge the "goodness" of published therapeutic recreation assessments?

Summary

This chapter provided a starting point for discussion about the improvement of therapeutic recreation assessment. The challenges outlined, including selecting and implementing assessments; specialist expertise; and instrument validity, standardization, and availability, point to the continued need to improve the current state of the art of therapeutic recreation assessment. This will happen only when each student and professional in the field meet the challenge of improving his or her or her own knowledge, skills and understanding of assessment and its crucial link to intervention programming. Are you up to the challenge?

References

Compton, D. M. (1997). *Issues in therapeutic recreation: Toward a new millenium* (2nd ed.). Champaign, IL: Sagamore Publishing.

Dunn, J. K. (1983). Improving client assessment procedures in therapeutic recreation programming. In G. L. Hitzhusen (Ed.), *Expanding horizons in therapeutic recreation X* (pp. 61–84). Columbia, MO: University of Missouri.

Dunn, J. (1984). Assessment. In C. A. Peterson and S. L. Gunn (Eds.), *Therapeutic recreation program design: Principles and procedures* (2nd ed., pp. 267–320). Englewood Cliffs, NJ: Prentice-Hall, Inc.

Dunn, J. K. (1987). Establishing reliability and validity of evaluation instruments. *Journal of Park and Recreation Administration, 5*(4), 61–70.

Dunn, J. K. (1989). Guidelines for using published assessment procedures. *Therapeutic Recreation Journal, 23*(2), 59–69.

Dunn, J. K., Sneegas, J., and Carruthers, C. A. (1991). Outcome measures: Monitoring patient progress. In B. Riley (Ed.), *Quality management: Applications for therapeutic recreation* (pp. 107–116). State College, PA: Venture Publishing, Inc.

Ferguson, D. (1983). Assessment interviewing techniques: A useful tool in developing individual program plans. *Therapeutic Recreation Journal, 17*(2), 16–22.

Horvat, M. and Kalakian, L. (1996). *Assessment in adapted physical education and therapeutic recreation* (2nd ed.) Madison, WI: Brown & Benchmark.

Howe, C. (1984). Leisure assessment instrumentation in therapeutic recreation. *Therapeutic Recreation Journal, 18*(2), 14–24.

Howe, C. Z. (1989). Assessment instruments in therapeutic recreation: To what extent do they work? In D. Compton (Ed.), *Issues in therapeutic recreation: A profession in transition* (pp. 205–221). Champaign, IL: Sagamore Publishing.

Katsinas, R. P. (1992). Social skills assessment for long-term care residents who have cognitive and multiple impairments. In G. Hitzhusen and L. T. Jackson (Eds.), *Expanding horizons in therapeutic recreation XIV* (pp. 193–224). Columbia, MO: University of Missouri.

Kinney, W. B. (1980). Clinical assessment in mental health settings. *Therapeutic Recreation Journal, 14*(4), 39–45.

Navar, N. (1991). Advancing therapeutic recreation through quality assurance: A perspective on the changing nature of quality in therapeutic recreation. In B. Riley (Ed.), *Quality management: Applications for therapeutic recreation* (pp. 3–20). State College, PA: Venture Publishing, Inc.

Olsson, R. H., Jr. (1992). Assessment and progress note writing: Skills needed for treatment documentation. In G. Hitzhusen and L. T. Jackson (Eds.), *Expanding horizons in therapeutic recreation XIV* (pp. 167–176). Columbia, MO: University of Missouri.

Perschbacher, R. (1995). *Assessment: The cornerstone of activity programs*. State College, PA: Venture Publishing, Inc.

Peterson, C. A. and Stumbo, N. J. (2000*). Therapeutic recreation program design: Principles and procedures* (3rd ed.). Needham Heights, MA: Allyn & Bacon.

Riley, B. (1991). Quality assessment: The use of outcome indicators. In B. Riley (Ed.), *Quality management: Applications for therapeutic recreation* (pp. 53–68). State College, PA: Venture Publishing, Inc.

Shank, J. W. and Kinney, W. B. (1991). Monitoring and measuring outcomes in therapeutic recreation. In B. Riley (Ed.), *Quality management: Applications for therapeutic recreation* (pp. 69–82). State College, PA: Venture Publishing, Inc.

Sheehan, T. (1992). Outcome measurements in therapeutic recreation. In G. Hitzhusen and L. T. Jackson (Eds.), *Expanding horizons in therapeutic recreation XIV* (pp. 177–192). Columbia, MO: University of Missouri.

Sneegas, J. J. (1989). Can we really measure leisure behavior of special populations and individuals with disabilities? In D. Compton (Ed.), *Issues in therapeutic recreation: A profession in transition.* (pp. 223–236). Champaign, IL: Sagamore Publishing.

Stumbo, N. J. (1983). Systematic observation as a research tool for assessing client behavior. *Therapeutic Recreation Journal, 17*(4), 53–63.

Stumbo, N. J. (1991). Selected assessment resources: A review of instruments and references. *Annual in Therapeutic Recreation, 2*(2), 8–24.

Stumbo, N. J. (1992a). *Leisure education II: More activities and resources.* State College, PA: Venture Publishing Inc.

Stumbo, N. J. (1992b). Re-thinking activity inventories. *Illinois Parks and Recreation Magazine, 23*(2) 17–21.

Stumbo, N. J. (1993/1994). The use of activity interest inventories in therapeutic recreation assessment. *Annual in Therapeutic Recreation, 4*, 11–20.

Stumbo, N. J. (1994/1995). Assessment of social skills for therapeutic recreation intervention. *Annual in Therapeutic Recreation, 5*, 68–82.

Stumbo, N. J. (1996). A proposed accountability model for therapeutic recreation services. *Therapeutic Recreation Journal, 30*(4), 246–259.

Stumbo, N. J. (1997). Issues and concerns in therapeutic recreation assessment. In D. M. Compton (Ed.), *Issues in therapeutic recreation: Toward a new millennium* (2nd ed., pp. 347–372). Champaign, IL: Sagamore Publishing.

Stumbo, N. J. (2001). Revisited: Issues and concerns in therapeutic recreation assessment. In N. J. Stumbo (Ed.), *Professional issues in therapeutic recreation: On competence and outcomes* (pp. 215–236). Champaign, IL: Sagamore Publishing.

Stumbo, N. J. and Rickards, W. H. (1986). Selecting assessment instruments: Theory into practice. *Journal of Expanding Horizons in Therapeutic Recreation, 1*(1), 1–6.

Stumbo, N. J. and Thompson, S. R. (1986). *Leisure education: A manual of activities and resources.* State College, PA: Venture Publishing, Inc.

Sylvester, C., Voelkl, J. E., and Ellis, G. D. (2001). *Therapeutic recreation: Theory and practice.* State College, PA: Venture Publishing, Inc.

Touchstone, W. A. (1975). A personalized approach to goal planning and evaluation in clinical settings. *Therapeutic Recreation Journal, 18*(2), 25–31.

Witt, P., Connolly, P., and Compton, D. (1980). Assessment: A plea for sophistication. *Therapeutic Recreation Journal, 14*(4), 3–8.

Student Exercises

Chapter 1

Discussion Questions

1. What role does client assessment play in the therapeutic recreation intervention program process?
2. Discuss the status of therapeutic recreation assessment within each of the purposes outlined in Table 1.1.
3. Compare and contrast the standards or competencies for assessment as given by the National Council for Therapeutic Recreation Certification, the National Therapeutic Recreation Society, and the American Therapeutic Recreation Association, as well as external accreditation bodies. How will you gain competence in these areas?
4. Compare the definitions of assessment outlined in Table 1.5.
5. What is the difference between intervention and nonintervention programs? What role does client assessment play in each?
6. Which of the principles of client assessment are most often violated and why?
7. Discuss the concepts of error and confidence as they relate to Table 1.7.
8. What other assumptions could be added to the lists found in this chapter?
9. What should client assessments in therapeutic recreation measure?
10. What are some measurement problems associated with client assessment?

Sample Test Items

1. One purpose of client assessment in therapeutic recreation is to:
   a. Analyze the properties of therapeutic activities.

   b. Place clients into programs based on their needs.

   c. Evaluate the effectiveness of the intervention for each client.

   d. Standardize programs aimed at achieving client outcomes.

2. All of the following are uses of client assessment EXCEPT:

   a. Gathering baseline information about the client.

   b. Monitoring client progress throughout the program.

   c. Analyzing the characteristics of activities.

   d. Providing research data about client changes.

3. The content of the client assessment should match the:

   a. Content of the therapeutic recreation programs.

   b. Specialist's areas of expertise.

   c. Standards of the Joint Commission.

   d. Protocols for community reintegration programs.

4. Clients should be placed in therapeutic recreation intervention programs based on:

   a. Need to fill programs.

   b. The mission of the agency.

   c. The standards of the National Council for Therapeutic Recreation Certification.

   d. Client need.

5. Client assessment information helps the specialist to:

   a. Develop goals and objectives for the clients.

   b. Create program protocols.

   c. Analyze which activities are best suited for client participation.

   d. Evaluate program or treatment protocols.

6. All of the following organizations have standards for therapeutic recreation assessment EXCEPT:

   a. Joint Commission on Accreditation of Health Care Organizations.

   b. National Recreation and Park Association.

   c. American Therapeutic Recreation Association.

   d. Rehabilitation Accreditation Commission.

7. What is likely to happen if the client assessment does not measure the right content?

   a. Clients are placed in the wrong programs.

   b. Clients with no need are placed into programs.

   c. Baseline information cannot be used to measure outcomes.

   d. All of the above

8. As opposed to nonintervention programs, intervention programs are specifically designed to:

   a. Improve clients' life satisfaction.

   b. Make decisions about clients.

   c. Reduce clients' leisure barriers.

   d. Address an area of client need.

9. What areas are likely to be included in a therapeutic recreation client assessment?

   a. Annual income and earning potential.

   b. Functional abilities and leisure patterns.

   c. Leisure theory and self-efficacy measures.

   d. None of the above.

10. What is likely to happen to clients when results from an assessment lead to incorrect program placement decisions?

   a. They achieve the goals documented in their treatment plan.

   b. They improve their functional abilities.

   c. They decrease the amount of services they receive.

   d. They receive the wrong or no services.

Sample Student Assignments

Professional Interview
Interview a practicing therapeutic recreation professional at his or her agency about how well the content of the client assessment matches the content of the program. Ask about the types of programs delivered for clients and how the assessment was developed or selected. Bring a copy of the assessment and program plan back to class for a comparison and discussion.

Programming Implications
Select a client group. Use the Leisure Ability Model and Table 1.7 to

describe scenarios for each of the four quadrants. What happens to clients in each of the four quadrants? What are the consequences of each quadrant?

Assessment Competencies

Review the standards that affect therapeutic recreation assessment from both professional organizations and external accreditation groups. Summarize the similarities and differences between the standards. Report your findings to the class.

Academic Preparation

Develop a list of 5 to 10 actions you will take to improve your knowledge and competence of therapeutic recreation assessment. Include both in-class and out-of-class experiences and both in-class and hands-on activities. Match each activity with the competencies that you plan to gain.

Assessment Summary

Most universities keep internship files in order for students to select their senior internship sites. Go to this file and review the client assessments. Compare the content of the assessments and the programs. Bring the information back to class for comparison and review.

University Websites

Look at university websites for therapeutic recreation curricula information. Find classes that address client assessment. From the content or assignments, create a list of competencies the enrolled students are likely to learn. Compare this list with NTRS, ATRA, or NCTRC standards and guidelines.

Other Professions

Interview individuals who work in disciplines besides therapeutic recreation (e.g., social workers, physical therapists, occupational therapists, speech pathologists, nurses) and ask to see copy of their assessments. Compare these with those used for therapeutic recreation. How well do the assessments complement each other? What does each add to the achievement of treatment goals for clients?

Answers to Sample Test Items

1. b; 2. c; 3. a; 4. d; 5. a; 6. b; 7. d; 8. d; 9. b; 10. d

Chapter 2

Discussion Questions

1. Discuss *error* and *confidence* in relation to assessment results.
2. Explain the differences between norm-referenced and criterion-referenced scores. Which type is most often used in therapeutic recreation?
3. What are ways to improve validity in assessment results? What are ways to improve reliability?
4. How does a developer gather evidence of content validity? criterion-related validity? construct validity?
5. Define validity in your own words and give two examples.
6. What factors may lower validity of an assessment's results?
7. How is evidence gathered to demonstrate reliability? How does this relate to validity?
8. Define reliability in your own words and give one or two examples.
9. How does a developer gather evidence of reliability?
10. What factors may lower reliability of an assessment's results?
11. What role do protocols play in client assessment? why are they necessary? why are they important?
12. Discuss ways to improve the fairness of assessments to a variety of groups, while being sensitive to validity and reliability issues.
13. Imagine you are building a new client assessment instrument. Describe how you would go about collecting validity and reliability evidence. How would you reduce error and improve confidence in the results?
14. The purpose of establishing validity and reliability indices is to increase the confidence placed in the assessment results, but we also know that there will be error in every score. What are the implications of score error for client assessment?

Sample Test Items

1. One of the first steps in developing a client assessment for therapeutic recreation is to:
   a. Write questions for the interview.
   b. Test the assessment on a small group of clients.
   c. Specify the client outcomes upon which the assessment will be built.
   d. Decide whether interviews or observations will be used.

2. Tess received the highest score on the Leisure Resources Knowledge Test. This statement uses which type of score interpretation?
   a. Norm-referenced.
   b. Criterion-referenced.
   c. Objective-based.
   d. Stability measures.

3. Validity relates to which of the following questions?
   a. How well does the assessment content match the program content?
   b. Does each client receive the same score?
   c. Is the assessment administered the same way every time?
   d. Are the two forms of this test similar?

4. All of the following are true statements EXCEPT:
   a. Validity is inferred by collecting evidence but is not directly measured.
   b. A test that is valid for individuals with mental retardation is valid for individuals with brain injury.
   c. A test instrument itself cannot be valid.
   d. Validity is important to the credibility or confidence placed in the results.

5. Which of the following is a method for improving evidence of content validity?
   a. Building a test blueprint or table of specifications.
   b. Conducting test–retest studies.
   c. Administering both forms of the assessment to one group.
   d. None of the above.

6. All of the following may lower validity of the assessment results EXCEPT:

    a. Unclear directions.

    b. Excessive interruptions during administration.

    c. Poorly constructed items.

    d. Assessment protocols.

7. Error variance or error of measurement can be defined as:

    a. How quickly a client finishes an assessment.

    b. How many mistakes there are on the assessment.

    c. The difference between a person's real ability and his or her obtained score.

    d. The number of attempts a client gets to answer a question.

8. Stability of assessment results over time can be tested by:

    a. Giving the assessment to a wide variety of audiences.

    b. Performing a test–retest.

    c. Administering both forms of the assessment to one group.

    d. Building a test blue print or table of specifications.

9. A correlation of +.80 means that:

    a. As one variable increases, the other also increases.

    b. 80% of clients answer the question incorrectly.

    c. The assessment is appropriate for 20% of the clients.

    d. The two variable have little or no relationship.

10. Measuring the internal consistency of an instrument is important when:

    a. The assessment has over 100 items.

    b. The test–retest showed poor results.

    c. People of various ethnic backgrounds will be taking the test.

    d. One test will be given one time to one group.

11. Interrater reliability is best calculated for which type of assessment?

    a. Record reviews.

    b. Interviews.

    c. Observations.

    d. Self-administered surveys.

12. All of the following may lower the reliability of assessment results EXCEPT:
    a. The test blueprint or table of specifications.
    b. Few number of items.
    c. Every client receives the same score.
    d. The client's anxiety of being interviewed.

13. Which of the following is the correct sequence of steps to develop an assessment instrument?
    I.   Determine the purpose of the assessment
    II. Develop the test specifications.
    III. Select and prepare appropriate items.
    IV. Validate items and the assessment.
    a. II, I, III, IV.
    b. I, II, III, IV.
    c. III, I, II, IV.
    d. None of the above.

Sample Student Assignments

Professional Interview
Interview a therapeutic recreation specialist about the "worst" and "best" client assessment he or she ever conducted. In the worst case, what types of things lowered the validity and reliability of the results? In the best case, what types of things improved the validity and reliability of the results? Report your answers back to class and compare.

Threats to Validity and Reliability
Make a list of at least 10 things that lower the validity and reliability of assessment results. For each item on the list, give two ways to improve it or lower its impact on the results. Bring your list to class and create one master list.

Validity and Reliability Information
From the information in Chapter 2, write a list of 20 to 30 things necessary to know about a client assessment before purchasing it for use in a specific therapeutic recreation program. Create an evaluation form or checklist from this list.

In-Class Assessment Descriptions

Select one therapeutic recreation assessment and develop a 5–7 minute in-class presentation, following the outline below. Additional information can be added. Prepare a 1–2 page handout following the outline below.

1. Description of assessment instrument/procedure
   a. Type (e.g., interview, observation, checklist)
   b. Basic constructs/ideas/content (How does it define or fit into TR services?)
   c. Purpose
   d. Background information on development
   e. Description of "forms," if applicable
2. Appropriate population
3. Appropriate agency
4. Validity, reliability, fairness, and usability information
   a. Directions
   b. Objectivity
   c. Validation studies
5. References, if any known, and how to order
6. Conclusions on development and usefulness
   a. What are your recommendations?
   b. How appropriate is this instrument for TR services?
   c. When would you recommend its use?

Assessment Reviews

Select any four commercially available assessments (e.g, LDB, LCM, BLRS, STILAP). For each, answer these questions (make sure to document your answers):

- Was the appropriate evidence gathered for validity?
- Was the appropriate evidence gathered for reliability?
- How much confidence would you place in the assessment results?
- For what type of program (content) might this assessment be appropriate?
- From the information given, how well could TRS across the country implement the assessment?

Bring this information to class and be prepared to critique the information you found.

Answers to Sample Test Items

1. c; 2. a; 3. a; 4. b; 5. a; 6. d; 7. c; 8. b; 9. a; 10. d; 11. c. 12. a; 13. b

Chapter 3

Discussion Questions

1. In your own words, explain the relationship between clients and programs depicted in Table 3.1.

2. Describe your own leisure lifestyle and that of someone you know well. How are they different and how are they similar?

3. What types of barriers to leisure may be felt by therapeutic recreation clients that are not experienced by individuals without illnesses and/or disabilities? What types of barriers are common to both groups?

4. In your own words, explain the Leisure Ability Model and its components. What types of therapeutic recreation programs might be provided using the Leisure Ability Model as the basis?

5. What are the advantages of depicting therapeutic recreation services through the Therapeutic Recreation Accountability Model? Explain each component and its relationship to other components.

6. What are the advantages of comprehensive program design? How does it benefit clients?

7. What is the relationship between program design and client assessment? How does one impact the other?

8. What role do program design and client assessment play in establishing and achieving client outcomes?

Sample Test Items

1. Programs that have been designed using the Leisure Ability Model might include all of the following EXCEPT:
   a. Functional participation.
   b. Functional intervention.
   c. Social interaction skills.
   d. Leisure resources.

2. Which of the following is a true statement about the concept of leisure lifestyle?

    a. People within a family unit have similar leisure lifestyles.

    b. Leisure lifestyle means spending the majority of one's time in leisure.

    c. People with illnesses and disabilities do not enjoy their leisure.

    d. Each person has a unique pattern of leisure within his or her life.

3. A person who has difficulty with his or her leisure may need the help of a(n):

    a. Social worker.

    b. Therapeutic recreation specialist.

    c. Occupational therapist.

    d. Activity director.

4. Which of the following contain goals and objectives derived from results of the client assessment?

    a. Treatment plan.

    b. Program protocol.

    c. Specific program.

    d. Client outcomes.

5. "Improved ability to initiate conversation" is an example of a:

    a. Treatment plan.

    b. Program objective.

    c. Client goal.

    d. Treatment protocol.

6. Which of the following is a true statement?

    a. Program design and planning are important to achieving client outcomes.

    b. Client assessment is optional for therapeutic recreation intervention programs.

    c. Therapeutic recreation is the only profession concerned with client outcomes.

    d. Activity analysis evaluates the leisure barriers perceived by clients.

7. Specific programs are developed for clients based on:
   a. Their leisure-related needs.
   b. Past leisure patterns and future potential participation.
   c. The results of the activity analysis.
   d. The delivery style specified in the treatment protocol.

8. Selecting programs that meet the intent of the comprehensive statement of purpose and goals is a major task in the _____ stage.
   a. Analysis.
   b. Conceptualization.
   c. Investigation.
   d. Determination.

9. Which of the following program titles would be most appropriate for the goal: "To provide programs that improve the clients' awareness of the need for leisure and its value in maintaining a healthy balance?"
   a. Functional intervention.
   b. Leisure attitudes.
   c. Social interaction skills.
   d. Recreation participation.

10. What is the major relationship between client assessment and intervention programs?
   a. Assessment places clients into services that address their needs.
   b. Intervention programs can be co-led with other disciplines.
   c. Assessment evaluates the properties of each activity to determine if it is suitable.
   d. Standardized intervention programs help assess staff competence.

Sample Student Assignments

Minipresentation
Create a 20- to 30-minute presentation on the relationship of program design, client assessment, and client outcomes in therapeutic recreation intervention programming as an in-service to other health care and human

service professionals. If possible, deliver the in-service to the staff at a local agency or a parents group.

Therapeutic Recreation Practice Models
Obtain copies of several commercial assessments. For each, compare the content with a therapeutic recreation practice model (see Ross and Ashton-Shaeffer, 2001). How many therapeutic recreation assessments are supported by one of the practice models? How well are the practice models represented?

Position Paper
Develop a 1–2 page position paper suitable for national adoption on the need for valid and reliable client assessment in therapeutic recreation intervention programming.

Professional Interview
Interview a therapeutic recreation specialist about his or her client assessment and therapeutic recreation program. Discuss how well the content of the assessment matches the content of the program. Discuss their plans for improving the assessment.

Answers to Sample Test Items

1. a; 2. d; 3. b; 4. a; 5. c; 6. a; 7. a; 8. d; 9. b; 10. a

Chapter 4

Discussion Questions

1. How do the Assessment Planning Model and the Assessment Implementation Model fit into the Therapeutic Recreation Accountability Model? How do models help you learn?

2. Why is it important to analyze the environment as the first step to assessment planning?

3. Think of three different disability groupings (e.g., traumatic brain injury, cancer, Alzheimer's) and discuss how this would affect the development and implementation of a client assessment.

4. What are some factors that influence the assessment implementation strategy?

5. List 8–10 questions you would want answered before purchasing a commercial assessment.

6. List 8–10 concerns you may have about developing an agency-specific assessment.

7. Discuss the importance of assessment protocols. What is their function and how do they relate to error and confidence?

8. Discuss 5–10 actions that can be taken to improve the confidence placed in an assessment's results.

9. How do assessment planning and implementation relate to program planning and implementation?

10. Why is it important to get an accurate and dependable baseline of information about a client before his or her participation in an intervention program?

Sample Test Items

1. When does the assessment planning process take place?
   a. Before the assessment is administered to clients.
   b. During program evaluation.
   c. Before activity analysis and modification.
   d. After efficacy research and quality improvement activities.

2. The purpose of defining parameters of the assessment is to:

   a. Analyze the characteristics of the agency, clients, and department.

   b. Understand why and what the assessment should do.

   c. Match client outcomes with treatment goals.

   d. Evaluate the effectiveness of the intervention programs.

3. If the therapeutic recreation program focuses on functional intervention, leisure awareness, social interaction skills, and leisure activity skills, the assessment should focus on:

   a. Leisure history, family structure, leisure interests, and leisure activity skills.

   b. Functional intervention, pain management, social networks, and leisure activity skills.

   c. Demographics, leisure history, leisure patterns, leisure interests, and leisure activity skills.

   d. Functional intervention, leisure awareness, social interaction skills, and leisure activity skills.

4. The four basic implementation strategies or ways to gather assessment data include all of the following EXCEPT:

   a. Interviews.

   b. Census data.

   c. Observations.

   d. Self-administered instruments.

5. A commercial assessment should be selected for use when it:

   a. Comes packaged with a test manual.

   b. Includes directions for scoring and interpretation.

   c. Is less expensive than an agency-specific assessment.

   d. Has been validated for the proposed use and client group.

6. The following are the major steps in developing an agency-specific assessment EXCEPT:

   a. Administering assessment protocols.

   b. Item writing.

   c. Item analysis and testing.

   d. Planning the assessment.

7. What is the purpose of assessment protocols?
   a. To demonstrate the variance of different client groups.
   b. To match the content of the assessment with the content of the program.
   c. To improve the consistency of assessment administration, scoring, and interpretation.
   d. To improve the intervention program delivery.

8. Reviewing a client's record before an assessment interview may help the specialist to:
   a. Observe dysfunctional family interactions.
   b. Complete the treatment plan prior to the interview.
   c. Establish rapport more quickly with the client.
   d. Ask more open-ended questions.

9. Reliable scoring procedures for client assessment are important because:
   a. Clients with similar scores should be placed in similar programs.
   b. Error in program placement can be increased.
   c. Confidence in the assessment's results can be decreased.
   d. Interviews yield open-ended information.

10. To use the same assessment to reassess a client for outcomes at the end of participation, the assessment must be:
   a. Widely used and accepted in therapeutic recreation.
   b. Administered to several groups of clients.
   c. Norm referenced.
   d. Valid, reliable, and measure small changes in the client.

Sample Student Assignments

Assessment Review
Review a copy of any assessment (commercial or agency-specific) and determine if it's function is to screen, identify problems, narrow problems, or reassess and monitor. What types of questions are included on the assessment? How detailed are they?

Client Assessment and Treatment Plan Practice
Use a commercially available client assessment in therapeutic recreation services to interview a friend, family member, or roommate. Use the results to create goals, objectives, and an action plan for that person's participation in a therapeutic recreation program. How well do the assessment results provide information for planning a person's treatment?

Assessment Planning Review
Obtain a copy of any commercial assessment for therapeutic recreation services. How much information is included about its development? Does it include training protocols for preparing the environment, and administering, scoring, interpreting, and reporting client assessment information? If not, develop a plan to validate the assessment and write a protocol for it.

Assessment Implementation Interview
Interview a practicing therapeutic recreation specialist and ask about his or her assessment implementation protocols. How are new staff and student interns trained to administer, score, interpret, and report assessment information? Is this likely to yield consistent information across administrations, clients, and specialists? What could be done to improve consistency?

Minipresentation
Create a 20- to 30-minute presentation on the client assessment process in therapeutic recreation intervention programming as an in-service to other health care and human service professionals. If possible, present the in-service to staff at a local agency or a parents group.

Answers to Sample Test Items

1. a; 2. b; 3. d; 4. b; 5. d; 6. a; 7. c; 8. c; 9. a; 10. d

Chapter 5

Discussion Questions

1. Why is selecting and implementing the right assessment just as important as selecting and implementing the right programs?
2. Describe the steps in the Assessment Planning Model and the Assessment Implementation Model. What are the critical decisions at each step?
3. To select an assessment, the therapeutic recreation specialist needs to be able to find and review several. Where can therapeutic recreation assessments be found?
4. Explain the similarities and differences between the selection steps outlined by Ward and Murray-Ward (1999), Gronlund and Linn (1990), and Dunn (1984).
5. By what criteria would you judge finding the "best" assessment for a certain program?
6. Explain the similarities and differences between the evaluation procedures outlined by Stumbo and Rickards (1986), Dunn (1989), Gronlund and Linn (1990), and Anastasi (1988).
7. What are the benefits of using a specific evaluation procedure when selecting assessment instruments?

Sample Test Items

1. Improving the confidence in assessment results means that:
   a. Therapeutic recreation will achieve equal status with other professions.
   b. Validity and reliability have been conducted.
   c. Error has been increased beyond chance alone.
   d. Clients are more likely to receive the services to meet their needs.
2. It is important to follow a systematic procedure for selecting therapeutic recreation assessments because:
   a. It improves the ability to make correct selection decisions.
   b. Interviews can be problematic for new therapeutic recreation specialists.

    c. Standards provide the minimal level of acceptable competence.

    d. Error can be increased beyond chance alone.

3. All of the following are important considerations when selecting an assessment procedure EXCEPT:

    a. The purpose of the assessment.

    b. How the results are to be used for client placement into programs.

    c. Client characteristics.

    d. Clinical management.

4. Which of the following is a possible source for locating therapeutic recreation assessments?

    a. Medical journals.

    b. Health care conferences.

    c. Therapeutic recreation journals.

    d. National Council for Therapeutic Recreation Certification.

5. When evaluating an assessment for use in a specific agency, which of the following best addresses the reliability of the assessment results?

    a. The content of the assessment matches the content of the program.

    b. The validation sample matches the population in the therapeutic recreation program.

    c. The consistency of results for similar clients.

    d. Adequate protocols for assessment administration, scoring, interpreting, and reporting.

6. When evaluating an assessment for use in a specific agency, which of the following is a major concern about the validity of the assessment results?

    a. The content of the assessment matches the content of the program.

    b. The validation sample matches the population in the therapeutic recreation program.

    c. The consistency of results for similar clients.

    d. Adequate protocols for assessment administration, scoring, interpreting, and reporting.

7. When evaluating an assessment for use in a specific agency, which of the following is a major concern about group it was tested on?

    a. The content of the assessment matches the content of the program.

    b. The validation sample matches the population in the therapeutic recreation program.

    c. The consistency of results for similar clients.

    d. Adequate protocols for intervention programs.

8. When evaluating an assessment for use in a specific agency, which of the following is a major concern about the assessment implementation?

    a. The content of the assessment matches the content of the program.

    b. The validation sample matches the population in the therapeutic recreation program.

    c. The consistency of results for similar clients.

    d. Adequate protocols for assessment administration, scoring, interpreting, and reporting.

9. When evaluating an assessment for use in a specific agency, the therapeutic recreation specialist would look for interrater reliability information if the assessment was:

    a. An observation.

    b. An interview.

    c. Used with clients with cognitive disorders.

    d. Used for research purposes.

10. Information about _____ would be appropriate to provide evidence about reliability.

    a. Internal consistency.

    b. Norm groups.

    c. Criterion-referenced interpretation.

    d. The constructs in question.

Sample Student Assignments

Assessment Evaluations
Use Tables 5.1, 5.2, 5.3, and 5.4 to evaluate any commercially available assessment. Report your findings to class. What are your overall conclusions about the assessment tool? What are its strengths and weaknesses?

Assessment Selections
Team up with a local therapeutic recreation specialist. Get to know his or her program well. Use Tables 5.1, 5.2, 5.3, and 5.4 to select a commercial assessment that matches his or her program and clients.

Assessment Comparisons
Review 3–5 commercially available assessments. Create a chart that compares their intended (validation) population, basic areas of therapeutic recreation content, evidence of validity and reliability, standardized protocols, cultural considerations, ease of use, and cost. Present this information to the class.

Answers to Sample Test Items

1. d; 2. a; 3. d; 4. c; 5. c; 6. a; 7. b; 8. d; 9. a; 10. a

Chapter 6

Discussion Questions

1. Describe the characteristics of an assessment that are important to consider prior to purchase.

2. Describe the practical considerations of an assessment that are important to consider prior to purchase.

3. Why are assessment protocols important?

4. Describe the technical considerations of an assessment that are important to consider prior to purchase.

5. Describe the summative considerations of an assessment that are important to consider prior to purchase.

6. What are the four categories of assessments outlined in this chapter?

7. Where can therapeutic recreation assessments be located or obtained?

8. Why are systematic critiques of commercial assessments important? Are they important for the therapeutic recreation specialist? for the therapeutic recreation program? for the client?

9. What is the relationship between systematic program design, client assessment, and client outcomes? How is this relationship strengthened?

10. Under what circumstances should a therapeutic recreation specialist develop an assessment rather than purchase one?

Sample Test Items

1. The purpose of the assessment directly affects:
   a. The types of items used.
   b. Its validity.
   c. The confidence in the consistency of results.
   d. The norm group.

2. One of the practical considerations in evaluating a commercial assessment includes:

    a. Evidence of validity and reliability.

    b. The availability of norm groups.

    c. The internal consistency of the tool over time.

    d. Required specialist qualifications, expertise, and training.

3. A therapeutic recreation specialist who uses an assessment without administration, scoring, interpretation, and reporting protocols is in jeopardy of:

    a. Introducing unwanted error into the process.

    b. Losing his or her professional certification.

    c. Placing the right clients in the right programs.

    d. Creating intervention programs to meet client needs.

4. As error increases, the _____ in the validity and reliability of results decreases.

    a. Confidence.

    b. Variance.

    c. Calculation.

    d. Evidence.

5. If the norm group used to validate an assessment is small and not representative of the population at the local agency, the therapeutic recreation specialist should:

    a. Create a protocol for administration, scoring, interpreting, and reporting the results.

    b. Select a different assessment.

    c. Evaluate the practical and technical aspects of the assessment.

    d. Use a different evaluation tool to review the assessment.

6. Which of the following is an example of collecting evidence of content validity?

    a. Giving the assessment two weeks apart to one group.

    b. Matching the content of the assessment with the content of the program.

    c. Creating two forms of one assessment.

    d. Calculating a correlation between an assessment score and a criterion score.

7. Which of the following is an example of collecting evidence of an assessment's stability?

a. Giving the assessment two weeks apart to one group.

b. Matching the content of the assessment with the content of the program.

c. Creating two forms of one assessment.

d. Calculating a correlation between an assessment score and a criterion score.

8. How many items should a therapeutic recreation services assessment have?

a. More than 20 items but less than 100 items.

b. 50 is an optimal number of items.

c. Enough to cover the content.

d. It does not matter.

9. Which of the following is an example of an assessment that includes leisure attitudes and barriers?

a. Comprehensive Leisure Rating Scale (CLRS; Card, Compton, & Ellis, 1986).

b. Comprehensive Evaluation in Recreation Therapy — Physical Disabilities (CERT—PD; Parker, 1977).

c. Leisure Competence Measure (LCM; Kloseck, Crilly, Ellis & Lammers, 1996).

d. Constructive Leisure Activity Survey #1 (CLAS #1; Edwards, 1980).

10. If an assessment was validated on a sample of adolescents with mental retardation, the assessment can be used with confidence for which of the following groups?

a. Adults with mental retardation.

b. Adults with cognitive impairments.

c. Children with mental illness.

d. None of the above.

Sample Student Assignments

Assessment Critiques

Use Tables 5.1, 5.2, 5.3, and 5.4 to evaluate any commercially available assessment. Report your findings to class. What are your overall conclusions about the assessment tool? What are its strengths and weaknesses?

Assessment Article Reviews
Use any published article (e.g., from the *Therapeutic Recreation Journal* or the *Annual in Therapeutic Recreation*) about an assessment. Note the intended population, the purpose of the assessment, its therapeutic recreation content, the reported evidence of validity and reliability, and plans for its further development. Report your findings to class.

Assessment File
Create a file of commercially available therapeutic recreation assessments. Include as much of their original documentation as possible.

Answers to Sample Test Items

1. a; 2. d; 3. a; 4. a; 5. b; 6. b; 7. a; 8. c; 9. a; 10. d

Chapter 7

Discussion Questions

1. Under what conditions should a therapeutic recreation specialist consider creating an agency-specific assessment procedure rather than purchasing a commercial assessment?
2. How does evidence-based practice relate to evidence-based assessment?
3. Choose a model of therapeutic recreation practice. List the content of assessments that match the content of that practice model.
4. For each area of content in question 3 create a general outcome and specific outcome statement.
5. How does the purpose of the assessment affect its development?
6. What advantage does starting with client outcomes have in the assessment development process?
7. What advantage does creating a table of specifications have in the assessment development process? Why is this step necessary?
8. For each type of item, practice writing a question related to social skills or leisure resources.
9. What are ways to collect evidence of validity for an agency-specific assessment?
10. What are ways to collect evidence of reliability for an agency-specific assessment?
11. How would you select a validation or norm group for an agency-specific assessment?
12. What types of documentation should accompany an agency-specific assessment?

Sample Test Items

1. The comprehensive program design for therapeutic recreation services at a particular agency is:
   a. Documented prior to the development of the assessment.

b. Not necessary for smaller agencies.

c. Created after the assessment has been selected.

d. Not required for one-person departments.

2. If the comprehensive program design contains services on stress management, functional intervention, leisure awareness, and leisure resources, the content of the assessment should include:

a. Leisure interests, leisure history, and leisure patterns.

b. Functional abilities, leisure awareness, stress management, and leisure resources.

c. Leisure interests, functional abilities, communication skills, and leisure resources.

d. None of the above.

3. All of the following are general outcomes of leisure resources EXCEPT:

a. To improve leisure activity skills that can be done alone.

b. To improve awareness of personal abilities and interests.

c. To improve utilization of community facilities.

d. To increase knowledge of leisure opportunities within the home environment.

4. When the therapeutic recreation specialist wants to know how a client responds to a certain stimuli or situation, he or she should administer a(n):

a. Interview.

b. Self-administered survey.

c. Records review.

d. Observation.

5. A(n) _____ is appropriate when the clients are cognitively intact and the therapeutic recreation specialist has a limited time to spend with each client.

a. Interview.

b. Self-administered survey.

c. Records review.

d. Observation.

6. In a table of specifications the number of items within each cell represents the weight that content is given in the therapeutic recreation:

  a. Comprehensive program design.

  b. Treatment plan.

  c. Written plan operation.

  d. Performance improvement plan.

7. Open-ended assessment items are best used for:

  a. Interviews.

  b. Self-administered surveys.

  c. Records reviews.

  d. Observations.

8. Rules for constructing rating items include all of the following EXCEPT:

  a. Match the item to specific client outcomes.

  b. Every response should have a descriptive "anchor" word.

  c. Allow the individual to check all that apply to him or her.

  d. Do not ask the question as a yes/no item.

9. The final number of items selected for inclusion on the assessment should match:

  a. Client needs and abilities.

  b. Results of the activity analysis.

  c. The requirements of the Joint Commission on Accreditation of Healthcare Organizations.

  d. The table of specifications.

10. The assessment documentation should include information on all of the following EXCEPT:

  a. The therapeutic recreation model upon which the assessment is based.

  b. The table of specifications.

  c. Critiques of the assessment.

  d. Characteristics of the norm or validation group.

Sample Student Assignments

Item Improvement

Use the principles of item construction in this chapter and others to improve the items located in Table 7.5 Bring your revisions to class and compare with others.

Item Development

Choose a population (e.g., individuals with physical disabilities or individuals with depression) and a specific content area of therapeutic recreation (e.g., leisure awareness or social skills). Develop 3 to 5 items for this content area that would be appropriate assessment questions for this population. Describe how their potential answers would lead to program placement.

Assessment Development

Create a plan to develop a client assessment that aligns with a therapeutic recreation program that you are familiar with. Outline the steps you would take in developing the assessment and collecting evidence of the validity and reliability of its results. Present your plan to the class.

Validating a Published Assessment

Locate a published therapeutic recreation assessment. Develop a plan to validate it for a different yet appropriate population than the one it was developed for. Outline the steps you would take in validating the assessment for this new population. Present your plan to the class.

Developing an Assessment Protocol

Locate a published therapeutic recreation assessment. Develop an assessment protocol for administering the assessment to a specific population of clients. Include a plan for staff and intern training on the protocol.

Answers to Sample Test Items

1. a; 2. b; 3. a; 4. d; 5. b; 6. a; 7. a; 8. c; 9. d; 10. c

Chapter 8

Discussion Questions

1. Discuss the purposes of interviewing as a method of therapeutic recreation assessment as outlined by Ferguson (1983).
2. Give examples of interviewing situations according to the seven different types described by Stewart and Cash (1988).
3. What are ways to develop rapport with clients at the beginning of interviews?
4. Discuss why open-ended questions are the best type to use for interviews.
5. Develop a list of open-ended interview questions based on a model of therapeutic recreation practice.
6. Develop a list of primary and secondary questions for social skills, leisure awareness, leisure activity skills, and leisure resources content.
7. Give two examples of each type of secondary question.
8. Give two examples of neutral and leading questions.
9. Develop sample interviews based on the five different ways to structure the body of an interview.
10. Develop two questions or comments based on each of the methods to close an interview.
11. Discuss the importance of the general rules for interviewing. What impact would each have on a interview with a client?
12. How can a student or a therapeutic recreation specialist improve his or her interviewing skills?

Sample Test Items

1. The primary time to use an interview is when the therapeutic recreation specialist wants to assess the:
   a. Strengths and weaknesses of the therapeutic recreation program.
   b. Leisure activity skills of the client.
   c. Leisure interests of the client.

    d. Client's thoughts, feelings, or perspective.

2. All of the following are ways to equalize power during an interview with a client EXCEPT:

    a. Allow the client to call you by your first name.

    b. Sit on the same side of the table or desk.

    c. Sit behind a table or desk as the client enters the room.

    d. Greet the client by name at the door.

3. Which of the following is considered a Level 1 question?

    a. Where were you born?

    b. How well do you interact with your relatives?

    c. What was your most traumatic experience in leisure?

    d. How does your physical ability compare with your peers?

4. The purpose of a primary question in interviewing is to:

    a. Make sure the client has nothing else to say on the topic.

    b. Introduce a new topic on the assessment.

    c. Create a feeling of trust with the interviewer.

    d. Clarify the client's response to a previous question.

5. The question "What else would you like to add before we move into the next section?" is an example of which type of secondary question?

    a. Nudges.

    b. Clearinghouse probe.

    c. Follow-up to irrelevant response.

    d. None of the above.

6. Which of the following changes the leading question "How wonderful do you think our therapeutic recreation program is?" into a neutral question?

    a. Our therapeutic recreation program is wonderful, isn't it?

    b. Can you tell me how wonderful you think our program is?

    c. Wasn't our program everything you wanted it to be?

    d. How well did the program meet your expectations?

7. Which of the following improves the question "How frequently do you participate in a social activity with friends?"

    a. How many times per week do you participate in a social activity with friends?

      b. How often do you participate in a social activity?

      c. How many friends do you have?

      d. What social activities do you frequently participate in with friends?

8. The opening of an interview can be used to:

      a. Orient the client to the program or department.

      b. Ask Level 3 questions.

      c. Ask clearinghouse probe questions.

      d. Evaluate the effectiveness of the intervention.

9. A body of an interview that uses a chronological time sequence for structure might include the following sequence:

      a. Childhood to young adulthood to adulthood leisure activities.

      b. Childhood problems and their causes.

      c. Childhood problems and their solutions.

      d. Adulthood problems, their causes, and their solutions.

10. A closing statement to an interview should:

      a. Discuss the treatment objectives developed from the assessment results.

      b. Include questions about the leisure behavior of the client.

      c. Summarize the interview, the information that was disclosed, and what happens next for the client.

      d. Be consistent with the client documentation used by other professionals.

Sample Student Assignments

Interview Development

Choose a population (e.g., individuals with physical disabilities or individuals with depression) and a specific content area of therapeutic recreation (e.g., leisure awareness or social skills). Develop 3 to 5 interview questions for this content area that would be appropriate for assessing this population. Describe how their potential answers would lead to program placement.

Interview Administration

Locate a commercially available assessment that uses interviewing. Pair with another student—as one observes, one interviews a "client" (friend, roommate, or family member). Both independently record the "client's" responses, score the assessment, and create a treatment plan. Compare your answers to check for consistency. Switch roles and repeat.

Videotaped Interview

Locate a commercially available assessment that uses interviewing. Create a videotape of an assessment interview with a "client." Have two other class members critique the interview, evaluating how well the protocol was followed, how rapport was established, how questions were delivered and how well they solicited information from the client, and how the interview was closed.

Developing an Assessment Protocol

Locate a published therapeutic recreation assessment that uses interviewing. Develop an assessment protocol for interviewing a specific population of clients. Include a plan for staff and intern training on the protocol.

Answers to Sample Test Items

1. d; 2. c; 3. a; 4. b; 5. b; 6. d; 7. a; 8. a; 9. a; 10. c

Chapter 9

Discussion Questions

1. Discuss the purposes of observation as a method of therapeutic recreation assessment.

2. Discuss the advantages and disadvantages of observations as assessments.

3. Discuss the advantages and disadvantages of direct versus indirect observations and obtrusive versus unobtrusive observations.

4. Where is error likely to be present in observations? How can this error be reduced?

5. What steps can be taken to improve the confidence placed in observation results?

6. Discuss the differences between accuracy and agreement in interrater observations.

7. Discuss the four observational recording methods and when each one is best used.

8. Discuss the four observational recording techniques and when each one is best used.

10. Discuss the importance of the general rules for observations. What impact would each have on an interview with a client?

11. How can a student or a therapeutic recreation specialist improve his or her observation skills?

Sample Test Items

1. Compared to interviews, the concern for the validity and reliability of an observation's results:
    a. Increases because of the subjective nature of observations.
    b. Remains the same.
    c. Decreases because observation methods yield better results.
    d. None of the above.

2. One major advantage of observations is that they record:

    a. Actual client behavior.

    b. What the client intends the specialist to see.

    c. What the client has done in the past.

    d. The client's motivations underlying his or her actions.

3. To get the most representative behavior of the client, the specialist should make observations:

    a. When the client has the most energy and enthusiasm.

    b. In the evening.

    c. Whenever it is convenient.

    d. In a natural setting whenever possible.

4. In what way can a therapeutic recreation specialist introduce bias during an observation?

    a. Have a reactive effect from being watched.

    b. Show favoritism toward certain clients.

    c. Record too many instances of the same behavior.

    d. Change his or her behavior depending on the location of the observation.

5. All of the following are ways to improve the confidence placed in the observation's results EXCEPT:

    a. Use two independent observers during the pilot test.

    b. Record behaviors as soon as possible.

    c. Decrease the number of observations.

    d. Describe the behavior as accurately as possible.

6. In calculating interrater reliability, the term _____ means that the two scorers mark the same score for a particular behavior.

    a. Accuracy.

    b. Agreement.

    c. Reaction.

    d. Consistency.

7. A checklist is best used when the behavior:

    a. Is either absent or present.

    b. Occurs to a degree or range.

    c. Is excessive.

    d. Is atypical.

8. When the antecedents, behavior, and consequences all need to be recorded, it is best to select _____ as the recording method.

   a. Checklists.
   b. Rating scales.
   c. Anecdotal records.
   d. None of the above.

9. When the number of times a behavior occurs within a given period is of interest, the best recording technique is:

   a. Frequency.
   b. Duration.
   c. Checklists.
   d. Interval recording.

10. All of the following are ways to improve the validity and reliability of observation results EXCEPT:

   a. Periodic training.
   b. Development and use of protocols.
   c. Interrater reliability checks.
   d. Change scoring based on need to fill programs.

Sample Student Assignments

Observation Development

Choose a population (e.g., individuals with physical disabilities or individuals with depression) and a specific content area of therapeutic recreation (e.g., leisure awareness or social skills). Develop 3 to 5 observation points for this content area that would be appropriate for assessing this population. Describe how their potential behaviors would lead to program placement.

Observation Administration

Locate a commercially available assessment that uses observation. Pair with another student—both observe a "client" (friend, roommate, or family member). Both independently record the "client's" behaviors, score the assessment, and create a treatment plan. Compare your observations to check for accuracy and agreement.

Videotaped Observation

Locate a commercially available assessment that uses observation or create one. Create a videotape* of a group of "clients." Have class members use the observation assessment while viewing the tape. Compare observations to check for accuracy and agreement.

*Can use a movie, such as the group treatment scene in *The Dream Team* or *One Flew over the Cuckoo's Nest*.

Developing an Assessment Protocol

Locate a published therapeutic recreation assessment that uses observation. Develop an assessment protocol for observing a specific population of clients. Include a plan for staff and intern training on the protocol.

Practice in Observation Tool Development

Choose a population (e.g., individuals with substance abuse issues, at-risk children) and a specific therapeutic recreation content area (e.g., functional intervention, social skills). Develop a sample assessment using each of the two observational recording methods. Create two questions using each of the four observational recording techniques.

Answers to Sample Test Items

1. b; 2. a; 3. d; 4. b; 5. c; 6. b; 7. a; 8. c; 9. a; 10. d

Chapter 10

Discussion Questions

1. Why has assessment been a continued source of concern for therapeutic recreation?

2. What affect do well-designed and implemented programs have on the assessment process?

3. What are concerns about assessment quality, and how can this be improved?

4. What are concerns about assessment resources, and how can this be improved?

5. What are concerns about therapeutic recreation specialist competence in assessment, and how can this be improved?

6. What are some assessment difficulties mentioned by Sneegas (1989) concerning the leisure behavior of individuals with disabilities and/or illnesses?

7. What are some of the problems associated with assessment planning and implementation? What can be done to improve it?

8. What are some of the problems associated with assessment scoring and interpretation? What can be done to improve them?

9. What are the effects of the problems noted in questions 7 and 8 on developing client objectives and treatment plans?

10. What will you do to improve the future state of affairs of therapeutic recreation assessment?

11. What should be done on the national level to improve the future state of affairs of therapeutic recreation assessment?

Sample Test Items

1. What role does client assessment play in the intervention process?

    a. It selects the right programs for implementation.

    b. It describes the client's leisure interests.

    c. It outlines the plan of action taken to reach the client's outcomes.

    d. It places clients in the right programs to meet their needs.

2. When an assessment is "borrowed' from another discipline for use in therapeutic recreation services, a problem that can result is:

    a. Clients react differently to being observed.

    b. The content does not align with the therapeutic recreation program.

    c. The interview questions can be leading and biased.

    d. A different sample of clients must be selected for the interviews.

3. Activity interest inventories are best used in programs that focus on:

    a. Social skill development.

    b. Acquisition of leisure skills.

    c. Functional intervention.

    d. Improvement of leisure awareness.

4. What actions can a therapeutic recreation specialist take to improve his or her competence in assessment?

    a. Read published articles in professional journals.

    b. Attend conference sessions.

    c. Network with fellow professionals.

    d. All of the above.

5. Why is leisure behavior hard to define for assessment purposes?

    a. It is unique to each person.

    b. It often presents problems for adults with addictions.

    c. It is less important than work and self-care behaviors.

    d. None of the above.

6. Assessment planning is an important step because it:

    a. Documents client outcomes.

    b. Reveals which activities are important to clients.

    c. Creates the foundation for the assessment to be built.

    d. Evaluates the effectiveness of the intervention.

7. An agency-specific assessment should be created only when:

    a. It is convenient to the therapeutic recreation specialist.

    b. Observations are the best method to collect assessment information.

    c. The cost can be justified to the agency's administration.

    d. A commercial assessment that produces valid and reliable results is not available.

8. The lack of an assessment protocol increases the likelihood of:

    a. Valid and reliable results.

    b. Activities being used as intervention.

    c. Periodic staff and intern training.

    d. Increasing error in the assessment results.

9. What is likely to happen when two specialists conduct the same assessment differently?

    a. Quadrant II and Quadrant III errors.

    b. Clients are able to express their individuality.

    c. The content of the assessment matches the content of the programs.

    d. Confidence in the results is improved.

10. Scoring of observations is made more difficult when the:

    a. Assessment lacks a scoring protocol.

    b. Specialist implements a diversional activity.

    c. Content of the assessment matches the content of the program.

    d. Opening fails to establish rapport.

Sample Student Assignments

Literature Review
Conduct a review of therapeutic recreation assessment literature and identify three barriers to conducting assessments that produce valid and reliable results. Document the sources and bring them to class.

Professional Interview
Interview a local therapeutic recreation professional to seek his or her views on the barriers he or she encounters concerning therapeutic recreation assessment. What actions have they taken to overcome these barriers? What actions do they plan to take?

National Agenda

Create a 1–2 page paper on how the profession of therapeutic recreation should address the shortcomings in assessment. Include realistic actions for improving the current state of affairs from a national level. Have the class create a national agenda and share it with the national professional organizations.

Resource List

Create a resource list concerning therapeutic recreation assessment. The list may include books, articles, websites, and individuals. Have each class member add to the list and make it available to the profession.

Answers to Sample Test Items

1. d; 2. b; 3. b; 4. d; 5. a; 6. c; 7. d; 8. d; 9. a; 10. a

Appendix
Therapeutic Recreation
Assessment Instruments

Leisure Attitudes and Barriers

Brief Leisure Rating Scale (BLRS)
Ellis and Niles, 1985

Ellis, G. and Niles, S. (1985). Development, reliability and preliminary validation of a brief leisure rating scale, *Therapeutic Recreation Journal, 19*(1), 50–61.

Ellis, G. and Niles, S. (1989). Development, reliability and preliminary validation of a brief leisure rating scale. In National Therapeutic Recreation Society (Ed.), *The best of the Therapeutic Recreation Journal: Assessment* (pp. 153–164). Alexandria, VA: National Recreation and Park Association.

Comprehensive Leisure Rating Scale (CLEIRS)
Card, Compton, and Ellis, 1986

Card, J., Compton, D., and Ellis, G. (1986). Reliability and validity of the comprehensive leisure rating scale. *Journal of Expanding Horizons in Therapeutic Recreation, 1*(1), 21–27.

Lindsey, S. P. and Card, J. A. (1990). Interrater reliability of the comprehensive leisure rating scale (CLEIRS). In G. L. Hitzhusen and J. O'Neil (Eds.), *Expanding horizons in therapeutic recreation XIII* (pp. 54–67). Columbia, MO: University of Missouri.

Leisure Attitude Scale
Beard and Ragheb, 1982

Ragheb, M. G. (1980). Interrelationships among leisure participation, leisure satisfaction and leisure attitudes. *Journal of Leisure Research, 12*, 138–149.

Ragheb, M. and Beard, J. (1982). Measuring leisure attitude. *Journal of Leisure Research, 14*(2), 155–167.

Leisure Diagnostic Battery (LDB)
Witt and Ellis, 1982

Dunn, J. (1986). *Generalizability of the leisure diagnostic battery.* Unpublished doctoral dissertation. University of Illinois at Urbana-Champaign.

Ellis, G. and Witt, P. (1982). *The leisure diagnostic battery: Theoretical and empirical structure.* Denton, TX: North Texas State University/ State College, PA: Venture Publishing Inc.

Ellis, G. and Witt, P. (1984). The measurement of perceived freedom in leisure. *Journal of Leisure Research, 16*, 110–123.

Ellis, G. and Witt, P. (1986). The leisure diagnostic battery: Past, present, future. *Therapeutic Recreation Journal, 20*(4), 31–47.

Ellis, G., Witt, P., and Niles, S. *The leisure diagnostic battery remediation guide.* Denton, TX: North Texas State University.

Witt, P. and Ellis, G. (1985). Development of a short form to assess perceived freedom in leisure. *Journal of Leisure Research, 17*(3), 225–233.

Witt, P. A. and Ellis, G. D. (1989). *The Leisure Diagnostic Battery: Users manual and sample forms.* State College, PA: Venture Publishing, Inc.

Witt, P. (1990). Overview and conclusions based on recent studies utilizing the Leisure Diagnostic Battery. In B. Smale (Ed.), *Leisure challenges: Bringing people, resources, and policy into play* (pp. 70–75). Waterloo, ON: Ontario Research Council on Leisure.

Leisure Motivation Scale (LMS)
Beard and Ragheb, 1983

Beard, J. and Ragheb, M. (1983). Measuring leisure motivation. *Journal of Leisure Research, 15*(3), 219–228.

Burlingame, J. and Blaschko, T. M. (1990). *Assessment tools for recreational therapy: Red book #1* (pp. 57–66). Ravensdale, WA: Idyll Arbor, Inc.

Leisure Satisfaction Scale (LSS)
Beard and Ragheb, 1980

Beard, J. and Ragheb, M. (1980). Measuring leisure satisfaction. *Journal of Leisure Research, 12*(1), 20–33.

Ragheb, M. G. and Beard, J. G. (1980). Leisure satisfaction: Concept, theory and measurement. In S. E. Iso-Ahola (Ed.), *Social psychological perspectives on leisure and recreation.* Springfield, IL: Charles C. Thomas.

Ragheb, M. G. (1980). Interrelationships among leisure participation, leisure satisfaction and leisure attitudes. *Journal of Leisure Research, 12*, 138–149.

Leisure Well-Being Inventory
McDowell, 1978

McDowell, C. F. (1978). *Leisure well-being inventory.* Eugene, OR: SunMoon Press.

McDowell, C. (1983). *Leisure wellness: Concepts and helping strategies.* Eugene, OR: SunMoon Press.

McDowell, C. (1986). Wellness and therapeutic recreation: Challenges for service. *Therapeutic Recreation Journal, 20*(2), 27–38.

Life Satisfaction Scale (LSS)
Lohmann, 1980

Burlingame, J. and Blaschko, T. M. (1990). *Assessment tools for recreational therapy: Red book #1* (pp. 75–78). Ravensdale, WA: Idyll Arbor, Inc.

Over 50
Edwards, 1988

Edwards, P. (1988). *Guide to over 50*. Los Angeles, CA: Constructive
   Leisure.

Perceived Competence Scale for Children/Self-
Perception Profile for Children
Harter, 1982/1983

Harter, S. (1979). *Perceived competence scale for children, Form O.*
   Denver, CO: University of Denver.
Harter, S. (1982). The perceived competence scale for children. *Child
   Development, 53,* 87–97.

What Am I Doing? (WAID)
Neulinger, 1986

Burlingame, J. and Blaschko, T. M. (1990). *Assessment tools for recre-
   ational therapy: Red book #1* (pp. 79–90). Ravensdale, WA: Idyll
   Arbor, Inc.
Hultsman, J. T. and Black, D. R. (1990). Baseline age norms for
   Neulinger's "What am I doing?" instrument. *Annual in Therapeutic
   Recreation, 1*(1), 37–47.
Hultsman, J. T. and Black, D. R. (1990). Baseline gender norms and cohort
   comparisons for Neulinger's "What am I doing?" instrument. *Annual
   in Therapeutic Recreation, 1*(1), 28–36.

Functional Abilities

Activity Therapy Assessment
Pershbacher, 1988

Perschbacher, R. (1989). *Stepping forward with activities*. Asheville, NC:
Bristlecone Consulting Company.
Perschbacher, R. (1993). *Assessment: The cornerstone of activity pro-
grams*. State College, PA: Venture Publishing, Inc.

Bond-Howard Assessment of Neglect in Recre-
ation Therapy (BANRT)
Bond-Howard, 1990

Burlingame, J. and Blaschko, T. M. (1990). *Assessment tools for recreational therapy: Red book #1* (pp. 189–194). Ravensdale, WA: Idyll
Arbor, Inc.

Bruninks-Oseretsky Test of Motor Proficiency
Bruninks and Oseretsky, 1972

Bruninks-Oseretsky Test Kit. Circle Pines, MN: American Guidance Service.

Burlingame Software Scale
Burlingame, 1980

Burlingame, J. and Blaschko, T. M. (1990). *Assessment tools for recreational therapy: Red book #1* (pp. 183–188). Ravensdale, WA: Idyll
Arbor, Inc.

BUS Utilization Assessment
Burlingame, 1989

Burlingame, J. and Blaschko, T. M. (1990). *Assessment tools for recreational therapy: Red book #1* (pp. 217–218). Ravensdale, WA: Idyll Arbor, Inc.

Communication Device Evaluation
Burlingame, 1990

Burlingame, J. and Blaschko, T. M. (1990). *Assessment tools for recreational therapy: Red book #1* (pp. 195–200). Ravensdale, WA: Idyll Arbor, Inc.

Comprehensive Evaluation in Recreation Therapy: Psychiatric/Behavioral (CERT: PB)
Parker, 1975

Comprehensive Evaluation in Recreation Therapy: Physical Disabilities (CERT: PD)
Parker, 1977

Burlingame, J. and Blaschko, T. M. (1990). *Assessment tools for recreational therapy: Red book #1* (pp. 107–116). Ravensdale, WA: Idyll Arbor, Inc.

Burlingame, J. and Blaschko, T. M. (1990). *Assessment tools for recreational therapy: Red book #1* (pp. 165-174). Ravensdale, WA: Idyll Arbor, Inc.

Parker, R. A. and Ellison, C. H., Kirby, T. F. and Short, M. J. (1975). The comprehensive evaluation in recreation therapy scale: A tool for patient evaluation. *Therapeutic Recreation Journal, 9*(4), 143–152.

Parker, R. and Downie, G. (1981). Recreation therapy: A model for consideration. *Therapeutic Recreation Journal, 15*(3), 22–26.

Parker, R., Keller, K., Davis, M., and Downie, R. (1984). *The comprehensive evaluation in recreation therapy scale—rehabilitation: A tool for patient evaluation in rehabilitation*. Unpublished manuscript.

Fox Activity Therapy Social Skills baseline (FOX)
Patterson, 1977

Burlingame, J. and Blaschko, T. M. (1990). *Assessment tools for recreational therapy: Red book #1* (pp. 129–144). Ravensdale, WA: Idyll Arbor, Inc.

Patterson, R. (1982). Development and utilization of an individualized assessment instrument for children and adolescents with severe and profound disabilities. In G. L. Hitzhusen (Ed.), *Expanding Horizons in Therapeutic Recreation X* (pp. 103–117). Columbia, MO: University of Missouri.

Patterson, R. (1985). *Activity therapy social skills baseline*. Dwight, IL: Wm. W. Fox Developmental Center. Unpublished manuscript.

Functional Assessment of Characteristics for Therapeutic Recreation (FACTR)
Peterson, Dunn, and Carruthers, 1983

Burlingame, J. and Blaschko, T. M. (1990). *Assessment tools for recreational therapy: Red book #1* (pp. 117-128). Ravensdale, WA: Idyll Arbor, Inc.

General Recreation Screening Tool (GRST)
Burlingame, 1988

Burlingame, J. and Blaschko, T. M. (1990). *Assessment tools for recreational therapy: Red book #1* (pp. 145–154). Ravensdale, WA: Idyll Arbor, Inc.

Idyll Arbor Reality Orientation Assessment
Idyll Arbor, 1989

Burlingame, J. and Blaschko, T. M. (1990). *Assessment tools for recreational therapy: Red book #1* (pp. 211–216). Ravensdale, WA: Idyll Arbor, Inc.

Idyll Arbor Activity Assessment
Burlingame, 1989

Burlingame, J. and Blaschko, T. M. (1990). *Assessment tools for recreational therapy: Red book #1* (pp. 257–274). Ravensdale, WA: Idyll Arbor, Inc.

Leisure Competence Measure (LCM)
Kloseck, Crilly, Ellis, and Lammers, 1996

Kloseck, M. and Crilly, R. G. (1997). *Leisure Competence Measure: Adult version professional manual and user's guide*. London, ON: Leisure Competence Measurement Data Systems.

Kloseck, M., Crilly, R. G., and Hutchinson-Troyer, L. (2001). Measuring therapeutic recreation outcomes in rehabilitation: Further testing of the Leisure Competence Measure. *Therapeutic Recreation Journal, 35*(1), 31–42.

Kloseck, M., Crilly, R., Ellis, G. D., and Lammers, E. (1996). Leisure Competence Measure: Development and reliability testing of a scale to measure functional outcomes in therapeutic recreation. *Therapeutic Recreation Journal, 30*(1), 13–26.

Maladapted Social Functioning Scale for Therapeutic Recreation Programming
Idyll Arbor, 1988

Burlingame, J. and Blaschko, T. M. (1990). *Assessment tools for recreational therapy: Red book #1* (pp. 201–210). Ravensdale, WA: Idyll Arbor, Inc.

Mundy Recreation Inventory for the Trainable Mentally Retarded
Mundy, 1966

Mundy, J. (1965). *The Mundy recreation inventory for the trainable mentally retarded*. Tallahassee, FL: Florida State University. Unpublished manuscript.

Ohio Leisure Skills Scales on Normal Functioning (OLSSON)
Olsson, 1988

Burlingame, J. and Blaschko, T. M. (1990). *Assessment tools for recreational therapy: Red book #1* (pp. 175–182). Ravensdale, WA: Idyll Arbor, Inc.

Olsson, R.H. (1990). The Ohio leisure skills scales for normal functioning: A systems approach to clinical assessment, In G. L. Hitzhusen and J. O'Neil (Eds.), *Expanding horizons in therapeutic recreation XIII* (pp. 132–145). Columbia, MO: University of Missouri.

Recreation Behavior Inventory (RBI)
Berryman and Lefebvre, 1981

Berryman, D. and Lefebvre, C. (1984). *Recreation behavior inventory*. Denton, TX: Leisure Learning Systems.

Recreation Early Development Screening Tool (REDS)
Burlingame, 1988

Burlingame, J. and Blaschko, T. M. (1990). *Assessment tools for recreational therapy: Red book #1* (pp. 155–164). Ravensdale, WA: Idyll Arbor, Inc.

Therapeutic Recreation Index (TRI)
Faulkner, 1987

Burlingame, J. and Blaschko, T. M. (1990). *Assessment tools for recreational therapy: Red book #1* (pp. 275–278). Ravensdale, WA: Idyll Arbor, Inc.

Faulkner, R. (1987). *TRI manual*. Seaside, OR: Leisure Enrichment Service.

Leisure Activity Skills

Cross Country Skiing Assessment
Peterson, 1990

Burlingame, J. and Blaschko, T. M. (1990). *Assessment tools for recreational therapy: Red book #1* (pp. 241–244). Ravensdale, WA: Idyll Arbor, Inc.

Downhill Skiing Assessment
Peterson, 1990

Burlingame, J. and Blaschko, T. M. (1990). *Assessment tools for recreational therapy: Red book #1* (pp. 237–240). Ravensdale, WA: Idyll Arbor, Inc.

Functional Hiking Technique
Burlingame, 1979

Burlingame, J. and Blaschko, T. M. (1990). *Assessment tools for recreational therapy: Red book #1* (pp. 227–236). Ravensdale, WA: Idyll Arbor, Inc.

Leisure Interests and Participation

Constructive Leisure Activity Survey #1 (CLAS #1)
Edwards, 1980

Constructive Leisure Activity Survey #2 (CLAS #2)
Edwards, 1980

Edwards, P. (1980). *Leisure counseling techniques: Individual and group counseling step-by-step.* (3rd. ed.) Los Angeles, CA: Constructive Leisure.

Edwards, P. and Bloland, P. (1980). Leisure counseling and consultation. *Personnel and Guidance, 58*(6), 435–440.

Family Leisure Assessment Checklist (FLAC)
Folkerth, 1978

Folkerth, J. (1979). Give the family flac. In D. J. Szymanski and G. L. Hitzhusen (Ed.), *Expanding horizons in therapeutic recreation VI* (pp. 174–179). Columbia, MO: University of Missouri.

Influential People Who Have Made an Imprint on My Life
Korb, Azok, and Leutenberg, 1989

Burlingame, J. and Blaschko, T. M. (1990). *Assessment tools for recreational therapy: Red book #1* (pp. 279–282). Ravensdale, WA: Idyll Arbor, Inc.

Joswiak's Leisure Counseling Assessment
Joswiak, 1979, 1989

Joswiak, K. (1975). *Leisure counseling program materials for the developmentally disabled.* Washington, DC: Hawkins and Associates.

Joswiak, K. F. (1980). Recreation therapy assessment with developmentally disabled persons. *Therapeutic Recreation Journal, 14*, 29–38.

Joswiak, K. F. (1989). *Leisure education: Program materials for persons with developmental disabilities*. State College, PA: Venture Publishing, Inc.

Leisure Activities Blank (LAB)
McKechnie, 1975

McKechnie, G. (1974). *Manual for environmental response inventory*. Palo Alto: Consulting Psychologists Press.

McKechnie, G. (1974). The psychological structure of leisure. *Journal of Leisure Research, 6*(1).

McKechnie, G. (1974). *The structure of leisure activities*. Berkeley, CA: Institute of Personality Assessment and Research.

McKechnie, G. (1975). *Manual for leisure activities blank*. Palo Alto, CA: Consulting Psychologists Press.

Leisure and Social Sexual Assessment
Coyne, 1980

Burlingame, J. and Blaschko, T. M. (1990). *Assessment tools for recreational therapy: Red book #1* (pp. 247–256). Ravensdale, WA: Idyll Arbor, Inc.

Leisure Interest Survey 2.0
Dixon, n. d.

Available at: http://www.computr.net

Leisure Pref
Edwards, 1986

Edwards, P. (1986). *Manual for leisure pref*. Los Angeles, CA: Constructive Leisure.

Leisurescope/Teenscope
Nall Schenk, 1983

Burlingame, J. and Blaschko, T. M. (1990*). Assessment tools for recreational therapy: Red book #1* (pp. 91–96). Ravensdale, WA: Idyll Arbor, Inc.

Nall, C. (1983). *Instructional manual for leisurescope.* Colorado Springs, CO: Leisure Dynamics.

Nall, C. (1985). *Instructional manual for Teen Leisurescope.* Colorado Springs, CO: Leisure Dynamics.

Recreation Participation Data (RPD)
Burlingame, 1987

Burlingame, J. and Blaschko, T. M. (1990). *Assessment tools for recreational therapy: Red book #1* (pp. 97–104). Ravensdale, WA: Idyll Arbor, Inc.

State Technical Institute Assessment Process
(STILAP)
Navar, 1980

Burlingame, J. and Blaschko, T. M. (1990). *Assessment tools for recreational therapy: Red book #1* (pp. 41–56). Ravensdale, WA: Idyll Arbor, Inc.

Navar, N. (1980). A rationale for leisure skill assessment with handicapped adults. *Therapeutic Recreation Journal, 14*(4), 21–28.

Navar, N. and Clancy, T. (1979). Leisure skill assessment process in leisure counseling. In D. J. Szymanski and G. L. Hitzhusen (Eds.), *Expanding horizons in therapeutic recreation VI* (pp. 68–94). Columbia, MO: University of Missouri.

Index

Books by Venture Publishing

Facilitation Techniques in Therapeutic Recreation
   by John Dattilo

File o' Fun: A Recreation Planner for Games & Activities, Third Edition
   by Jane Harris Ericson and Diane Ruth Albright

The Game and Play Leader's Handbook: Facilitating Fun and Positive Interaction
   by Bill Michaelis and John M. O'Connell

The Game Finder—A Leader's Guide to Great Activities
   by Annette C. Moore

Getting People Involved in Life and Activities: Effective Motivating Techniques
   by Jeanne Adams

Glossary of Recreation Therapy and Occupational Therapy
   by David R. Austin

Great Special Events and Activities
   by Annie Morton, Angie Prosser, and Sue Spangler

Group Games & Activity Leadership
   by Kenneth J. Bulik

Hands on! Children's Activities for Fairs, Festivals, and Special Events
   by Karen L. Ramey

Inclusive Leisure Services: Responding to the Rights of People with Disabilities
   by John Dattilo

Innovations: A Recreation Therapy Approach to Restorative Programs
   by Dawn R. De Vries and Julie M. Lake

Internships in Recreation and Leisure Services: A Practical Guide for Students, Second Edition
   by Edward E. Seagle, Jr., Ralph W. Smith, and Lola M. Dalton

Interpretation of Cultural and Natural Resources
   by Douglas M. Knudson, Ted T. Cable, and Larry Beck

Intervention Activities for At-Risk Youth
   by Norma J. Stumbo

Introduction to Recreation and Leisure Services, Eighth Edition
   by Karla A. Henderson, M. Deborah Bialeschki, John L. Hemingway, Jan S. Hodges, Beth D. Kivel, and H. Douglas Sessoms

Introduction to Writing Goals and Objectives: A Manual for Recreation Therapy Students and Entry-Level Professionals
   by Suzanne Melcher

Leadership and Administration of Outdoor Pursuits, Second Edition
   by Phyllis Ford and James Blanchard

Leadership in Leisure Services: Making a Difference, Second Edition
   by Debra J. Jordan

Leisure and Leisure Services in the 21st Century
   by Geoffrey Godbey

The Leisure Diagnostic Battery: Users Manual and Sample Forms
   by Peter A. Witt and Gary Ellis

Leisure Education I: A Manual of Activities and Resources, Second Edition
   by Norma J. Stumbo

Leisure Education II: More Activities and Resources, Second Edition
  by Norma J. Stumbo

Leisure Education III: More Goal-Oriented Activities
  by Norma J. Stumbo

Leisure Education IV: Activities for Individuals with Substance Addictions
  by Norma J. Stumbo

Leisure Education Program Planning: A Systematic Approach, Second Edition
  by John Dattilo

Leisure Education Specific Programs
  by John Dattilo

Leisure in Your Life: An Exploration, Fifth Edition
  by Geoffrey Godbey

Leisure Services in Canada: An Introduction, Second Edition
  by Mark S. Searle and Russell E. Brayley

Leisure Studies: Prospects for the Twenty-First Century
  edited by Edgar L. Jackson and Thomas L. Burton

The Lifestory Re-Play Circle: A Manual of Activities and Techniques
  by Rosilyn Wilder

Models of Change in Municipal Parks and Recreation: A Book of Innovative Case Studies
  edited by Mark E. Havitz

More Than a Game: A New Focus on Senior Activity Services
  by Brenda Corbett

Nature and the Human Spirit: Toward an Expanded Land Management Ethic
  edited by B. L. Driver, Daniel Dustin, Tony Baltic, Gary Elsner, and George Peterson

Outdoor Recreation Management: Theory and Application, Third Edition
  by Alan Jubenville and Ben Twight

Planning Parks for People, Second Edition
  by John Hultsman, Richard L. Cottrell, and Wendy Z. Hultsman

The Process of Recreation Programming Theory and Technique, Third Edition
  by Patricia Farrell and Herberta M. Lundegren

Programming for Parks, Recreation, and Leisure Services: A Servant Leadership Approach
  by Donald G. DeGraaf, Debra J. Jordan, and Kathy H. DeGraaf

Protocols for Recreation Therapy Programs
  edited by Jill Kelland, with the Recreation Therapy Staff at Alberta Hospital Edmonton

Quality Management: Applications for Therapeutic Recreation
  edited by Bob Riley

A Recovery Workbook: The Road Back from Substance Abuse
  by April K. Neal and Michael J. Taleff

Recreation and Leisure: Issues in an Era of Change, Third Edition
  edited by Thomas Goodale and Peter A. Witt

Recreation Economic Decisions: Comparing Benefits and Costs, Second Edition
  by John B. Loomis and Richard G. Walsh

Recreation for Older Adults: Individual and Group Activities
  by Judith A. Elliott and Jerold E. Elliott

Recreation Programming and Activities for Older Adults
  by Jerold E. Elliott and Judith A. Sorg-Elliott

Reference Manual for Writing Rehabilitation Therapy Treatment Plans
  by Penny Hogberg and Mary Johnson

Research in Therapeutic Recreation: Concepts and Methods
  edited by Marjorie J. Malkin and Christine Z. Howe

Simple Expressions: Creative and Therapeutic Arts for the Elderly in Long-Term Care Facilities
  by Vicki Parsons

A Social History of Leisure Since 1600
  by Gary Cross

A Social Psychology of Leisure
  by Roger C. Mannell and Douglas A. Kleiber

Steps to Successful Programming: A Student Handbook to Accompany Programming for Parks, Recreation, and Leisure Services
  by Donald G. DeGraaf, Debra J. Jordan, and Kathy H. DeGraaf

Stretch Your Mind and Body: Tai Chi as an Adaptive Activity
  by Duane A. Crider and William R. Klinger

Therapeutic Activity Intervention with the Elderly: Foundations and Practices
  by Barbara A. Hawkins, Marti E. May, and Nancy Brattain Rogers

Therapeutic Recreation: Cases and Exercises, Second Edition
  by Barbara C. Wilhite and M. Jean Keller

Therapeutic Recreation in Health Promotion and Rehabilitation
  by John Shank and Catherine Coyle

Therapeutic Recreation in the Nursing Home
  by Linda Buettner and Shelley L. Martin

Therapeutic Recreation Protocol for Treatment of Substance Addictions
  by Rozanne W. Faulkner

Tourism and Society: A Guide to Problems and Issues
  by Robert W. Wyllie

A Training Manual for Americans with Disabilities Act Compliance in Parks and Recreation Settings
  by Carol Stensrud

Venture Publishing, Inc.
1999 Cato Avenue
State College, PA 16801
Phone: (814) 234–4561
Fax: (814) 234–1651
http://www.venturepublish.com